3900

To Sis & Math with love from
Ann & Jack.

Sale

Christmas 1955.

BRITAIN IN PICTURES

BRITISH CRAFTSMANSHIP

A

COMPANION VOLUMES

THE BRITISH COMMONWEALTH AND EMPIRE
FIRST PUBLISHED 1943   REPRINTED 1945

IMPRESSIONS OF ENGLISH LITERATURE
FIRST PUBLISHED 1944   REPRINTED 1945 AND 1947

THE ENGLISHMAN'S COUNTRY
FIRST PUBLISHED 1946   REPRINTED 1946

NATURE IN BRITAIN
FIRST PUBLISHED 1946

BRITISH ADVENTURE
FIRST PUBLISHED 1947

ASPECTS OF BRITISH ART
FIRST PUBLISHED 1947

The Editor is grateful to all those who have helped in the selection of illustrations, especially to officials of the various public Museums, Libraries and Galleries and to all others who have generously allowed pictures and MSS. to be reproduced

BRITISH CRAFTSMANSHIP

INTRODUCTION BY W. B. HONEY
EDITED BY W. J. TURNER

WITH
48 PLATES IN COLOUR
AND
152 ILLUSTRATIONS IN
BLACK & WHITE

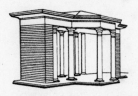

COLLINS · 14 ST. JAMES'S PLACE · LONDON
MCMXLVIII

PRODUCED BY
ADPRINT LIMITED LONDON

PRINTED IN GREAT BRITAIN BY
CLARKE & SHERWELL LTD NORTHAMPTON
ON MELLOTEX BOOK PAPER MADE BY
TULLIS RUSSELL & CO LTD MARKINCH SCOTLAND

BRITISH
CRAFTSMANSHIP

—

CONTENTS

—

BRITISH CRAFTSMEN BY THOMAS HENNELL: PAGE 9

BRITISH FURNITURE MAKERS BY JOHN GLOAG: PAGE 59

ENGLISH GLASS BY W. B. HONEY: PAGE 107

ENGLISH POTTERY AND PORCELAIN BY CECILIA SEMPILL: PAGE 157

BRITISH CLOCKS AND CLOCKMAKERS BY KENNETH ULLYETT: PAGE 207

ENGLISH POPULAR AND TRADITIONAL ART BY ENID MARX

AND MARGARET LAMBERT: PAGE 257

INTRODUCTION

IT is well known that people come to value a thing at its true worth only when they are on the point of losing it. This is notably the case with the handicrafts in England. The coming of the machine in so many departments of life and industry has rendered obsolete, by sheer pressure of economic forces, much that was of great human and aesthetic value. The basic achievement of the Englishman, here as elsewhere, was unassertive, seldom an affair of a newly created decorative style setting a European fashion, like the arts of Renaissance Italy or of France in the seventeenth and eighteenth centuries. It was often no more than a traditional skill in the handling of tools and materials, flowering on rare occasions into ornament which was no more than a gesture of workmanlike pride. That skill was at the disposal of the fashionable designers, with their Baroque and Rococo and Neo-Classical styles, curbing their extravagance and giving firmness to their wilder fancies, persisting like a ground through all the changes of fashion. That skill was a guarantee of quality—the trustworthy and lasting quality for which English goods have always been valued. Fine quality in workmanship, with commonsense and efficiency in

5

use, rather than art in the customary sense, have been the mainstay of our reputation.

The coming of the machine and the spread of mass production threaten, where they have not already destroyed, all that proud workmanlike skill. The mastery of the potter throwing vessels on the wheel is no longer necessary when they can be made more accurately in a tenth of the time by casting. The beautiful art of the glass-blower, with his rhythmical movements and dexterity, is obsolete where bottles can be made by thousands a day on a machine that hardly requires tending at all. With a tractor a man can plough, or with a combine-harvester reap and thresh, in a day, fields which formerly called for weeks of labour. That these things are exploited for profit, for quicker returns, should not blind us to the potential benefit to the human race represented by the machine. In a world where a living has always been hard to win and desperately insecure, any device that will save time and drudgery and guard against insecurity should surely be welcomed, even though its adoption means the loss or disuse of a valuable sort of craftsman's skill.

Before the general introduction of machinery, when hand-labour was almost universal, only a relatively few could enjoy life in an England that was hardly "merrie." The others lived their lives brutalised by toil, decimated by diseases brought on by hardship, with a population kept down by an appalling death-rate. Such was the price paid in suffering by the common people for a social order in which the craftsman was necessary. The immediate effect of the Industrial Revolution was of course a worsening. But that was no more than the result of a licence which allowed men to prey on their fellows, in harmony with a "nature" that is a welter of mutual devouring. The "dark Satanic mills" of William Blake were indeed a blot on what in a superficial view was "England's green and pleasant land." But the real offender was not the machine itself, but a commercial morality, capable not only of exploitation but of declaring that to make an article to last is bad for trade ! Such a declaration implies a treachery to the machine, which with responsible forward-looking control could produce goods as efficient in use, as enduring, and as well designed as any hand-made article.

The design of machine-made goods naturally belongs, of course, to an order entirely distinct from that of hand-made objects. It is in the first place the work of an external designer, impersonal, with a hard but delicate precision, but lacking the "organic" freedom and irregularity of objects individually wrought to the design of a craftsman-maker. This is of course nothing new. The drawing-office was not unknown to the furniture-makers of the eighteenth century, while architecture and book-production supply familiar parallels. There is every reason why the native English sense of proportion, mechanical genius and restrained fancy should excel in this new order of design.

6

Yet the old craftsmanship will survive. There is room and need for it in the modern world. Not only does it provide aesthetic education and a delight beyond the range of machine-made things, gratifying a sensuous longing, but it may satisfy also a "skill-hunger" in us which modern life and labour are apt to starve: so that the man who builds a boat for his own sailing, and the woman who embroiders a quilt for her own home, are getting a satisfaction far beyond that given by any passive pleasure. Making things is a good life. But those men live in a fool's paradise who seek to revive obsolete modes and make by hand for everyday use things that are now normally made with a new kind of excellence by the machine. Apart from all question of contemporary style (and such craftsmen are apt to be backward-looking) the work of these diehards must stand accused of an economic unreality, since their patrons must be rich men and their work a luxury art. Some have thought to throw a bridge between handicraft and the machine. Walter Gropius, for example, has said that "the field of handicraft will be found to lie mainly in the preparatory stages of evolving type-forms for mass production"; but this would hardly work, since the handworker's tools and his whole attitude towards his materials differ fundamentally from those of the designer for the machine. So it must remain, unless the breakdown of our Western civilisation prevents all large-scale co-operation and brings poverty again for most of us.

Meanwhile we may enjoy the lovely work of bygone times to which the contributions to this book are chiefly devoted. They record not only the major handicrafts, but certain lesser-known arts until lately surviving in the market-place and fair-ground, as well as those minor crafts, perhaps the most interesting of all, which are still practised in remote country places. Here are displayed in pictures the virile art of the English potter, ranging from the noble vessels made in mediaeval times down to the essentially modern cream-colour of Josiah Wedgwood and his followers; the dying art of hand-blown glass; the exquisite art of the clockmaker, as much science as handicraft; and the work of the joiner and cabinet-maker in a procession of styles coming down to that modern stage when, in Mr. Gloag's words, "we may even outgrow the use of wood" altogether. We have in England no peasant art, but in many toys and trinkets sold for a few pence was embodied a true native English taste, racy and extravagant where academic art is apt to be tame and timidly correct. This is the traditional popular art so happily described by Margaret Lambert and Enid Marx; while Thomas Hennell devoutly celebrates the humble country crafts, of saddler and wheelwright and builder of carts; of blacksmith and carpenter, mason, bricklayer and pargeter, down to the thatcher, whose once indispensable task it was to cover in and protect the newly harvested stack of hay or corn, adding to each an ingeniously-woven straw idol, or "dolly," as a rite of exorcism and a gesture of craftsmanlike mastery.

W. B. HONEY

BRITISH

CRAFTSMEN

BY

THOMAS HENNELL

PREFACE

AS common crafts grow scarce and die out, it occurs vividly to some people that here is something precious; though hitherto it has always been taken as a matter of course, and of little consequence to any save those whose living it had been. But now it will be missed, for nothing of the same kind is growing up to fill its place. The old tree is half-dry and tottering; a few hands would pluck the branches of experience to strike them, if possible, in some sheltered spot.

Yet, as often happens, the impulse which gave the old life harmony with its surroundings is ever active. The new plant, though not vigorous and fruitful as the old has been through many centuries, may yet become so: then let those who have eyes and understanding train it to future fruitfulness. To change the metaphor, we have a new language of technics to learn; but for a long while to come the old language may provide a basic grammar. Our school subjects are now more numerous and complicated than they were in the days of master and apprentice. It may be difficult to put so much heart in them, or to pursue our task with so much devotion and satisfaction. But it is our fault if they spread uselessly. It is no easier and no more difficult to become a master, except in special ways, than it ever has been.

I have divided my book into eleven sections, with a brief conclusion. I start with the Crafts of Stone as being among mankind's earliest activities and then proceed, in what may seem a capricious, but is nevertheless not an undesigned, sequence in which the intention has been to give the reader a vivid set of illustrations of the life and conditions of the craftsman rather than a text-book exposition of the theory of handicrafts.

9

The relics of man's early weapons are an index of the age of the human race, which some say can thus be traced back for fifty and even seventy thousand years. The brown 'eoliths' with their nibbled edges, and the much later struck flakes and nicks, are quite plentiful in our fields in North Kent. People went on using flints for striking a light; at first on pyrites and later on steel. No doubt the knack of flaking and striking flints survived quite widely until recent times. Thirty years ago the stone-breaker was to be seen (as he still may be seen in Ireland) with his wire spectacles and his long hammer, breaking flints for road-surface. At Brandon, Suffolk, flint-knapping is still an industry practised by one or two families, who make gun-flints for the African trade, and 'quarries' (square-faced flints) for church-building. It is a direct survival of the neolithic craft, but that iron hammers and 'anvils' (made from old files) are used for striking and shaping the flakes. The flints used are dug from pits at a depth of thirty to fifty feet; they split and flake more cleanly when 'green' than when seasoned for some time above the surface. These flints tend to be smooth nodules somewhat flattened like a home-baked quartern loaf.

The knapper first lays the flint on his leather apron and cracks it in two with a six-pound hammer, then he strikes off the crust with successive blows round the edge of the fracture—it is like a wasteful way of peeling a potato. But it leaves a series of plane surfaces, so that the next strokes detach long thin flakes which can be reduced, in a second process, to the squares and sizes that are needed. At last only the polygonal 'core' of the original half-flint is left.

The working of freestone developed greatly in the bronze age. A metal edge, not necessarily a sharp or toothed one, can be used with sand and water to saw the blocks accurately and without waste: this is the method still used. Stone can most readily be shaped when 'green,' but is then liable to be damaged by frost. In places where it is quarried underground (as at Box, near Bath) the block, after being partly excavated from the seams with the pick, partly cleft with wedges, is rough-hewn with a sort of axe, and not brought to the surface till summer. In the underground 'roads' of the quarry the air is damp and tepid: it varies little in winter or summer. The great blocks are not used in modern buildings, and, after they have seasoned for some years, they are sawn into slabs of from three to seven inches in depth. Even in this country, stone-quarrying and masonry are crafts much older than the cathedrals. But the use of cement and steel structures in cities, and of cheap and light substitutes, such as breeze-blocks in country which once built with its native stone, have reduced stone-masonry to the secondary rank of a decorative craft. A less excusable injury has been done to the English mason by the wholesale importation of Italian marble monuments—a trade based on no sound

MEDIAEVAL BUILDING
Illumination from the Guthlac Roll, late 12th century

values, either religious or aesthetic. So the stone-mason has been degraded to the manufacture of bird-baths and sundials.

We need imagination as well as patience to form a reasonable idea of the great history of stone-masonry and stone-carving in this country, which flowered so magnificently and so profusely in the twelfth and thirteenth centuries. We do not know the names of the sculptors of such rich and lovely works as Kilpeck Church, or St. Mary's, Lavenham. And though Gothic mouldings and decoration have been profoundly studied, compared and systematised, few if any restorers can do more than a dull, laborious counterfeit, because such restoration cannot recover the under-

lying impersonal conviction, the sense of beauty, the free and spirited fancy that were the birthright of those stone-carvers; which, like Abel's faith, "being dead, yet speaketh." It is a virtue which never asserts itself as brilliant and original, which may easily be passed over and dismissed as ordinary: we realise it only in tranquillity and as it were unawares.

The best stone-carver of modern times, Eric Gill, was well aware that his craft was not an accomplishment but a life and all: he began at the beginning with letter-cutting, and faith was not less essential than practice to his calling.

The life of a traditionary stone-worker is chronicled by Eric Benfield in *Purbeck Shop*. He tells of the family-owned quarry, of the solitary underground daily toil with its difficulty and danger; which yet came to have a grip on those who were bred to it, so that they sought no other nor easier job. They spoke little, and spent little, except in the way of candles, blacksmiths' bills and beer. The stone firms which gave them credit for their output and marketed it as needed, provided the stone-workers' families with such things as clothing, boots and groceries. It must have been a life almost as single-minded and simple as that of the men who built the Gothic churches—"wandering about in sheepskins and goatskins, of whom the world was not worthy," as Blake curiously wrote on his print of Joseph of

12

PURBECK QUARRYMEN
Line engraving by Stanley Anderson

13

Arimathaea. Many of those who work among the Rocks of Albion are intensely religious men: a pity if their calling can only serve mean uses.

There are a few local stone-builders, and a few architects who encourage them. In the Cotswolds one or two are left who make 'roofing slats' of the laminated stone which is found near the surface. These are worked in a succession of sizes—a V-shaped 'crest' on the ridge, the smallest and lightest next beneath it; the largest at the eaves. They are known by queer names: cocks, cuttings, mobbities; becks, bachelors, nines and wibbuts; elevens to sixteens, follows and eaves. The making and use of such slats has not been carried on for a thousand years and more without developing a truly scientific perfection. And yet reputable modern architects ignore the tradition and order their slats all of one size. Those stone roofs are not only strong and durable against storm and weather; they are organic forms like the covering of creatures. They are as much part of the landscape as shepherd and flock, fields and ploughman.

Here again is a close partnership: the carpenter who frames the stout roof with the 'slatter' who hangs the stones: there is the field-gate hinged to a stone post and the stone 'hedge' built by a dry-waller. Here one sees walls and barns with mortarless joints; yet houses and churches must be more draught-tight, so perhaps with the mason and plasterer the lime-burner (whose trade is indispensable to them) may claim a place.

SOME CRAFTS OF FIRE

Lime can be burnt from chalk as well as from limestone, but the forms of kiln are different. The chalk-kiln is conical, or shaped like a straw bee-hive. Stone-lime, however, with washed sharp sand, makes the strongest building mortar. The stone-kiln is built into a mound, or at the end of a cutting, and it is like an egg-cup in section, whose rim is at the upper surface of the mound. There is an upright opening or oven-door into the stem of the egg-cup from the cutting; in here a fire is lit, and the cup is filled from above with thin layers of slack coal and heavy layers of broken limestone laid alternately. As the mass burns, the lime and ashes work through, are carried out below, sifted and carted away, and more coal and limestone added above. A cart-track leads from the top opening to the quarry. At one of these kilns in Somerset there were many great fossil shells called ammonites, such as are often built into walls for a 'fancy'; some were as big as barrow-wheels. The quarryman came up with a fresh load of stones and enquired what I thought of them. What was his opinion? I asked. "Well," said he, "I reckon God put them there at the Flood." He called the lime-kiln "an unfruitful place."

No doubt when coal was not carried everywhere the lime-burners made shift with wood or charcoal. The charcoal burner can still be found, although

MASONRY
Etching from W. H. Pyne's *Microcosm*, 1806

there are modern methods of reducing wood and saving the by-products. But he needs no equipment beyond shovel, rake and sacks. The rest is all home-made. He sleeps in a shelter by his fire, which he builds round a core of sticks, laying the lengths of 'cordwood' on end in a circle, their heads inclined inward: then another layer, set more obliquely above them. This pile (a flattened cone) is covered with straw, ashes and earth which is kept damp and frequently patted down: it takes three or four days to burn through. Meantime there must be no direct draught: the wind is kept off by means of thatched hurdles or 'looes.' When the fire is taken down, all the wood is burnt to black glistening charcoal: there should be no white ash.

The brickmaker's is another ancient trade, much changed by machinery. There were (and may still be) brickmakers who travelled about to places where houses were needed. They tested the local clay, treated or blended it, and could adapt their processes to its nature. The selected clay was washed to remove flints, allowed to settle again and thicken; then kneaded in the pug-mill (as it were in a fixed churn containing rotating forks), then shaped in moulds and set to dry—or in a later process cut off by lengths from a squeezed-out ribbon. The old blind horse which used to go round and round at the pug-mill was replaced by steam-power and later by oil-engines. The steam-tackle in some deserted brick fields at Bromley must

15

have been among the most cumbersome ever designed by man. The great art is in building the brick-stack so that the bricks are burned evenly.

Such crafts as pargeting (a pretty way of finishing outside walls in East Anglia) and the more primitive wattle-and-daub; the Dorset walls of beaten clay and straw, called wichut in Thames Valley (there is also cob in Devon and clay lime in Norfolk), often plastered and thatched over in a ridge; the pebbly walls of North Norfolk; the woven panelling of cleft oak used on farm-buildings in Hereford, and the squared chalk or 'clunch' used in Thanet; with Norfolk reed-thatching (still in a flourishing way); oak-shingles—not to mention weather-vanes of a hundred forms—each local branch and appendage of the builder's craft deserves a monograph. The works of the old builders keep us in mind of the past, their example should make us conscious of the future. "Trifle not," run the words under Graves-end Church clock, "thy time is short."

SECTION OF A LIME KILN
From the *Compleat Body of Husbandrye*

WOODEN ROOFS

Next to stone, oak was the chief glory of Gothic buildings. The gradual development of stone vault building from Romanesque to Perpendicular was paralleled if not preceded by refinements in wooden roof-framing. The cambered-beam, at first spanning the walls and immediately supporting the roof, was succeeded by the tie-beam roof with king-post or queen-posts; then by the collar-beam, scissors-truss and hammer-beam types. There are many variants and hybrid types, and it is unsound to regard them as so many steps in evolution; for much depended on local fashion and on the

By courtesy of Canon F. Harrison and the Studio, Ltd.

AN ENGLISH STAINED GLASS WINDOW, C. 1400
Detail from the Jesse window in the Choir of York Minster

SLIPWARE DISH MADE BY SAMUEL MALKIN, BURSLEM, STAFFORDSHIRE, C.1726

By courtesy of the Fitzwilliam Museum, Cambridge

richness of the building. The ancient, doubtless Saxon, form known as cruck, which consists in framing wall and roof together, from foundations to apex, with great curved baulks, survives in modified form in arch-braced roofs, and is even suggested in the arch-ribs of Westminster Abbey. (There is in Cheshire a timber barn of crucks, and cruck cottages are not very rare.)

The intention of those elaborate difficult structures, the double and compound hammer-beam roofs, was to give apparent height and mystery. As the roof-space became larger so that no oaken beams would span it, it had been necessary to carry the tie-beams on posts, with an aisle or double-aisle at the sides: and this greatly interrupted the space, and its properties of accommodation, sight and hearing; so that by building the roof as it were on stepped arches or bridges, a far grander effect was obtained. And in such lofty roofs was great scope for enrichments of carving. The hammer-beams may end in carved angels (as at Westminster) or their pendentives be transformed into sculptured bosses.

The roof of Westminster Hall, of length 238 feet and 68 feet in span, which was begun in 1394, is the largest and "the greatest triumph of mediaeval carpentry which England has ever possessed." It was built of Sussex oak. It is formed of thirteen roof-trusses, each with a pair of hammer-beams and hammer-posts, of which a single timber weighs three-and-a-half tons and must have required an oak of four feet diameter.

It may not be fantastic to consider that, since oaks known to have been planted in Queen Elizabeth's reign have sometimes attained this size, the tree can be said to survive much longer in a building than the time it has taken to grow to maturity. And therefore it should be profitable for the State to plant oaks, and to discourage (instead of compelling) the cutting of oaks at sixty years or less. Wasteful felling of oak-trees is a crime against the community which ought to be heavily penalised.

It is not so easy to guess the date of a wooden roof as of a stone building, whose mouldings date it; for the masons who built and adorned the stone churches and most of the rich and comfortable houses (as distinct from purely military defences) were craftsmen from the monasteries. Their handiwork is recognisable in the fine finish, the correct detail and occasional ornament which may be seen in small manor-houses and even in tithe barns, such as those of Bradford-on-Avon and Glastonbury. But the wood-builders were less closely organised, and their work was constantly needed for useful and ordinary purposes. So, though the monastic style of architecture came to an end with the Dissolution of Monasteries about 1540, we may say that the Gothic tradition in wood can be traced, in the framing of timber barns, at least till the eighteenth century. In a sense the ship-wrights continued to keep alive the Gothic principles as long as ships were built of wood: and their craft, so essential to Britain's resources and defence, had acquired a whole universe of basic design between the discovery of the New World and Trafalgar. Then the tradition of adapting old ships'-

timbers to barn building, a very old one, continued to be useful until steam-threshing replaced flail-labour, for which the old barns, with their great 'mows,' threshing-floor and waggon-door, were designed.

The timber building must be braced together, firmly as a chair or table, to support the roof's weight, and to withstand wind and weather: its timbers being pegged into tenons with oaken pegs, not nailed. The posts must not be planted in the ground, but carried on piers above the level of rot. The side-walls, of uprights weather-boarded with elm, are set into wall-plates upon a low outer wall of flints or brick carrying very little weight. The roof is supported on two rows of posts, joined with transverse beams: and upon these again are upright king-posts, which carry a sort of backbone down the length of the barn, whose horizontal ribs bear the purlins and rafters. This was an arrangement common in Kent. The uprights and horizontals are braced together with 'quarter-bars' mortised diagonally, so that the framework may not twist. To the horizontal battens which cross the rafters is sewn and pegged a covering of thatch; or tiles, stone or slate are hung. Despite the immense weight of such a roof the strain upon individual timbers is less than in the living tree, under its load of twig, leaf and acorn, or standing naked to the winter wind.

COUNTRY WOOD-CRAFTS

A wooden roof framed by intersecting timbers—the purlins keyed into the rafters or ribs—is called a waggon-roof. It is as old a principle as the Egyptian harrow. And the wainwright's or wheelwright's trade of the Gothic tradition is of great interest in that it is not yet absolutely extinct. Though his work serves rougher uses than did that of the Church craftsmen, it has maintained for centuries longer the essentials of structural soundness and decorative fitness. These must survive as long as the thing made is useful, necessary and done with pride. It requires great knowledge to choose and season the right timber for each purpose: especially so in the times before iron fittings and castings could be easily procured to get over difficult details such as the wheel-bearings and the struts which hold the built-out lades.

What is striking is that these carpenters have never worked from plans or drawings; they work directly in the wood and think of their work in no other way. The parts of waggons and carts (even of the lighter sort) are first fitted together 'in the square,' then chamfered up and carved so as to give the maximum of lightness with strength, and at the same time a decorative finish.

Never was painting done more soundly and permanently than by these tradesmen, especially by the fine coach-builders who spared no pains to make their work beautiful and lasting. John Crome of Norwich and his friend Ladbrook were coach-painters' apprentices, so was Caravaggio; and

ROOF OF WESTMINSTER HALL
Detail from a coloured aquatint by Pugin and Rowlandson, 1809

Velasquez knew the virtue of carriage-painter's varnish. Philip Webb imitated the waggon-builder's methods in a ponderous and indestructible piano-case which is in the Victoria and Albert Museum: but Burne-Jones and Rossetti, who painted the panels of it, had not mastered the tradesman's practice, and their work has blackened.

The country millwright's trade was a more elaborate one than the wheelwright's and it too developed from the sixteenth to the nineteenth centuries, as an evolutionary stage of machinery or 'technics.' The great windmill in the Oostpleine at Rotterdam was one of the world's largest and most beautiful examples. It was of seventeenth-century design throughout; a 'smock-tower' of wood upon three storeys of stone, with wooden-framed canvas sails and wooden lantern-pinions to drive the stones. The part below the gallery was a stone-walled tower, which was originally the dwelling-house of the miller and his family. At the time it was built, the English millwrights were not nearly so advanced; but they were less conservative and they progressed along half-a-dozen provincial traditions, especially during the late eighteenth and early nineteenth centuries when the use of cast iron was introduced and the miller's was a prosperous occupation.

The miller required nerve and resource especially in emergency—to stop or check the mill in a storm, or when by a sudden change of wind after a calm it became 'tail-winded' and ran the wrong way! But the millwright's man had sometimes to perform astonishing feats as a steeplejack. Or else he might have weeks of interminable drudgery—sitting hour upon hour (from six in the morning till seven at night, or longer)—in a cramped, ill-lit space, pitching and trimming wooden mill-cogs in the circumference of a ponderous oaken brake-wheel. The cogs themselves were carefully shaped from hornbeam, beech or apple-wood. Dressing the mill-stones was harder still. They had sometimes to be 're-draughted,' then levelled, then the ridges and furrows made sharp and equal. An old stonedresser's hands and wrists were 'peppered' as though by small-shot, from fragments of steel which had flown from the edge of his mill-bill, in this work.

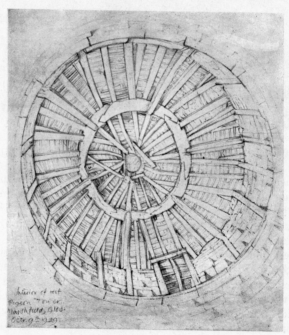

INTERIOR OF PIGEON HOUSE ROOF
Pencil drawing by T. Hennell, 1929

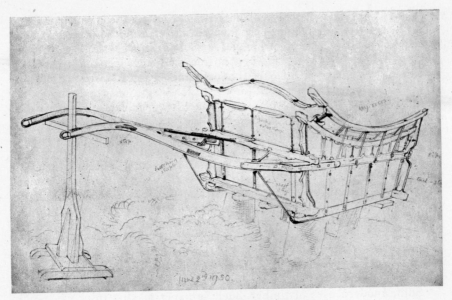

FARM CART UNDER CONSTRUCTION
Pencil drawing by T. Hennell, 1930

BRITISH TIMBER

"In the earliest of the three periods of the Machine Age," says Lewis Mumford, "wood was the universal material of economy. Houses were built of wood: the stones of the Gothic churches, whose piers stood like forests, were raised with wooden scaffolding and cranes. Tools were of wood, but for the last cutting edge: the rake, the oxyoke, the cart, the waggon, were of wood: so was the washtub in the bathhouse: so was the poor man's shoe. Wood served the farmer and the textile worker: the loom and the spinning-wheel, the oil presses and the wine presses were of wood, and a hundred years after the printing-press was invented, it was still made of wood. The very pipes that carried water in the cities were often tree-trunks; so were the cylinders of pumps. One rocked a wooden cradle: one slept in a wooden bed, and when one dined one 'boarded.' One brewed beer in a wooden vat and put the liquor in a wooden barrel."

These uses of wood, each highly developed and connected with larger enterprises—with timber ships and barges; piers, barns and buildings, windmills and watermills—were the parts of a well-wrought, balanced civilisation which reached its most perfect development in seventeenth-century Holland—a form adjusted to a steady, businesslike and dignified mode of living which has been slow to change.

23

Nor in Britain are many of these uses of wood truly obsolete. With each of them (and many more) are involved the traditions of as many living crafts. Railway-sleepers, pit-props, sectional buildings consume great quantities of wood every year. Though no more wooden ships, yet there are yachts, barges and smaller boats. The windmiller and watermiller, and the country millwright whose work for them was mainly in wood, the cooper and the waggon-builder : theirs may be 'dying trades'—though by no means so the undertaker's. And there is the pattern-maker whose work is the preparation for metal castings in the engineers' shops, and calls for as fine and accurate handling of the material as any. In a still broader sense the joiner is the means of effecting a technical transition. Parts of aeroplanes, as of vessels, for which at first wood was indispensable, are progressively replaced by suitably designed metal. In furniture, steel chairs and table-tops of bakelite are seen—on the other hand cast-iron seats and tables, and marble-topped washstands, tend to be superseded: metal bedsteads have not acquired the popularity of wooden ones. There is still plenty for the expert cabinet-maker to do, and the possibilities of many beautiful colonial woods (such as used to be exhibited in the Imperial Institute) have by no means been worked out.

Some modern uses of timber, such as paper-making from wood-pulp and artificial silk from wood-fibre, destroy its integral nature; and since trees cannot be grown nearly quickly enough to balance the demand, these industries involve the destruction of natural capital resources. We must learn through necessity to plan and economise such timber resources as we have, and their waste products, and to replace our ephemeral needs of silk stockings and daily papers in some less wasteful way. In the seventeenth century a kind of paper was made from nettles; and also a sort of hemp from stalks of nettle and agrimony. A tendency to waste characterises the transitional stages of technics. The chemists and industrial economists have taught the wasteful blast-furnace owners how to use up their slag-heaps and keep the air clean—converting waste products to wholesome and profitable use: the same process must be taught in rural economy by biologists, botanists and bio-chemists.

It is generally but falsely assumed that the use of local building materials is uneconomical. There has been a want of individual enterprise in using them; but mainly because the local contractor cannot compete against the capitalised organisation which sells concrete, galvanised iron, breeze blocks, patent bricks and the like, he takes to using these in the end to save trouble.

The old craftsmen understood empirically (by instinct and practice) the nature and right use of their material—whether it was wood or metal, glass or colours—and of the power developed from currents of wind and water; and these things are learned again scientifically.

HAPPY THE MAN WHOSE WISH AND CARE
A FEW PATERNAL ACRES BOUND.

CONTENT TO BREATHE HIS NATIVE AIR
IN HIS OWN GROUND.   POPE

THE WHEELWRIGHT
Line engraving by Stanley Anderson

25

The woodman who had a whole idea of his job wasted nothing, except the root of the tree, which would not repay the trouble of excavating. He knew each kind of tree and what it was good for: its right age and season for felling. He put by the pieces of timber for the shipwright and the builder whose natural growth was most suited to their needs: of posts and beams, straight planks, or crooked 'knee-timber.' To-day, the offals of the tree-carcase are burnt and wasted—then, twigs were made into faggots for the baker and the bark was stripped for the tanner.

FURNITURE

The native toughness of oak agrees well with the massive forms and bold designs which were slowly shaped under the tools of primitive English carvers. Yet this toughness, not easily splintered, was as well able to sustain the intricate fret and foliation of the most elaborate rood-screens and canopies of the last Gothic period. But the finer later work is not, like modern church-furniture, made up of thin panels and small posts and quoins; but carved continuously from massive timbers, and so it has a greater dignity and solidity. Other English woods were used—deal and elm, beech, poplar and ash; but owing to its proved durability, oak was used for the richest work until the latter half of the seventeenth century, when walnut began to be used alternatively for furniture, and woods of softer and more even texture for ornamental carving.

Meantime there had been great social and economic changes and the craftsman had passed through great vicissitudes.

"The fifteenth century and the first quarter of the sixteenth were the golden age of the English labourer," reckoning, that is, the wages by their purchasing value of the necessaries of life. The yearly store, which in 1495 was purchased with fourteen weeks' wages, in 1690 costs £14 11s. 6d. and the skilled artisan's wages are only £15 13s. a year and those of a farm hand are about £10 8s. or less. In 1725 the artisan's wages are £15 13s. the year, but the cost of the 1495 subsistence standard is £16 2s. 3d.

From 1805 to 1830 pauperism, which was unknown in the fifteenth century, was common. The Speenhamland Act and the Poor Laws of the early nineteenth century were needed, not to relieve the unemployed, but to relieve those whose full employment did not bring them a living wage.

Until the Reformation, the tradition of carving in wood and in stone, and of the fine crafts generally, was largely the Church's possession. The monasteries had the time, endowment and organisation to practise and teach these crafts: there was constant occasion for their employment, better taste and judgment than can usually be attained by the individual artist or his patron. But now the monks were turned out, each man (if he were lucky) "with a gown and two pounds," to do the best he could in the world.

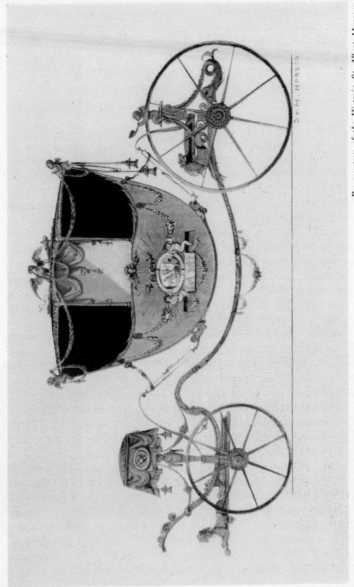

DESIGN FOR A COACH
Late 18th Century

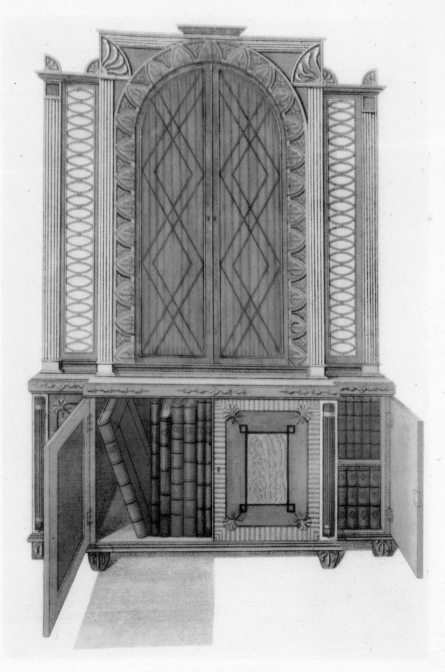

DESIGN FOR A BOOKCASE
Coloured engraving from T. Sheraton's
The Cabinet-Maker, Upholsterer and General Artist's Encyclopaedia, 1804

CEILING DECORATION AT 20 PORTMAN SQUARE, LONDON
Designed by Robert Adam, 1775, and probably painted by Angelica Kauffmann

From about 1540 to 1560 was "a depraved period, when the former Gothic designers were roaming the highways or lurking in the forests of England as vagabonds and outlaws."

Though thus, for want of patronage or teaching, the best part of the tradition was necessarily wasted, there did begin to be some interest in rich furniture, such as hitherto only the houses of the Church had possessed. But those who now had money were ignorant profiteers who did not know how to use it. Next after the Church, the Merchants of East Anglia were the most generous and enlightened builders: they were the next to be ruined by Henry VIII's unscrupulous greed. The silver currency was debased, in 1546, at the rate of eight ounces of alloy to the pound troy: with the result that the wool trade with the Netherlands, which had been the means of building not only many magnificent churches in Norfolk and Suffolk, but town halls and houses of almost equal splendour, was at an end.

There was an end of such magnificent works as the Angel Roof of Blythburgh Church, in which carving and painting together produce a noble effect: it is as though the great beings, whose wings are made like the sides of boats, are sailing through a snowstorm. But alas for the workmen bewitched by Tudor taste, it would be harder to find a much uglier pretentious job than the painted roof of Bere Regis Church, which perpetuates the memory of Cardinal Morton.

The best work of Elizabethan times was incidental to domestic building and furniture. The tendency to barbaric ornament, that is to say rich and gorgeous but comfortless, which is essentially feudal, became modified to a degree of utility and convenience—Elizabethan church-monuments are stiff yet apparently weightless—the surfaces meticulous yet inexpressive. For important works of architecture and decoration foreign artists were employed, of whom the most wholesomely influential seem to have been the French carvers, through whom the spirit of the Renaissance was assimilated, notably in the church woodwork of Devon. The common English work of the time, such as the painted patterns which were a usual adornment of room-walls, was direct and unpretentious, there is no mistaking its native character.

With Inigo Jones (1573-1652) and a generation later Sir Christopher Wren, what may be called the educated style of English Renaissance came to perfection: and their school provided a clearer, more intelligent level of taste than the clumsy imported Baroque. With Wren is associated the most illustrious of all English woodcarvers, Grinling Gibbons. He is said to have been of Dutch extraction, and to have first attracted Royal attention by an immense carved copy, in high relief, of Tintoretto's Crucifixion, with over a hundred figures. To the purist in styles this may seem a flagrant example of a wrong use of wood-carving—but Gibbons was a virtuoso, and was able, by exuberance of fancy and a masterly understanding of

TUDOR PAINTING TO IMITATE CARVING

30

PARGETING ON AN ESSEX HOUSE
Drawing by Mary Cregan

natural forms and of composition, to carry off such *tours de force* as would
have defeated another man. He carved in St. Paul's and in seven City
churches. "Nearly all the mansions of the nobility at this time were decorated to some extent with carvings executed under Gibbons"; who, like
Raphael and Rubens, was not only a supreme master but a successful
organiser of many assistants. Gibbons used principally lime-tree and plane,
and must have handled them with a painter's fluency.

By this time (as readers of John Evelyn's *Silva* are aware) almost every
English forest-tree was known for some useful purpose to the craftsman
or the tradesman—uses which had been learned slowly from French,
German, Flemish and Dutch sources, beside our native traditions. Walnut
was coming to be valued for its beautiful quality either carved or plain, in

31

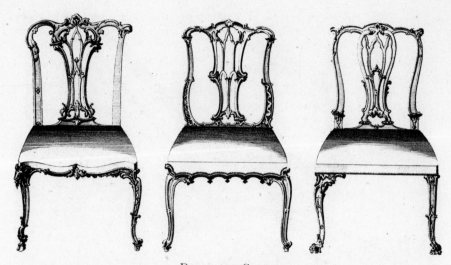

DESIGN FOR CHAIRS
Engraving from Chippendale's *Gentleman and Cabinet Maker's Director*, 1762

the time of Charles II; and in its carving Spanish as well as Flemish influence is to be seen. The art of wood-turning, for balusters and chair- and table-legs, reached its most perfect development in the reign of William and Mary.

This period was notable for another decorative use of wood which, though not newly-invented, was now developed to an extraordinary fineness, and began to predominate over carving: the use of inlay, veneer and marqueterie. This very fine and elaborate surface-decoration was associated with a taste for severe simplicity of general outline and proportion. The work of the great clock-makers, such as Tompion and Knibb, is of this period. But the best clocks are characteristically the plainest.

The extraordinary fashion for Chinese lacquer-painting was developed by English furniture-makers during the eighteenth century. There were perplexing associations of 'Chinoiserie' and romantic Gothic, though of course respectable designers did not mix their styles. The most learned and severe of late eighteenth-century designers is Sir John Soane. But the mind of the time is more typically expressed in the suave and practicable adaptation by the Brothers Adam of Classic ornament to English homes. More than a touch of softness and sentiment is given to some of their best interiors by the decorations of Angelica Kauffmann and Cipriani, whom they employed: while another Italian designer, Pergolesi, produced many of the intricate ornaments known as 'Adam.' The style of the Brothers is not profound in structural principles, but it seems to us, like Jane Austen's, to reflect perfectly the best manners and culture of the day. They had, too, a sound and liberal idea of what was wanted, and their designs which were

BED HANGING

Designed and embroidered by Miss Morris, daughter of William Morris

FORGING BILLHOOKS, SHEFFIELD

Water colour by Thomas Hennell

circulated in the country had a wide influence; though they came in for fierce criticism in their own day. In the same way the great names in furniture, Chippendale, Heppelwhite and Sheraton, are famous not because of particular pieces which can be assigned to their workshops in London, but because they published and circulated pattern-books which were eagerly used by the provincial cabinet-makers. And in those days not only country towns, but even large villages, had their furniture-maker and clock-maker. It was an age when good taste in the ordinary details of life was the rule, and good materials and workmanship were expected before cheapness.

In the period when Burke and Pitt could stir the Commons to deep emotion by an apt line of Latin verse, there was a standard of culture which could afford to use classic allusions for the adornment of living. But not so with the merchant princes who succeeded the old gentry in the main responsibilities of ruling and spending. They were inclined to prefer the Gothic forms to the Grecian, as being appropriate to the industrial feudalism which they maintained. But they had a strong instinct for 'improvement,' for the gorgeous and massive.

Every effort was made to please the new taste. Mahogany had 'come in,' and ormolu, and they soon lost their elegant French airs. Furniture, hangings and upholstery grew more and more impressive, chairs and whatnots, carpets and wallpapers assumed an aggressive, dominating air. They did not need to satisfy contemplation, but they must excite sensations, whether of curiosity, astonishment or intimidation.

This character reflects perhaps the mind of the craftsman, who made the Victorian furniture, no less than that of the patron. The hardest patronage to serve is that which knows not its own mind, which is ambitious and inarticulate, insisting on discordant features which would cover its poverty and ignorance of taste with the appearance of richness and the pretence of learning. The craftsman is irked; he knows not what irks him, but his handiwork communicates the irk. And the Victorian workmen did their best with that willing pride in almost insuperable undertakings which was characteristic of their faith: which made unity of style, of which they were not ignorant, seem of much less consequence to them than it now seems to us, who seek to recover it through perplexity and confusion.

CRAFTS OF IRON

The typical craftsman is master of a whole job. Such a man is Mr. Brunt. His daily work consists of ordinary jobs such as come to the country farrier. But there is a masterly touch about it, which involves a knowledge and sympathy which is rare not only in blacksmiths but in veterinary surgeons. He is great at putting right other men's mistakes. The horse which has been pricked by an unskilful smith, or wrongly doctored, he handles with a steady confidence which seems never to go wrong. He looks after a dozen things beside: the sawmill, carpentry and wheelwright's shop, undertaking and ladder-making, repairing carts, threshing-machines or old lorries, buying bits of junk at country sales and making them work; the small hardware shop where you may buy brushes, paraffin, boot-protectors, kettle-menders and rawlplugs. Other members of the household help to do these things, but Mr. Brunt is there, if necessary, to do any of them as well or rather better.

Then I have in mind another smith, this time a town craftsman; a specialist, yet one whose range is nearly as wide but more concentrated. His work is done in a little stone-built smithy, surrounded on all sides by slag-heaps, furnace-chimneys and vast factories. A hundred years ago, no doubt, there was a heath at this place, traversed by the main road from Sheffield to Dronfield, a hamlet noted then as now for the manufacture of billhooks and axes, and from whence the axe with which Charles I was beheaded is said to have come. This main road passes close beside the smithy, but on a higher level: a steep winding lane which crosses a walled brook, connects them. A few yards beyond is a great viaduct carrying four lines of railway. But the smithy has stood there longer than any nearby building except the ancient Swan Inn, and the still more ancient, and more distant parish church on the hill. A sign-board upon the wall of the smithy which fronts the road, bears this inscription:

ARTHUR HOLMES.
ANVIL FORGER.
HOES, WEEDHOOKS TURNIP-KNIVES
CHISLES ECT.
AGRICULTURAL IMPLIMENTS &
COLLIERY REPAIRS: GENERAL IRONWORK.

Surely a reasonably full list of different jobs to be carried out in a single-room smithy with only one forge, by father and son without any other assistant. And not quite full either, for this smith learnt to shoe horses also within the last four or five years, having had no previous occasion for such work. The 'anvil forger' means one who works upon an anvil, not one who makes anvils. (One may see anvils made at Peter Wright's of Stourbridge and elsewhere: great masses of iron are forged into shape by a drop-hammer in the open air.) All the same, this 'anvil forging' is strenuous and accurate work. Mr. Holmes held the record among Sheffield smiths for making hoes, at the rate of three thousand in a week. The blade of the hoe, and its shank and socket, are wrought from lengths of iron bar: a stout template (made by the smith) is used to form the 'swan-necks' to the right size and curve, and the socket, having been spread flat from the shank, is hammered over an iron mandril to the hollow form that will fit over the wooden handle. Five 'welding-heats' are necessary to complete the union of the

WOODEN DOOR WITH WROUGHT IRON HINGES, 14TH CENTURY
Probably from Dunnington Church, Yorkshire

blade with the shank and socket. When light pieces of metal are heated so much as this, there is the risk of spoiling the work by burning. So the iron is 'soaked,' that is to say heated all through with borax, which prevents it from catching fire.

In this work many objects of the same standard have to be made by hand—for example, several dozen hoes—and the smith saves time by carrying them all through one stage of their making before proceeding to the next. His forge is maintained at the right heat; his tools and materials all ready to hand: his assistant knows exactly what is coming. Then there are some parts which the assistant can do alone, and so make up for his slower working: and they can finish the hoes in collaboration. Where smiths

37

FACE OF A ONE-HAND CLOCK BY BENJAMIN HIGHWORTH, 1740

work like this, the making of each single article becomes a formula—a certain number of blows in accurate sequence of time and direction. All the time the smith watches his material, correcting accidental deviations and when necessary rejecting a faulty piece. He knows his work by heart and, in a great workshop, the sound of other workmen's tools which chime with his own; where each pair of hands carries a certain piece of work through a certain stage only in its making.

Supposing in such a great workshop a machine should go wrong and show signs of inaccuracy or loosening: there will be one of these men at hand who can lay aside his routine job, examine and diagnose the trouble, and with secure confidence make good the damage, even to the extent of making a heavy forging, cutting and fitting it accurately. This man, whose confidence and skill are adaptable to an emergency, will always justify the name of craftsman. But in a little business, and especially where there is accurate work to do, he needs such qualities continually. Not far from the smithy a small factory for aeroplane accessories has been set up. It is well equipped and contains what is called a 'high-speed steel plane.' This often requires new blades—they are like carpenters' plane-irons but must withstand intensely harder strain. A well-tempered blade will last a week or two; a bad one be useless after ten minutes' work. In the factory which makes them they are chilled by a forced blast of cold air. Mr. Holmes

WROUGHT IRON GATE, EARLY 18TH CENTURY

39

ART OF MAKING CLOCKS AND WATCHES
Engraving from the *Universal Magazine*

managed to temper such blades by taking them out of his forge at the right moment of heat, and holding them outside in the tongs, when the right north-east wind was blowing. The craftsman who can thus recognise the simple properties of things, is not to be put out of business by machinery.

All perfectly accurate work has to be done by human hand and eye: the machine can only copy the first accuracy that man has set it to. The copy (like a cast from sculpture) nearly always loses something of the sharp perfection of the original. The maker of the very finest watch, clock, musical or mathematical instrument, or of the best gun, is usually a master working in close contact with a group of very highly-skilled specialists. With so complicated and exact a machine as a watch, over a hundred such specialists were needed in the early nineteenth century, not only because there are many different techniques of handling required, but simply in order to make enough watches, and quickly enough, for the work to be profitable. There are a few famous clocks whose movements have been so abstruse and manifold that the secret of keeping them in order has died with the maker: no succeeding artificer having been able to follow it. As early as the reign of Richard II, an astronomical clock was made by the abbot of St. Albans. "It represented the revolutions of the sun and moon, the fixed stars, and the ebbing and flowing of the sea. When he had finished it, so deficient were we at that time in the knowledge of mechanics, that he was obliged to compose a book of directions for managing and keeping it in order, lest it should be ruined by the ignorance of the monks." In the eighteenth century several church-tower clocks were made by country blacksmiths; there is one in the fine steeple of Ross-on-Wye. The most famous of all clock-makers, Thomas Tompion (who died November 20th, 1713), was originally a farrier.

SILVERSMITH'S WORKSHOP
17th century engraving

INDUSTRIAL REVOLUTION AND DECLINE OF CRAFTS

Through the Industrial Revolution (as Chesterton points out) the word 'master' ceased to mean a man who was master of his craft and came to mean one who was master of others. The meaning of 'shop' changed too. In the eighteenth century a shop was a place where things were made. By degrees the shop-window acquired importance, as the place where goods were put to sell, or at least to attract attention: it assumed and amplified the function of the old hanging signs. Still the work was done on the premises; the master attended to all that was made in the shop and was able to do it himself.

After this came the partnership between this master-craftsman and a business man, who took no part in the actual making, but attended to the very necessary work of book-keeping, reckoning costs and prices, paying accounts and wages, organising the firm's output and extending its connexions. With the introduction of factory machinery and the immense improvement of transport (canals and railways) the labour of those who, with simple methods, had done piece-work in their homes became organised under the direction of the more able and enterprising master-men. With the increasing competition in cheap production which followed, it was almost necessary for the master to expand his business by means of borrowed capital. So, from a partnership of several business men who were not craftsmen, arose the Limited Liability Company.

Thenceforth the character of productions and of producers changed greatly and rapidly. The workman may well be content to work for a master whom he knows, and especially if that master knows how to employ his best abilities. Taking the greater share of gain, the master in return shoulders the major responsibility. If sometimes conscious of injustice, the workman will be jealous for his master's repute. But with him who serves a Limited Company it is otherwise: the character of the work he does may be destroyed, the materials he handles be replaced by inferior ones which are not pleasant to handle, the designs be chosen in ignorant inferior taste; and there is no longer one master to answer for it but a group, and none of them having common ground with him in the Trade.

The Trade Union was the very slow and moderate, but logical answer to the Limited Company and suffers from most of its faults. It gave the workman a defensive weapon of a sort, but at a deplorably heavy cost to his individuality in his calling. He did not necessarily do his work worse, but the work was less interesting, he could not make so much of it. And so he wanted to make out of it, not simply a living, but profits. The manufacturer had become a financier, and presently the workman became a legislator.

These effects of the Industrial Revolution have however their bright and promising aspects. In many ways the large public company is the best employer. Its directors know very well that good working conditions are essential to their standards of work and to their economy. They have gone far to clear up the muddle of the transitional stage of technics. They exceed the requirements of the law in eliminating dangerous and unwholesome employments—whose exploitation was the curse of nineteenth-century industry. Their factories are well-lit and ventilated, their housing is well planned, they contribute to excellent schools, they provide for exercise and amusement on a grand scale—and they stamp out with unbelievable ruthlessness any 'quite legitimate' competition (*e.g.*, the country miller and the

THE CHARCOAL BURNER
Water colour by Vincent Lines

A BLACKSMITH'S FORGE

Water colour by C. Conway

milling combines). In all these things they differ as widely as possible from the magnates who grew rich, or are supposed to have grown rich, upon unending acres of slum, whose corner-stones are the taverns and pawnshops.

Of course no one builds a slum. But it takes us time to realise that a group of makeshift cottages built among the fields, with others added as needed, does at last become a foul area: and that decent houses in a district which has 'declined' from residential to industrial, may, when divided and sub-let by petty usurious landlords, become an even more horrible scandal to the community. These processes of slum-making are by no means abolished. And the small exploiter whether of his premises and capital, or of the labour of others, is the most ruinous and the hardest to control. The petty master, the family company, tend to spend up to their incomes in good years, and to economise in bad years: the great companies through better economy can keep a steadier level and they are better employers.

I have said that, through the nineteenth century, the craftsman's tendency was to lose interest in his work. Yet in many respects the standards of efficiency were improved. Based on science and invention, technical excellence is not only another thing from craftsmanship; it may be even a destroying factor, because it substitutes a mechanical for a human standard. But in a more complete development of technics this fault seems to be righting itself. The worker is better adjusted to the perfection of his machine; the physical as well as the chemical properties of his material (its 'nature' in fact) are more completely understood. But an immense bulk of work produced between 1860 and 1914 and believed to be the best in its day, is only gradually discerned to be in most deplorable, perverted taste. These heavily-capitalised industrial systems have in turn a greater enemy in the State—in the nationalised industries which offer them the alternative which they have offered the small tradesmen: either to be ruined and bought up, or to be salaried managers under the larger unit.

The town of Jarrow became ruined and derelict because the iron-works closed: but total nationalisation is the ruin of continents.

In a famous chapter of *Vision and Design*, Roger Fry makes an analysis of the 'art' which he finds in a railway refreshment room. All that incredibly futile yet incredibly laborious elaboration of ornament in things which would better have been left plain, was done, as Mr. Fry shows, not because its making or contemplation gave pleasure to anyone, but because its absence would be resented by the average man who regards a large amount of futile display as in some way inseparable from the conditions of that well-to-do life to which he belongs or aspires to belong. Yet, he adds, "After years of a purely commercial standard, there is left even now, in the average workman, a certain bias in favour of sound and reasonable workmanship as opposed to the ingenious manufacture of fraudulent and fatuous objects; and if we suppose the immediate pressure of sheer necessity to be removed, it is probable that the craftsman, acting through his guild

45

organisations, would determine to some extent the methods of manufacture."

But, trustworthy and intelligent as the individual workman may prove in his job, he may yet be incapable of guiding his destinies, or bringing in a reform to his ultimate advantage. It is much easier, apparently safer, to patch and compromise with what we have, than to foresee and build a clearer, more purposeful future.

TILE
Designed by William Morris

SOME MODERN REVIVALS: MORRIS AND CO.

William Morris made himself a suit of armour, which (once at least) he wore at dinner with his friends, to their great admiration. This suit of armour has been called, by one who has knowledge in the subject, a tawdry amateur production. But the virtue lay not in the armour, nor yet in the Renascence of Chivalry nor even in Craft Socialism: but in Morris's animating presence inside them, which could make anything convincing. Morris may not have been a good critic of himself, but he had skill in many things, and a whole-hearted regard for any carpenter, weaver or dyer who was truly master of his job.

"It seems to me," said Morris, "that the real way to enjoy life is to accept all its necessary ordinary details and turn them into pleasures by taking interest in them: whereas modern civilisation huddles them out of the way, has them done in a venal and slovenly manner till they become real drudgery which people can't help trying to avoid." This may be a commonplace truth, but it is one which the industrious Victorians were slow to grasp: if ever a man put his principles into practice and enjoyed his work it was Morris. His printed books have lost their hold on a generation brought up to admire self-conscious simplicity. It needs a fresh imagination to feel their magic, their intricate exuberance of decoration. The style and manner of Moxon which corresponded in printing to that of Pugin, Street and Scott in architecture, is more to our taste. But Morris's textiles, the carpets made at Hammersmith and the fabrics woven, dyed and printed at Merton Abbey, do fuller justice to his purely decorative genius. The best of them are the fine flower of their day, the work of one who was by temperament, research and practice a great colourist, unique in his generation. "He actually did create new colours," says a pupil of his, "in his amethysts and golds and greens; they were different to anything I have ever seen; he used to get a marvellous play of colour into them. The amethyst had flushings of red; and his gold (one special sort), when spread out in the large rich hanks, looked like a sunset sky . . . when he ceased to dye with his own hands I soon felt the difference. The colours themselves became perfectly level, and had a monotonous prosy look; the very lustre of the silk was less beautiful. When I complained, he said 'Yes, they have grown too clever at it—of course it means they don't love colour, or they would do it'."

The imitators of Morris's patterns infallibly preferred the subdued and degraded tones of his earlier makeshifts (before he could get the pure and permanent vegetable dyes that he wanted) to his successes—and these degraded imitations found a readier market with well-to-do householders. Morris described an imitation of one of his wall-papers as "a mangy gherkin on a horse-dung ground."

Such imitations are always damaging to works of original and vital design. Writing on an entirely different subject (Paper on Westminster Abbey for Society for Protection of Ancient Buildings, 7th March 1892, quoted by Mackail) and yet to the point, Morris says, "It may seem strange that whereas we can give some distinguished name as the author of almost every injury it has received, the authors of this great epic have left no names behind them. For indeed it is the work of no one man, but of the people of South-Eastern England. It was the work of the inseparable will of a body of men who worked, as they lived, because they could do no otherwise, and unless you can bring these men back from the dead, you cannot 'restore' one verse of their epic. Rewrite the lost trilogies of Aeschylus, put a beginning and an end to the Fight at Finsburg, finish the Squire's Tale for Chaucer, and if you can succeed in that, you may then 'restore' Westminster Abbey."

Morris understood the value, beyond scholarship, of the living tradition and practice. His workmen went through storms with him, they experienced outbreaks of uncontrolled wrath (as did customers sometimes) but they kept lifelong faith to the firm. Even after the designs in use had run to seed, with quite lifeless imitations of Burne-Jones, there was a man at Merton Abbey who could cut and lead in those pieces of gorgeous glass with unrivalled skill; there were dyers who used the deep stone wells of indigo; there was a workman named Chippendale. The firm's affairs, though informally conducted, were not exclusively in the hands of artists and craftsmen. An efficient business manager reckoned its costs and expenses and regulated its prices on an economic scale. Morris left £30,000—the same sum which he had inherited from his father. In the latter days of the firm (the Merton Abbey Works were closed in 1939) the outward symbols of the founder lingered, the patterns that he had designed were still printed, occasionally a tapestry was commissioned for some temple or chapel in America. But the mysteries were growing savourless; the spirit was given over to church-furnishing.

WEAVING AND FABRIC-PRINTING : INDIVIDUAL CRAFTSMEN

Between the time when English weavers abandoned their spinning-wheels and cottage looms, to tend the power-loom and the spinning-jenny in the cloth-mills, and the time when interest in hand-weaving revived, there was a long gap. Meantime much had changed. The introduction of cotton, demanding a mechanised spinning, hastened the Industrial Revolution. Flax no longer was grown and dressed in England: the arts of spinning it and weaving linen by hand had died out too. Fustian (or cotton-and-shoddy) was worn by labourers instead of the linsey-woolsey of two generations earlier. The only obtainable wool-yarn was chemically dyed and machine-spun. The finer sorts of cloth, made in the West of England and at Norwich, were replaced by the products of the Yorkshire cloth-mills. The only traditional hand-weavers to survive in Great Britain were the crofters of Lewis and Harris, and their tweeds had not then been brought into demand in London by West-End tailors.

Morris had not done his own spinning at Merton Abbey, nor weaving except for the silk-tapestry. His Hammersmith carpets were made under the instruction of a carpet-knotter from Dundee. Towards the end of the nineteenth century, weaving began to be revived as a handcraft by Luther Hooper. Already there was hardly an English loom to be found: for these, being made of substantial timbers and requiring as much space as four-poster beds, when they went out of use were soon broken up. Hooper, perhaps naturally following Morris's Norse sympathies, adopted the Swedish loom which has ever since been the one most used by English revivers of weaving.

An Englishwoman who deserves mention here is Miss Hobhouse, who devoted her life to reconstruction after the Boer War. She taught spinning to the homeless Dutch girls in orphanages which were then founded: and for this purpose a shipload of old family spinning-wheels was collected and sent to her from Switzerland. But of her teaching and influence there remains, it is said, not a trace.

Perhaps Luther Hooper's revival might have faded likewise, but for one or two vigorous successors. Hooper had woven on a warp of mercerised

48

TAPESTRY DESIGNED AND WOVEN BY WILLIAM MORRIS

cotton; he had stuck to Swedish patterns such as the 'Rosepath' and 'Honeysuckle'—which, though charming in their original vitality, became presently insipid through repetition, patterns being made and sold for 'students'' copies. Mrs. Ethel Mairet (whom Hooper taught to weave about 1900) delved more deeply to the roots of the subject and, in finding out about hand-spinning, came to recognise the still living traditions of Central Europe as more vital and important than the Swedish.

Mrs. Mairet has broken fresh ground in spinning and weaving in wool, silk—even in cellophane: her exquisite taste and great knowledge are further expressed in her writing.

Miss Jean Milne is a really important weaver of rugs: the process is slow and therefore her rugs are rare. Her vegetable dyes are of the very best, pattern and technique of the first order. Some years ago she started a village industry in Skye: rugs in natural colours, called Shiant Rugs. Messrs. Kilbride and Brocklehurst, who weave church vestments, Elizabeth Peacock, and many other good weavers, are working in England to-day.

Miss Kendon of Uckfield, like Cecil Sharpe in music, has collected folk traditions in her craft; and by visiting the last surviving spinners and weavers of Wales, Ireland and Scandinavia, she has acquired their several methods in spinning and weaving, and in making and using vegetable dyes. In this way, methods on the point of extinction, yet still capable of beautiful development, are kept alive: such craftsmen may seem unpractical (as the early technical inventors seemed) but they are the pioneers of a new impulse in culture and in education.

In a letter about the gap between the weaving tradition and the revival, Miss Kendon writes:

"I really think we are too near it to see it properly. It seems to me that ever since Morris (and I think Ruskin tried to do something with the Lakeland spinners didn't he?) there have been various groups of people such as the Rural Industries Bureau, the Red Rose Guild, Omega Workshops, Dartington, Artificers' Guild, Guild of Weavers and Spinners, etc., etc., who have all tried in various ways to fit the craftsman, traditional or otherwise (there's the Highland Home Industries for traditional work), into the present state of affairs. Although all of these groups may have had their uses, not one of them seems to me ever to have pulled anything off, therefore we have reached no sure land from which we can look back to view the gap. (I don't, of course, include Morris and individual people in that sweeping statement.) I suppose not one of us is making anything which, to the superficial eye, cannot be made more cheaply by machine, therefore we appear as 'something fancy.' I think that one day, of necessity, we shall fit in again. And when things happen of necessity it is because the time is really ripe. In the meantime I think there is no need to fear starvation—or perhaps the more one is a craftsman the less one fears it.

"Then, thinking particularly of the weavers. Although, since we were the first country to become mechanized, the gap has been long, and we have lost much of the technical skill of the traditional weavers, I think no mere lapse of time could ever kill in us our inherited feeling for wool. It has been an unbroken growth since the Norman Conquest, or if you like, since we were rid of wolves, and it persists in the cloth woven in the West of England Mills still, as well as in individual weavers. One only has to handle a countryman's covert shooting jacket, the pink coat of a huntsman, and the cloth of a billiard table to realise that. There is no cloth in the world to touch it, except Rodier's stuffs which, being French, don't come into the question. After all, it is a great thing to have inherited an understanding of one's raw material. Given that, the gap in technical knowledge matters really very little."

By specialising within narrow limits in work for which they discover a peculiar gift, artists succeed occasionally in placing their work above commercial competition. Miss Barron and Miss Larcher produced their hand-blocked linen, which used occasionally to be exhibited in London, at

BLOCKS CUT FOR TEXTILE PRINTING
Designed by P. Barron and D. Larcher, using felt on wood, lino on wood,
wood and rubber blocks

Painswick, Gloucestershire, until 1940. In their way they had no rivals. Deeply learned in tradition, in dye-substances, and in printing from every kind of block—from the early French pearwood studded with brass pins to modern cuts from rubber—they could produce perfectly all the effects proper to their materials. And, which makes them important as interior decorators, they can evolve a print which is exactly right for the scale and character of any particular room.

Allan Walton is well known as a designer of fabrics: Paul Nash is a distinguished designer for this and other industrial uses, including patterned glass and typography. Enid Marx has engraved lovely patterns on wood: her end-papers for the Curwen Press are familiar as book covers. That firm made a trial of printed wall-papers from the designs of chosen artists. The painter Edward Bawden, who made some outstanding ones, later experimented independently; cutting the blocks, grounding the rolls of cartridge-paper with distemper beautifully laid in the tradition of the eighteenth century, and printing by hand. He was joined by another landscape-painter of Bardfield, John Aldridge. There may yet be a revival of interest in this least expensive and potentially lovely form of wall-decoration.

Aldridge's sober harmonies of ivy-blue and brown-purple, of lilac and cream, are peculiarly agreeable to English eyes: till 1941 he made designs for printed fabrics, using floral and organic forms with sensitive vigour.

51

Given encouragement, no doubt British designers can do at least as well as any to be found in Europe.

The last important move however to establish artists as industrial designers was made in 1935 by Mr. T. A. Fennemore of Messrs. Brain Ltd., Stoke-on-Trent (who has since become Director of the Central Institute). Some beautiful china-ware was exhibited at Harrods: artists such as Sutherland and Ravilious had engraved their own designs, which were printed as transfers. But the movement was opposed by other large London stores, which did their best to put off the market what might reduce the demand for their regular stock. The fashion was being changed too quickly.

POTTERY AND THE OMEGA WORKSHOPS

While the last descendant of the last Spitalfields weaver was weaving the last Burne-Jones tapestry at Merton Abbey, in France a Post-Impressionist painter, Dufy, was producing designs of astonishing vigour and beauty for the silk-weavers of Lyons. In England, habits of taste and the fallacious axioms of commerce have hindered us from appreciating good designers and from introducing them, as the French have done, into our manufacturing firms. Good artists are not unemployable, though to employ them wisely and profitably may require special patience and intelligence.

Josiah Wedgwood, by getting Flaxman to design some of his choicest pieces, set an example to the Staffordshire pottery firms which they have not yet forgotten. From time to time his example has been followed, but not always successfully. The artist ought to be allowed to work directly, and to teach what other hands may do: for his designs when translated by the busy accustomed hand of the shop-engraver and the china paintress lose their forceful spirited character, acquiring the look of stock productions. This obviously wastes the expense and the point of employing good artists.

Although during the nineteenth century, after the Exhibitions of '51 and '62, art was distrusted by manufacturers—or rather, what was called 'art' produced forms of complicated exuberance, as though workmanship were to be stimulated by being made more difficult of execution—there were outstanding individual exceptions; attempts from time to time to revive and reanimate the making of beautiful things which, if never common, were once the crown of common things, but which now are rarities whose place in life is hard to find. Alfred Stevens, who improved his native gift by seven years' single-minded study in Italy, until he was our greatest sculptor and decorative designer, not only planned great monuments and paintings which he was seldom allowed to carry out; but he designed plates and vases for Messrs. Minton, silver-work, architectural ornament, even carrying the nobility of classic design into the stoves and fire-irons which were produced by several Sheffield firms about 1851.

Design for a Covered Vase
Water colour drawing by Alfred Stevens

Another great Victorian artist, Watts—whose taste was formed by study in Italy—made a more impersonal and in a sense more permanent contribution to industry. With Mrs. Watts' very active help, he established a village industry at Compton, Surrey, where it was his aim to produce such vessels and ornaments of ordinary use as are made by village craftsmen in Italy, much as they were made in the days of the High Renaissance. The Compton pottery and terra-cotta industry still survives. There were some associated crafts, embroidery, plaster-work and stencilling. But it needs a very vigorous and independent genius to enlarge the scope of such an industry beyond the imitation of ancient or foreign patterns, and where the craft is so definitely organised it may well remain limited, overshadowed by the tutelary reputation.

Meanwhile there are a number of British traditions in village crafts—such as King's Pottery, Verwood, Hampshire, where earthenware vessels, pitchers and mugs are made as they were made in Queen Elizabeth's day. At Winchcomb, Gloucestershire, is another old pottery which was taken over and completely reanimated by the genius and enterprise of a Cornish potter, Michael Cardew.

Other English potteries which once produced homely yet beautiful vessels of brown 'salt-glaze' have been degraded by close competition till now they only make drain-pipes or ginger-beer bottles. Such manufacture requires even more exact control to make every article uniform, but the workman's fancy, and apparently all scope for enjoyment of the work, is sacrificed to efficiency in a narrowly commercial sense. But perhaps this dullness is transitory; some very splendid earthenware vessels have been made for use by Imperial Chemical Industries. These mark a stage in the adjustment of good design to large-scale economic production.

To satisfy the very limited demands of careful taste in the potter's art, Messrs. Staite Murray, Bernard Leach and Kenneth Murray have developed stoneware pottery, from the practical study of Oriental methods. Their works are characteristic products of the best contemporary English culture and feeling. No longer, however, are these arts limited by national or even European traditions. We may seek inspiration equally from Mexico or Korea, from Benin or Hawaii. No sooner is the cult extinct of those gods of wood and stone, which two generations ago we should most zealously have destroyed, but we learn to read in them the handiwork of vigorous primitive artists, and they become the models and the inspiration of our more advanced art. We send our best potters to re-instruct the Gold Coast natives, instead of sending them missionaries. Perhaps, in return, these Africans may send us the next messengers of Christian revival.

So great has been the circulation and exchange of works of art internationally, both of current and historical examples, that local classification becomes impossible. Royal Academicians may maintain an attitude of provincial isolationism, but many provincial and colonial artists are abreast of modern exploration and well informed as to what has been and is being done. There is, too, more intelligent curiosity about art than there was some years ago. People are no longer scandalised, or moved to fury or ridicule about works which they have not learned to understand; they are more willing to look and to understand. In adult education, many societies and councils have been active in stimulating interest; and slowly, very slowly, the appreciation of unfamiliar art, and even the exercise of an unwanted faculty, is roused and directed. From about 1925, there was a great change in the attitude of the Board of Education to the subject of art teaching and pictures in schools. Hitherto the inspectors of schools had bowed to the opinion of 'eminent artists' and had chosen works which were to form the taste of the rising generation for the sake of subject rather than treatment. Their standard was that of the Chantrey Bequest selectors between 1890 and 1914, with some illustrations of natural history and a leavening of Old Masters in the form of Medici colour prints. But now the professional artist began to be 'debunked'; not only were painters beginning to be accepted whose intentions and methods had lately been thought outrageously bad and incompetent, but children were found able to produce pictures and designs which by the initiated were found no less exciting and 'alive.' The effects were not exclusively academic. A Manchester firm produced some cotton-prints from patterns which had been cut by children.

54

BOWL DECORATED BY ERIC RAVILIOUS AND PLATE BY MICHAEL CARDEW
Oil painting by Beryl Sinclair

For a moment it seemed that an ideal was coming true: that art, instead of being the occupation and amusement of a few individuals, was a common right, a common power, if only it might be allowed to live.

One of the immediate inspirers of this minor revolution in taste was Roger Fry, whose Omega Workshops were an outstanding experiment in

BLUE GLAZED COVERED BOWL
Designed and made in the Omega Workshops

producing works of domestic utility to which the skill and taste of the best available artists had been devoted. Fry's genius was more successful in planning and inspiring than in maintaining what he had established, and after his works, opened in 1913, had survived the war of 1914-1918, he closed them in 1919, when the experiment no longer seemed to him worth the effort; though probably a more efficient business man would have succeeded in it.

Fry's idea was that the furniture, fabrics and interior decoration under-taken by himself and his colleagues should be carried out with pleasure to themselves, and that thus it should not only be in good taste, but should communicate the joy of artistic creation. His capital being narrowly limited he paid his colleagues at a very low rate, and this, with the fact that such work brought them no personal reputation, caused a secession of his first disciples. There were many jobs which none of them could do. They could not make chairs and tables, but had to contract for them with small trades-men in by-streets; and then the surfaces of wood were painted in the shops. Sometimes the making was shoddy, and sometimes the methods of decora-tion were not all they should have been—but this amateurishness was gradually righted. One who worked in Omega during its last two years

56

declares that both the structure and decoration of its furniture were by then of the best and soundest that could be procured.

The Omega fabrics, which included rugs, embroidery, woven and block-printed patterns, were an intelligent and spirited application to domestic use of some special decorative qualities of Post-Impressionist painting. Some were inspired by those forms based on Negro art which Picasso had developed in painting about 1905-1912. Half a dozen distinguished painters were among their designers; they showed interest in surface ornament rather than in design of structural utility. Fry's personal touch found most favourable scope in making and decorating pots. He learned the methods at Poole Potteries and such were his instinct and his taste that pieces which the professional potter would have rejected as not accurately conforming to his standard became in Fry's hands objects worthy of any museum.

CONCLUSION

A revival must essentially be the work of individuals, finding for themselves the thing they seek. It cannot be imposed from without. One cannot endow a revival; except to the extent of providing open opportunities for the individual. Craftsmen cannot be recruited by public advertisement nor by asking men about to be demobilised to write their names on a list: for if so the standard of work will not be high enough to make the revival succeed. There are also economical methods which can be applied within a group of efficient craftsmen, and which can defeat the outside pressure of the commercial system. Such a group needs a good clerk and accountant, but there is no room for usurers and manipulators.

The crafts which are taught in art and technical schools are subsidised by the trades which are to employ the craftsmen. The trades are advised as to what is wanted by their commercial travellers; and thus is determined the character of the work favoured by the teachers. These teachers mainly do nothing but teach; they are rarely practical designers. Only a small proportion of their students do ever become industrial designers; of these a few are strong enough to follow their own convictions. In the exceptional cases where really good practising designers have given part of their time to teaching, the students' work has been admirably transformed, and such practice ought to be the rule. Fine pieces of craftsmanship of the great periods of art ought to be accessible: in order that they may instruct students' taste, and be regarded as things possible to make, not simply as museum exhibits. Taste can only develop slowly and with difficulty: it is even less likely to be found in advisory committees of taste than in the juries of the Royal Academy or the Salon.

Reform of taste begins only in life—the world to-day has to live more dangerously, more realistically, closer to the roots of production, than it has lived for more than a century. At the moment when domestic life has greatly deteriorated, communal life becomes possible and organised: a common active need (though one of self-defence) replaces the axioms of waste leisure, and may go some way towards shaming the false and venal out of existence—in art, music and literature. Investments have become less substantial; work, especially in farm and field, has become again a common and wholesome means of livelihood: one which must quicken our sense of values.

The true master of his craft is one who has a comprehensive and at the same time simple idea of it, so that first things come first and other things in due order of importance, for in machinery as in the other arts harmony of the whole is much more important than elaboration of particular details. The great surgeon John Hunter, if he could return to practice, would no doubt be required to spend several years in bringing his technical knowledge up to date, before he was allowed to perform an operation. Yet it would be much easier for him to learn this, than for a modern specialist to acquire Hunter's essential scope of idea. In the same period of time man has, by applying the sciences of mathematics, physics and chemistry, immensely extended his accurate control of matter. He can determine, measure and utilise materials and temperatures which are far beyond the immediate range of his senses.

So it may appear that the craftsman's skill finds its place to-day in proving and perfecting what may be called the hand and eye of the machine. Great mechanical skill exists, but it is much rarer than two or three centuries ago, and it seems less adaptable, and less often associated with great inventive powers. The individual does not recapitulate all the steps of evolution. The old blacksmith, when set the riddle, "How did they make the first hammer?" replied at last, after deep thought, "They must have found an old un." The London mechanic to-day, who could probably give a better account than this of technical evolution, may none the less feel that he has lost something good which the country workman possesses. He may lack the immediate sense of his materials, the readiness to turn them to whatever use the occasion demands. The hand of the craftsman is recognisable in the quality of life and the unity which develops under it.

BRITISH

FURNITURE MAKERS

BY

JOHN GLOAG

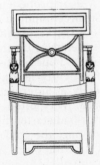

THE BACKGROUND OF SKILL

FOR many centuries woodworkers in England have established and enlarged a reputation for skill. They began to acquire a mastery of their craft many generations before the Norman Conquest, and from the pooled knowledge of woodman, shipwright and carpenter arose a profound and enduring comprehension of the characteristics of timber. In a country with many large forests, the woodman, or wood-reeve, was a highly skilled judge of the merits of the raw material available for architecture and shipbuilding; while the carpenter and the joiner were the principal craftsmen, for nearly everything was built of wood, and the abundant forests of Britain provided such sturdy and lasting timber as oak and ash. Century after century, the woodworker's knowledge of his material deepened; he acquired a sympathetic understanding of its limitations and possibilities; unlike European craftsmen, he never willingly forced it to perform highly decorative tasks that disguised or ignored its natural qualities. The influence of that ancient partnership with the woodman remained. In periods when the furniture craftsman has been allowed to solve problems in his own simple, direct way, and to make the best use of the materials that grew in the English countryside—not only oak and ash, but yew, elm, beech and such fruit woods as cherry and apple—he has produced tables and chairs and chests that reflect the pride and pleasure he took in his work, and the serene satisfaction of living fully that such work provided. Consequently the furniture of those happy and far-off times when the craftsman was left to himself, has a rich and unmistakable humanism; not the scholarly humanism of the accomplished designer, dedicated to the service of classical taste; not the self-conscious rusticity imposed by some passing fashion; but an honest and consistent acknowledgment of the needs of good living and common sense.

Unfortunately the furniture-makers have seldom been left to their own skilled ways. Fashions have been imposed on them from abroad; modish freaks of taste have battened on their skill; wealth has outrun education, and patrons have insisted on vulgar profusion, and this latter disaster has happened twice during the last three hundred and fifty years—at the end of Elizabeth's reign and throughout the Victorian period. After the late seventeenth century, the town craftsmen gave up the struggle for independence: thereafter they were the humble and obedient servants of fashion, their skill directed by designers who, frequently lacking an intimate knowledge of materials, used craftsmen merely as interpreters of ideas that were born and bred on the drawing board. Very often these master designers were architects, like William Kent, or had started life as craftsmen, like Thomas Chippendale. Thus began not only the golden age of the great cabinet-makers, but the separation of drawing office from workshop which at first limited the craftsman and eventually eliminated him from the main development of the furniture industry. To-day he survives only as a copyist, using his skill to imitate antique models, or as an isolated artist-craftsman, designing and making original furniture for a few discriminating patrons, and acting, unconsciously, as a research worker in design. Only the country craftsmen retained their independence throughout the eighteenth and early nineteenth centuries: they created their own variations and simplifications of town fashions, still using the timber of the countryside, oak, ash, elm and the fruit woods, while the great cabinet-makers of London were producing luxurious and lovely things in walnut and mahogany or, towards the end of the golden age, in satinwood and rosewood.

From the days of the mediaeval makers of benches and chests to the close of the Georgian period, standards of furniture design were developed in England that have not yet been surpassed, nor even equalled. It is the purpose of this book to indicate the rise, decline and revival of skill in the making and designing of furniture from the Middle Ages to our own century. The story lies mainly in England, for during the Middle Ages the need for fortification gradually diminished, architectural knowledge increased, and town and country houses were built for comfort rather than for safety, thus giving English woodworkers opportunities for furniture making that were denied to such regions as Scotland and Wales, where the rigours of militarised life still oppressed lord and peasant alike, long after the moats of fortified manors in England had been filled in and transformed into gardens, and their windows broadened to let in light.

17TH CENTURY CHAIR OF RAISED VELVET
IN THE CARTOON GALLERY AT KNOLE
Drawing by H. Shaw from Meyrick's *Specimens of Ancient Furniture,* 1836

COMMODE BY ROBERT ADAM
IN THE COUNTESS OF DERBY'S DRESSING ROOM, OSTERLEY PARK
Coloured engraving by B. Pastorini, 1770
From *The Works in Architecture of Robert and James Adam, Esqs.*
By courtesy of the Trustees of the British Museum

THE AGE OF THE CRAFTSMEN

Sixteen hundred years ago, when Britain was a Roman province, houses had been furnished with luxury and provided with nearly every modern convenience, from hot and cold running water to central heating. The type of furniture used in Romano-British homes is recorded on various sepulchral monuments. Those preserved in the Yorkshire Museum show couches and tables with curved legs, and on one, inscribed to Julia Velva, there is a figure seated in what appears to be a basketwork armchair. But the material accomplishments of Roman civilisation in architecture and furnishing never became part of our English heritage: they did not survive the barbarian invasions and settlements of the fifth and sixth centuries. After this period of barbarism civilisation gradually recovered, but many generations passed before it rose again above a crude agricultural level. Five hundred years later Geoffrey of Monmouth mournfully records in his *British History* that the country "was formerly adorned with eight and twenty Cities, of which some are in Ruins and Desolate" and Gerald de Barri—Giraldus Cambrensis—also writing in the twelfth century, describes the ruined baths, temples and palaces in the deserted Romano-British city of Caerleon.

For over four centuries before the Conquest the English kingdoms were established; and it was during those centuries that the foundations of English craftsmanship in wood were laid. Even Danish raids, and the overthrow of the great artistic culture of Northumbria, did not arrest this steady growth of skill. Much of it was devoted to the building of ships and churches; houses were either military strongpoints or glorified huts; only the simplest type of furniture was made and it was generally built into the framework of the house. For example, beds were mere bunks built against the wall, "shut-beds" as they were called, for they had heavy wooden shutters which could be closed and fastened at night. The independent bedstead was a rarity, even in Norman times.

The earliest piece of independent furniture was the chest; this was usually of the dug-out type, hollowed or burnt out of a single log, and fitted with a lid. When chests became a little more elaborate, the carpenter and the smith worked as partners, the former shaping the necessary boards, the latter making iron bands to hold them together, also hinges for the lid and a strong lock for fastening it down. Chests were used not only as receptacles, but as seats. The only other seats were benches and stools. Tables were either chunks of wood, rather like butchers' blocks, or else boards elevated on trestles.

Only in the palaces and castles of the nobility was there any suggestion of elaboration in furnishing, and few people apart from the great ecclesiastics had any pretensions to taste in such matters. But as law and order were established in Norman England, and the anarchy that had

63

followed the Conquest was replaced by stable conditions of life, the military aspect of building became less important. Furniture design has always been influenced by architecture, and the opportunities of furniture makers for experiment have been conditioned by the opportunities given to architects and builders; so in the thirteenth and fourteenth centuries, furniture emerges from a crude utility period, becomes stiffly dignified, luxurious only in terms of decoration, but remains uncomfortable.

In the fifteenth century, chairs appeared, rigid, box-like designs, with high backs; but another type of chair with an X-shaped frame came into use during the fourteenth century. (An example of this type was preserved in the vestry of York Minster.) The X-shaped frame supported a cushioned seat, and the back was framed by a piece of stretched fabric. It was the first structural partnership between wood and textiles; it was the great-ancestor of every comfortable chair in use to-day; but it was three hundred years before its possibilities were appreciated.

By the close of the fifteenth and the beginning of the sixteenth century, town and country houses were conveniently equipped: beds were comfortable, independent pieces of furniture, though bedding was often used without a framework, the bed being made up direct on the floor. Trestle tables and benches were still used, and chests had become larger and better finished, and were supplemented by standing cupboards.

The front panels of chests were sometimes elaborately carved, and they often reflected the characteristic lines of contemporary architecture, reproducing the severe geometric tracery of Perpendicular Gothic windows. That witty and most readable authority on costume and fashion, James Laver, has suggested that many parallels exist between the costume and architecture of a period. He tells us that "the fifteenth century pointed shoe and the so-called 'steeple' head-dress echo the Gothic pointed arch." He develops this theory in a paper on *Fashion and War*, read before the Royal Society of Arts, March 1, 1944, and quotes several other supporting examples. But there has always been an even greater affinity between furniture and architecture. Those "blind" Gothic windows on the fronts of fifteenth century chests and standing cupboards and on tall chair backs were not the only ornamental forms employed by furniture makers at the end of the Middle Ages. Occasionally the fronts of chests were embellished with heraldic devices, geometric roundels of chip carving, and, more rarely, hunting or battle scenes. The linenfold pattern was extensively used, this representing the severely formalised folds of the linen which a chest so often accommodated. In many of these early chests, a ledge is found near the top, for the dried herbs, lavender or woodruff, which were used for scenting the contents.

Most of this late mediaeval and early Tudor furniture was made in oak, though other woods were used, such as elm, ash and beech. By the end of the fifteenth century, a recognisable English style was emerging, sturdy,

OAK CHEST, THIRTEENTH CENTURY
Said to have come from a Church in Hampshire

simple, and appropriately ornamented. But its development was checked, and its forms distorted, by the first of a series of invasions by foreign fashions.

Only furniture made for the farmhouse or cottage was immune from the effect of the "Italianate" fashions that began to attract the English nobility and which wholly dominated their taste during the latter part of the sixteenth century. Reluctantly, English craftsmen were compelled to abandon their native ideas: the formalised beauty of the linen-fold pattern, the flowing lines of the vine leaf ornament, the subtle use of tracery, the skilful employment of the chamfer to break the variation of surface between a panel and the framework that enclosed it, the freedom to use wood to the best advantage and to use ornament for emphasising the lines which structural necessity had determined—all such knowledge and liberty of invention arising from the practice of a craft, were discarded. The craftsman was having his first taste of the serfdom that fashion imposes, and if we may judge from his rendering of the forms demanded by modish taste, he was actively rebellious. The classical architecture of Rome had been revived in Italy, and the effect of the Italian Renaissance had spread across Europe, but in England neither architects nor craftsmen understood its real significance. They were unaware that the classic orders of architecture represented a system of design, and for over a century they regarded those orders, Tuscan, Doric, Ionic, Corinthian and Composite, as so much material for decoration. They never mastered their proportions, and corpulent variations of them masqueraded as table legs and bed posts, and disfigured the massive heads of beds.

In the palaces of the nobility, and in the great country houses of the new rich merchant class, furniture became more plentiful. Chests and tables were elaborately decorative: there were standing cupboards, sideboards or buffets, stools and benches. Chairs were still rare. All this furniture was of oak, much of it was overloaded with carving, but the article which attained the greatest elaboration was the bed. This was more than a piece of furniture; it was almost an independent building, and it provided a room within a room. Its heavy canopy, or tester, was supported by tall posts in front, which bore a bloated resemblance to Ionic columns, and the head was a framework of oak enriched with carving, the upper part of it often filled by arcaded panels, separated by boldly carved figures on the uprights of the framing. From the tester, curtains were hung, and at night the occupants were enclosed in this airless cave of wood and fabric. The tradition of the Anglo-Saxon "shut-bed" was thus perpetuated; it survived until late in the nineteenth century. This excessive devotion to stuffiness, which used to be called cosiness, may be partly attributable to the climate, and partly to the draughts which have always haunted the rooms of English houses.

Like the beds, sixteenth century tables were massive and the early Tudor trestle form was abandoned in favour of four, six or eight legs according to the length. These legs, like the bed posts, would reproduce the vague likeness of an Ionic column, but they would swell out into melon-shaped bulbs, which would be covered with elaborate carving. The simple functional solution produced by furniture makers in the late fifteenth and early sixteenth centuries, of two legs which supported the table top, and gained their stability by being set solidly into broad bases, horizontally tied by stretchers, was replaced by the clumsy, many-legged table required by fashion, which provided the maximum discomfort for those seated at it, but also provided the maximum possibility for the ornate semi-classical carving which was so popular with the new rich. By the opening of the seventeenth century, wealth had outrun education, and taste was dominated by a desire for vulgar display.

Only in country homes, farmhouses and small manor houses was furniture to be found which still preserved the satisfying early Tudor simplicities of form, uncomplicated by foreign influence. Here, trestle tables and stout stools called "joyned" or joint stools would furnish the great kitchen-living rooms of the farm. Chests that had been in the family for generations would still be in use, and new furniture would be made by the local carpenter as need arose. The competence of the local craftsman was impressive: he could turn his hand to any kind of woodwork, from the oak framing necessary for a complete house, to the simple turned work needed for the legs of a stool. William Harrison, in his *Description of England*, praises English carpenters, and says they are "worthilie preferred before those of like science among all other nations." Another contemporary tribute, concerning the pleasantness and general equipment of the English home, comes from a Dutch

CARVED OAK BEDSTEAD, MIDDLE OF THE SEVENTEENTH CENTURY
From Queensbury, Yorkshire

physician, Dr. Levinus Lemnius, who wrote an account in Latin of a visit to England, which was translated and published in London in 1581 under the title of *The Touchstone of Complexions*. He said, among other complimentary things: "the exquisite finenisse, the pleasaunte and delightfull furniture in every poynt for household, wonderfully rejoysed mee . . ." His visit took place before the exuberant love of colour and decoration that characterised the Elizabethan period had degenerated into an urgent appetite for visible riches.

Between 1580 and 1630, large town and country houses were furnished with chests, sideboards, buffets, court cupboards, joint stools, and tables with turned legs, wooden armchairs, and even small chairs with upholstered seats and backs. These small chairs were originally designed to accommodate that extravagant garment, the farthingale. They were without arms, so that ladies encircled by that spreading cartwheel of fabrics could sit without discomfort. This was one of the first examples of the direct influence of costume on furniture design, and no doubt drew a fresh grumble from sorely tried craftsmen.

67

Apart from the farthingale type, chairs made no concessions to the human form or the extraordinary clothes that bedecked it. Seats were hard, backs were upright, and although they were less heavy and clumsy than the early Tudor box-type, they lacked elegance. Even the upholstery on the farthingale chair was greatly inferior to the deeply-sprung heavily-stuffed upholstery of modern times. There was one luxurious development: the X-shaped type of chair that had appeared in mediaeval times was revived, broadened, fitted with a deep, loose cushion, and covered completely, back, underframe and arms, in velvet or some other rich material. Tasselled fringes trimmed the seat and arms, and the close-covering fabric was secured to the framework by round-headed nails of gilded brass. Such chairs were seldom seen outside palaces: they had a regal air, and Charles I sat in one of this type during his trial.

The court cupboard was not unlike an enclosed buffet or sideboard, but instead of having three open shelves, supported by columns, it had a big cupboard in the lower part, and small cupboards above, set back to form a shelf. Above these small cupboards, the top projected like a canopy, and was sometimes upheld by columns rising from the shelf. The huge bedsteads became still more elaborate, bearing an ever increasing load of carved ornament. It almost seemed as though nobody could bear the sight of an empty space on any piece of furniture.

Chests became more commodious, and presently the mule chest evolved. This had two drawers fitted in the base, with the usual lidded receptacle above. It was the forerunner of the chest of drawers. During the 1620's, the gate-legged table was invented, an ingenious combination of hinged flaps and hinged legs, which developed many variations during the seventeenth century.

The Puritan period, through which England passed in the middle of the century, had a great effect upon the form of all furniture. Fashion and luxury were considered officially sinful, and to the prying bureaucrats of the Commonwealth highly ornamented furniture was indisputable evidence of sin. Furniture makers everywhere were released from their perplexing thraldom to alien forms of ornament. Once again, the native genius of the English craftsman was released to work in its own way, with inspired common sense and with an unshakable respect for fitness. Even under a Puritan government, some concessions were made to ornament, for ornament is an old human need, and cannot be denied satisfaction. Great developments took place in turning, and chair legs and table legs assumed many delicate and delightful shapes, including the famous "barley sugar" twist. Bobbin turning was a favourite form of ornament for table legs, and split bobbins were sometimes applied to the face of chests and cupboards. Of all the misunderstood architectural forms which had afflicted furniture in the late Elizabethan and early Stuart periods, only arcaded decoration remained in favour, and usually took the form of panels filled by round arches.

OAK GATE-LEGGED TABLE, SEVENTEENTH CENTURY

Early in the seventeenth century, a new technique of decoration came into use. Patterns were formed on chair backs and occasionally on panels and friezes of cupboards by inlaying such woods as holly and sycamore. The standard of finish for such work was rather crude, except with "None-such" chests. The front panels of these chests were embellished with highly conventionalised pictures of the Royal Palace of Nonesuch at Cheam in Surrey, formed by inlays of decorative woods. This famous building, with its pointed towers, was as familiar to Englishmen in the sixteenth and seventeenth centuries as the Crystal Palace was to later generations. It is not certain that these Nonesuch chests were of English workmanship, though they may have been made in this country by French or Flemish craftsmen. The development of this form of inlaying, known as marquetry, was delayed until late in the seventeenth century; its progress was checked by the Puritan ban on luxury and ornament. The Puritans liked austerity for its own sake. They stopped the use of costly embroidered fabrics, trimming braid and tasselled fringes. But the period was not without benefit. Apart from liberating the natural inclinations and abilities of woodworkers, it purified taste by encouraging a return to the bare structural bones of such articles as chairs and tables.

69

During the middle years of the century, a new type of chair was produced, a combination of wood and leather. The seats and backs of such chairs were formed by leather, stretched across the wooden framework, and nailed to it with brass-headed nails. Although rather severe in aspect, they were comfortable, and the seats were slightly wider than the hard-seated oak chairs of late Elizabethan times. In addition to the gate-legged table, other space-saving devices were invented; for example, the table-chair, which was an armchair with a hinged, circular back. This back could swing over and lie supported on the arms, thus forming a small table.

With the end of the Puritan period, we come also to the end of the great period of English furniture making in oak. So far as personal craftsmanship was concerned, it was the true end of the Middle Ages. Thereafter, woods of richer decorative qualities, English walnut and mahogany from the New World, replaced the material with which the English craftsman had served his long apprenticeship. Oak was still used in the country, and many a fine manor in the eighteenth century retained its earlier furnishing; and in the cottages, oak chests and stools, benches and tables, were handed down from father to son, generation after generation. That boisterous advocate of everything English, William Cobbett, was still praising the durable qualities of oak some hundred and seventy years after the end of what has been aptly called "The Age of Oak." In his *Cottage Economy*, published in 1822, he wrote, "In *household goods* the *warm*, the *strong*, the *durable*, ought always to be kept in view. Oak-tables, bedsteads, and stools, chairs of oak or of yew-tree, and never a bit of miserable deal board. Things of this sort ought to last several life-times. A labourer ought to inherit something besides his toil from his grandfather."

NONESUCH CHEST, LATE SIXTEENTH CENTURY
Oak, inlaid with Marquetry

70

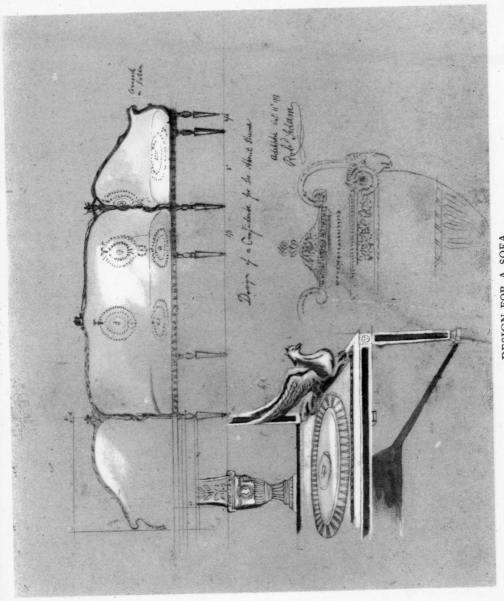

DESIGN FOR A SOFA

Drawing by Robert Adam, signed and dated, 1777

By courtesy of Dr. H. Burg

DRESSING TABLE IN SATINWOOD

Coloured engraving from Sheraton's *The Cabinet Maker and Upholsterer's Encyclopædia*, 1804

By courtesy of the Victoria & Albert Museum

THE GOLDEN AGE OF DESIGN

In that great period of accomplishment in design, between the 1650's and the 1820's, furniture makers were serving two separate civilisations—the breathless, exciting, fickle and increasingly complex civilisation of the fashionable world, and the rich, satisfying, common-sense civilisation of the farm, the cottage and the small country town. After the Restoration of Charles II, furniture makers were permanently saddled with fashion, and continually plagued by imported, foreign notions. It was some time before they acquired a facility for extracting the best from a foreign idea, and comfortably anglicising it: but they had abundant opportunities for thus "naturalising" some mode thrust upon them by the taste of the court, or some innovating and all too well travelled nobleman. During the Puritan interval, hundreds of English gentlemen had gone abroad, and back they came with their heads full of foreign notions, just like their great-grandfathers, who had travelled in Europe during the rapturous and intoxicating Italian Renaissance.

French, Spanish and Dutch ideas filtered into the country; the marriage of Charles II to Catherine of Braganza encouraged a temporary popularity for Portuguese taste; a craze began for oriental objects, and screens and cabinets of Chinese lacquer were shipped from the Far East, the latter being displayed on intricately carved stands, which were gilded or silvered. The desire for beautiful and highly decorative things attained the most extravagant dimensions: it expressed the joyful appreciation of freedom from Puritan regulation and repression, but it also indicated a new and sometimes rapacious appetite for precious and costly articles of furniture, which affected both design and the materials used by makers. Oak and walnut were not good enough for those who wanted their surroundings to proclaim the wealth or the royal favours they enjoyed. John Evelyn's description of a visit to the Duchess of Portsmouth illustrates the reactions of an educated gentleman to this variety of taste. His curiosity was engaged by "the rich and splendid furniture of this woman's apartment, now twice or thrice pull'd down and rebuilt to satisfie her prodigal and expensive pleasures . . ." He writes of "Japan cabinets, screenes, pendule clocks, greate vases of wrought plate, tables, stands, chimney furniture, sconces, branches, braseras, etc., all of massive silver, and out of number . . ." (*Diary*, October 4th, 1683.) But the taste of the fashionable world in the years following the Restoration was educated: the King's mistresses might cram their houses with furniture and fittings of precious metals, but they were merely banking in terms of furniture, and showing off the extent of the infatuation they inspired; other people were more discriminating, and the form of furniture was never debased in the interests of ornament, as it had been at the beginning of the century. The new refinements in architecture that had followed the work of Inigo Jones—the first architect in England to understand

DAY BED IN WALNUT
Late Seventeenth Century

the real significance of classic architecture—had a widespread effect upon the design of houses and what went into them in the shape of furniture and equipment. Towards the end of the seventeenth century the influence of architectural taste began to regulate the lines of large pieces of furniture; but in the transitional period, from the decline of the craftsmen's influence to the establishment of the fashionable furniture designer, many admirably proportioned things were made.

The preoccupations of Charles II's court were reflected by a generous use of amorini in decoration. Puffy-limbed, lascivious cupids lurked on the cresting of chairs, on the framework of mirrors and on a variety of other articles. The day-bed was invented; a light and graceful piece of walnut furniture, with a seat of woven canework, and a head filled by a panel of the same material. It was really an armless chair with a greatly elongated seat. Another piece of furniture typical of this period was the "love-seat"; a small settee, richly upholstered, with just enough room for two people to sit side by side.

Chairs acquired a new dignity; the backs were high, surmounted by carved cresting—with floral or heraldic devices, the almost inevitable amorini acting as supporters—the arms curving out and ending in scrolls, the legs also enriched with scrollwork, which foreshadowed the lines of the cabriole leg. Chair legs were still braced by underframing, and the stretcher

74

that tied the front legs together was enriched with carving. All this carved ornament on furniture was gay and fluent; it was part of a design conceived as a whole, not an afterthought applied to placate modish ideas. This masterful handling of ornament, and the new inventions and materials that became available, constitute the main difference between the luxurious furniture of the Restoration and that of the late Elizabethan and Jacobean periods.

In the last third of the seventeenth century the inventive gifts of furniture makers increased the comfort and convenience of town and country homes. Mirrors were no longer rarities, and they were set in deep frames of walnut, sometimes edged with narrow bands of blue glass. Clocks were beginning to claim the skill of the cabinet-maker, for the small, compact, brass "lantern," "bird-cage" or "bed-post" clocks, as they were variously called, which were formerly perched on brackets projecting from the wall so that their weights could hang free, were now enclosed in wooden hoods, and those hoods eventually stood upon tall boxes, which accommodated weights and pendulum. Thus the long-case or "grandfather" clock evolved. Chests with two, three or four sets of drawers were elevated on stands with turned or twisted legs. From the wooden settle, the settee was developed, with a high back and winged sides; and from this in a few years arose that superb draught-excluding and most comfortable of seats, the winged or "grandfather" chair. Upholstery was improved, and there was a lavish use of fabrics, not only on chairs, stools and settees, but on beds, which had grown larger and loftier. No particle of the wooden framework of beds was visible; it was covered in velvet or damask, and the curtains depended from deep cornices, which elaborated the moulded detail of this architectural feature.

In the country furniture acquired a few distinctive regional characteristics. For example the Yorkshire chair was clearly recognisable, with its turned legs and the crescent-shaped cross rails of the back. These rails were often heavily carved, and the upright members of the back terminated in scrolls, curving inwards. Another local chair type came from Lancashire, not unlike the Yorkshire, though of stouter build and less ornamental. The back was formed by a solid panel, with a semi-circle of carved cresting above, and the legs were turned. From the hands of Welsh craftsmen came solidly-made oak furniture, abundantly ornamented with rather coarsely carved geometrical patterns, such as interlaced semi-circles. Naturalistic *motifs* were sometimes used, birds and foliage, executed with spirit but without departing from stiff, conventionalised forms; but it was in the representation of heraldic and fabulous monsters that the Welsh carver excelled. The queer, suppressed magic of an ancient land quivers in the lines of such decoration; it recalls the tales and legends of the *Mabinogion;* small wonder that no trace of foreign influence, no concession to any form of taste but local taste, appears in this work. Welsh culture has resisted every invasion,

75

WRITING CABINET, INLAID WALNUT
Made by Samuel Bennett, c. 1700

Welsh crafts have stubbornly endured, and a few have survived even in our commercial machine age, Welsh furniture remained simple stuff for satisfying rustic needs: dressers and chests and cupboards were still being made in oak throughout the eighteenth and early nineteenth centuries, and there was little change in the form of such things. English furniture-makers in the country also continued to use oak, but they made simplified versions of town fashions in that material; their Welsh contemporaries ignored those fashions.

Scotland produced no furniture during the seventeenth century, and Dr. Johnson's comments on this inability to master the arts of life are illuminating. During his travels in Scotland with Boswell in 1773, he wrote: "I know not whether it be peculiar to the Scots to have attained the liberal, without the manual arts, to have excelled in ornamental knowledge, and to have wanted not only the elegances, but the conveniences of common life." He praises their literary accomplishments and records that "from the middle of the sixteenth century, almost to the middle of the seventeenth, the politer studies were very diligently pursued." (*A Journey to the Western Islands of Scotland.*)

But Dr. Johnson did not draw a significant conclusion from an observation made early in his tour, when he said: "A tree might be a show in Scotland as a horse in Venice." There was no great tradition of forestry and woodworking as in England, and after the Union when some furniture was made in Scotland, the prevailing fashions of the South were adopted and produced with minor local variations. The principal contribution of Scotland to furniture making was the influence of those master architects, Robert and James Adam, in the latter part of the eighteenth century. But like many other talented Scotsmen, they exerted their influence and improved their fortunes in the South, and there was nothing distinctively Scottish in their work, for they were concerned with designing everything, from great fashionable town houses down to the knife-boxes on sideboards, in the purest classical taste.

That pure classical taste, which was first introduced by Inigo Jones, was established by Sir Christopher Wren and his brilliant contemporaries between the Restoration and the beginning of the long Georgian period. Wren liked to design buildings "after a good Roman manner," to use his own words, and by the opening years of the eighteenth century, that "Roman manner" was leaving its improving mark on many pieces of furniture. After the close of the Stuart period, and during the reigns of William and Mary and Queen Anne, such commodious articles as bureau-bookcases and knee-hole writing desks were introduced, and a greater refinement of form was apparent in chairs and tables. An early eighteenth century example of the architect's influence on furniture design is a writing cabinet which was acquired in 1924 by the Victoria and Albert Museum, and is perhaps the first signed work of an English furniture-maker, for it bears the inscription: "Samuel Bennett, London, Fecit." The upper part is framed by correctly

TOP OF A WALNUT TABLE
Marquetry, c. 1680

proportioned fluted pilasters, and the whole character of the cabinet is architectural. The "good Roman manner" has been used with judgment and comprehension, and worked out in wood as admirably as Wren, Gibbs, Hawksmoor and Vanbrugh were expressing it in stone and brick. It is not too fanciful to suggest an affinity between the steeples Wren designed and the long-case clocks that towered up in the nobly proportioned rooms of Queen Anne and early Georgian houses.

The cabinet-maker spent much of his time executing interior woodwork, panelling, door and window architraves and mantelpieces to the designs of architects; so he was well schooled in the details of the classic orders; he attained a mastery over their proportions, and had abundant opportunities for study, for books and sheets of detailed drawings of architecture began to appear. The Earl of Burlington published the *Designs* of Inigo Jones and the *Antiquities of Rome* by Palladio; a contribution to the education of taste that moved Pope to apprehensive reproof:

> "Yet shall (my lord) your just, your noble rules
> Fill half the land with imitating fools;
> Who random drawings from your sheets shall take,
> And of one beauty many blunders make . . ."

78

WALNUT CABINET IN DECORATED MARQUETRY, C. 1700

WINGED ARMCHAIR UPHOLSTERED IN NEEDLE-WORK, C. 1700

There was far more intelligent interpretation than foolish imitation; for to the good sense of the English craftsman and his sympathetic knowledge of the materials he used, was added the enlightenment derived from ably directed architectural studies. Town and country furniture-makers were inventing and improving and absorbing new ideas.

The cabriole leg was used in the closing decades of the seventeenth century, and during the reign of Queen Anne it attained a simple and graceful form: it outgrew the floreated decoration and the scrollwork that in the previous reign had obscured its lines. It was used on chairs, tables, stands for cabinets, stools, settees and bureaux. The development of this form had been indicated earlier in the legs of some Carolean chairs; but its origin was ancient, and was derived from formalised representations of animals' legs. The cabriole leg, or something very like it, was known in Roman Britain, if the table sculptured on the monument to Aelia Aeliana, now in the Yorkshire Museum, is typical. Roman furniture in stone and bronze from Pompeii shows how the cabriole form arose from the crouching sinewy legs of some beast of prey, supporting a table top and resting naked claws upon the ground. Such features returned in Queen Anne and early Georgian times, and the cabriole leg, curving gently outward from the chair seat or table top, and then inwards, so that it formed a knee, would terminate in a claw or a hoof. Sometimes those claws would grasp a ball, and the claw-and-ball foot became a favourite device in the reigns of the first and second Georges. Chairs were now made without stretchers; the legs were independent, and the backs were slightly curved to form a comfortable support for ladies and gentlemen who were sitting bolt upright, for lounging is a modern habit. Designed in sets, there would be ten or more single chairs and a couple of elbow chairs; their seats covered in needlework, their frames of golden-hued walnut, until the seventeen-twenties and thirties when mahogany began to be used extensively.

The influx of French ideas that had followed the Revocation of the Edict of Nantes in 1685 and the consequent settlement of Huguenot refugees in England, and the enormous influence of Dutch taste in the William and Mary period, had great and improving effects upon the work of the furniture-makers who catered for fashionable folk. From France came a new conception of the decorative significance of upholstery; the backs as well as the seats of chairs and couches were upholstered; rich fabrics glowed everywhere; while an injection of fresh talent from Holland extended the scope of cabinet-makers. The Huguenots founded the silk industry at Spitalfields. The Dutch cabinet-makers introduced the highly skilled craft of veneering. The fronts of drawers and cupboards, table tops, bureaux and cabinets, were clothed by thin veneers of beautifully figured walnut, enriched with floral patterns and arabesques of marquetry. Apple, pear, holly, box, sycamore, yew and beech were the woods used for marquetry inlay on those veneered surfaces; Dutch and English craftsmen mingled their skill; and during the Queen Anne period the English genius for common sense and fitness in the shape of things was re-asserted. Dutch taste was inclined to be ponderous; it encouraged the use of gross and heavy shapes; but in the hands of Englishmen such shapes grew slim, and the furniture that is associated with the name of Queen Anne is perhaps the most agreeable that has ever been made in wood. The form of the chair at that time reached a singular and unforgettable beauty; with its cabriole legs, accommodating arms and back, and its fluid curves, it was perfectly fitted for its purpose, the light touch of carved ornament on the knees and the back appropriately embellishing the design. Ornament had been relegated to its proper place; and until the disastrous Victorian period it seldom obtruded. Ornament might be elaborate, it might be used lavishly, as indeed it was in the designs of William Kent and Thomas Chippendale, but it was never allowed to obscure the form or to mar the proportions of English furniture during the eighteenth century. By dispensing with straight legs and the stretcher, chair-makers had to solve a difficult constructional problem, for a curved wooden leg or arm was liable to fracture. "Wood with its straightness of grain demands a rectangular construction," as Mr. R. W. Symonds points out in *Masterpieces of English Furniture and Clocks*. He tells us that "The eighteenth century chairmaker . . . tried to overstep this limitation; the unskilled craftsman by making the curved arm, leg or upright unduly thick or heavy; the skilled craftsman by using the finest quality close-grained timber." The introduction of that stalwart wood, mahogany, enabled furniture-makers to carry the process of refining the structural lines of chairs, stools and settees still further, until they achieved the tapering legs and almost spidery framework that distinguish the seating accommodation of the late eighteenth century.

Throughout that century, country furniture-makers had been inventing things without reference to town fashions. In many Buckinghamshire villages, chair-making had become established as an industry, for the beech woods that clad the Chilterns provided turners with material for chair-legs and spindles. These legs and spindles were turned in clearings in the woods; the turners (or "bogers" as they were called) working under rough shelters formed by interlaced boughs, daubed with mud. Their work would be assembled by chair-makers, and this chair-making industry grew steadily, the market town of Chepping Wycombe, or High Wycombe, becoming its centre. It was from this rural industry that the countryman's own special arm-chair came; a typically English piece of furniture; comfortable, sensible and displaying those individual mutations of form that reflect the diversity of national taste and character. It may have evolved from the simplest type of three-legged stool; but whatever its origin, it represented a masterly handling of the simple forms provided by the turner. This stick-back or Windsor chair had a seat of elm or oak, shaped from a clay mould, which had recorded the curved indentations made by a well-built man when seated; the legs were turned in beech, and the back was formed by spindles of beech, set into the seat, flanking a flat, central splat; both spindles and splat being socketed into a head of oak or into a bow-frame of yew. The rake of the back and the height of the arms were adjusted to provide comfort; and for those who still sit upright in an age of lolling and sprawling, no seat is as comfortable to-day as the Windsor chair. There was no upholstery, nor did the chair need cushions: the English furniture-maker had solved this particular problem of comfort with his own chosen and familiar materials. As the eighteenth century advanced, the Windsor chair acquired touches of town taste; its front legs would follow the cabriole form; while the back splat might resemble a Queen Anne splat in outline, but pierced ornamentally in a manner that borrowed something from later fashions. The rural craftsman was generally fifteen to twenty-five years behind the modes of the town, unless he was working directly under the orders of an architect, imported by the local nobleman or squire for the re-building and re-furnishing of his country house. Other simple chair types were invented; in

MID-EIGHTEENTH CENTURY WINDSOR CHAIR
Yew and Oak

the north of England the ladder-back chair was made; and all over the country rush seating was used in conjunction with frames of oak, cherry-wood, elm or beech.

As walnut was gradually replaced by mahogany, the fashionable furniture-makers gave their customers many things that in earlier periods would have been deemed unnecessary. To-day we marvel at the bland perfection of those mid-eighteenth century designs for chairs and tables, bookcases, bureaux, mirror frames, beds, and all the hundred and one exquisite things fashioned in ruddy mahogany and enriched with delicate lines of gilded carving, that adorned the rooms of a gentleman's house. Their urbanity reflected the educated patronage that encouraged their makers; for a gentleman's education then included a critical knowledge of architecture, and in acquiring that knowledge he also gained discreet judgment of the proportions of furniture and its background, and an eye for appropriate decoration. "The practice of architecture," wrote Edward Gibbon, "is directed by a few general and even mechanical rules." It seemed as simple as that to the nobility and gentry of the Georgian period. The Earl of Burlington's "just" and "noble rules" had improved the taste of his own and succeeding generations. It was essentially an age of gracious living and large leisure for the well-to-do, and all classes enjoyed a reasonable though unequally distributed abundance. The people who set the fashions in that great period of English furniture design had plenty of time; they lived in larger houses and larger rooms than their latter-day descendants; their lives were unhurried, their privacy uninvaded, and as architecture and such ancillary arts as furniture-making invariably reflect the quality of life in any period, we must conclude from the evidence left by designers and craftsmen, that eighteenth century England had attained a much higher level of civilisation than we enjoy. A compact picture of the life of educated and moderately prosperous people appears in the warmly human and unaffected *Memoirs of William Hickey*. The home life of a gentleman named Smith, whose income was £2,000 a year, is thus described:

"He had a noble house upon the border of the river, a little above the town of Battersea, where he lived in the true style of old English hospitality in the midst of a happy family consisting of a wife, one son, and one daughter, entertaining his numerous friends with a warmth and cordiality that never was exceeded, seldom equalled. After a liberal quantity of the best port and madeira, which followed an excellent dinner, himself and guests adjourned to the billiard table, or Bowling Green, according to weather, or the season of the year. From either of those amusements they went to the drawing room, where tea and coffee being served, music filled up the space till ten, at which hour supper was served, and at eleven everybody retired to their homes, or if his guests for the night, to their chambers, where every comfort awaited them." (*Memoirs of William Hickey*, 1749-1775. Edited by Alfred Spencer. Chapter VII, page 75.)

And "every comfort" would include a four-post bed that had lost the monumental clumsiness of sixteenth and the awesome stateliness of seventeenth century beds, though the slender turned columns of mahogany still upheld a tester, and curtains still depended from the cornice. The bedroom furniture—chairs, dressing table, mirror, chest of drawers or that accommodating double chest, the tallboy—would be complementary to the painted panelled walls of the room, and mouldings that appeared on the cornices of bed and tallboy and on the edges of the table top would have a classical elegance of line, in keeping with the moulded detail of door and window architraves, and the cornice that ran above the panelled walls. By all these happily related features was the influence of the architect made manifest; by mastering "a few general and even mechanical rules" and applying them with imagination, he could create harmonious associations

84

FURNITURE FROM DAVID GARRICK'S BEDROOM
Painted in the Chinese manner, c. 1770

of form; he had at his service the finest craftsmen in Europe, and he was sustained and encouraged by the most enlightened patronage. The architect was thus established as the master designer, and he maintained that position from the early Georgian to the early Victorian period, when patrons ceased to be educated, and the supply of imaginative architects diminished.

Furniture-making for the Georgian world of fashion was directed and controlled by two types of designer: the architect, whose drawings were interpreted by craftsmen; and the craftsmen-designers, who like Robert Gillow and Thomas Chippendale founded cabinet-making businesses, designing and organising the production of furniture, with, of course, an alertly deferential eye on the prevailing taste in architecture. Some architects and many craftsmen-designers issued books of designs for interior woodwork and furniture, and from these books the country maker could copy up-to-date ideas, modifying and occasionally improving them in the process. Chippendale, when he published *The Gentleman and Cabinet-Maker's Director*, in 1754, said in his preface that he had included "no design but what may be executed with advantage by the hands of a skilful workman. . ." One of the earliest craftsmen-designers of whom adequate records exist was Robert Gillow. The date of his birth is uncertain, but he died in 1773.

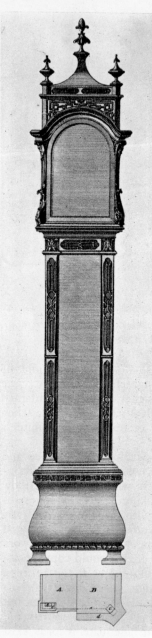

CHIPPENDALE CLOCK-CASE

He founded a firm of cabinet-makers at Lancaster, whose books begin in 1731. His eldest son, Richard Gillow (1734-1811) was an architect, and was taken into partnership when he was twenty-three, ultimately succeeding his father. The firm became Gillow and Barton, and in 1761 a London branch was opened in Oxford Street—a site continuously occupied from that date until 1906.

The outstanding name among eighteenth century furniture-makers is that of Thomas Chippendale. He established himself in London, and before 1750 had premises in Long Acre, eventually moving to St. Martin's Lane. It was at one time supposed that he came from Worcestershire; but his Yorkshire origin is now generally accepted. There is a record of his baptism at Otley on June 5th, 1718; and some documents are preserved in the West Riding Registry at Leeds, concerning a messuage, gardens and orchards, in Broughgate, Otley, in which "Thomas Chippindale, of St. Martin's Lane, London, cabinet maker" is mentioned, together with his uncles, William, Benjamin and Joseph, the date being April 30th, 1770. Various other facts confirming his Yorkshire origin appeared in an article on "The Chippendale Family," based on information provided by his greatgreat-grandson, Mr. John Chippendale, which was published in *The Cabinet Maker*, March 31st, 1923, and the documents mentioned are referred to in an article on Thomas Chippendale by J. S. Udal, F.S.A., published in *Notes and Queries* during 1922.

His abilities as a designer were considerable; but he was too good a craftsman, too well grounded in the exacting crafts of chairmaking and cabinet-making, to allow the ambitious exuberance of his fancy to entrap him into the follies committed by his French contemporaries. Also, he knew that while his customers expected a certain ornate extravagance in the decoration of furniture, they

CLOTHES PRESS
Engraving after a design by Thomas Chippendale
from *The Gentleman and Cabinet Maker's Director*, 1754

liked no more than a flavouring of foreign taste. "The parlour was (ill) furnish'd in the modern taste, with French chairs, festoon'd curtains, and puff'd bell ropes. . ." Thus did that critical observer, the Hon. John Byng, who became the fifth Viscount Torrington, record his dislike of modish innovations, after an inhospitable reception at a small country house, during one of his rambling tours in the west country in 1781. (*The Torrington Diaries*, Volume I.) "Modern" taste in English furnishing has so often meant "foreign" taste to those who liked to be a little ahead of the fashions; but Chippendale could give his customers genuine

RIBBON-BACKED CHAIR
In the manner of Thomas Chippendale, c. 1760

native modernity. On the title page of his *Director* he describes the contents as "a large collection of the most elegant and useful designs of household furniture in the Gothic, Chinese and Modern taste." The array of articles portrayed in the 160 "neatly engraved" copper-plates illustrate the growing complexity of life, and the author declared that his plates were "calculated to improve and refine the present Taste, and suited to the Fancy and Circumstances of Persons in all Degrees of Life." They included "book-cases, commodes, library and writing-tables, buroes, breakfast-tables, dressing and china-tables, china-cases and hanging-shelves, tea-chests, trays, fire-screens, chairs, settees, sopha's, beds, presses and cloaths-chests, pier-glass sconces, slab-frames, brackets, candle-stands, clock-cases, frets and other ornaments."

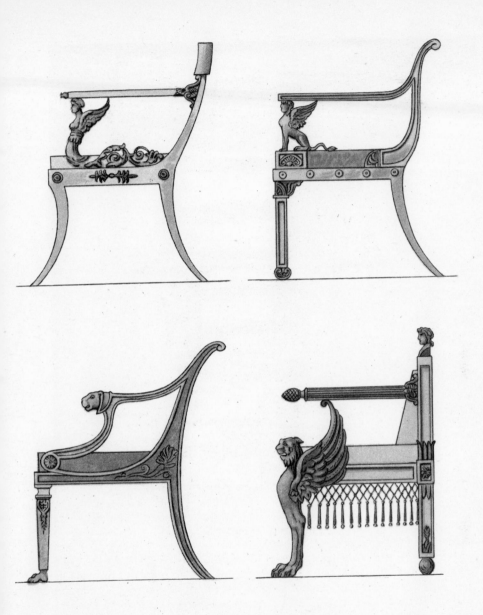

DRAWING ROOM CHAIRS

Coloured engraving from George Smith's *A Collection of Designs for
Household Furniture and Interior Decoration,* 1808

MUSIC GALLERY IN THE ROYAL PAVILION AT BRIGHTON

Coloured engraving by John Nash, 1824

Perhaps Chippendale's outstanding achievement as a designer was his ribbon-back chairs, those miracles of controlled intricacy, as blithely ornamental as the snowy lace that poured over the wrists of the gentlemen who sat in them after dinner, laying up gout for their old age. His chief material was mahogany; but much of his furniture was painted, particularly his Chinese designs, and he used gilding extensively on pier glass frames and fire screens, and on what he described as French chairs, which were the least satisfactory examples of his work. His business also carried out work for architects, and he made the furniture designed by Robert Adam for Harewood House, in Yorkshire. Robert Adam and Chippendale were both members of the Society of Arts which was founded in 1754, and the membership included other famous architects, among them Sir William Chambers, George Dance, and James Paine.

Thomas Chippendale died in 1779, and his business was carried on under the title of Chippendale, Haig & Co. until 1796. The influence of his work was considerable during and long after his lifetime. "Chinese" Chippendale furniture showed how ideas which Sir William Chambers and other travellers had imported from the Far East could be naturalised by English skill, and Chippendale's *Director*, with its gay treasury of pagoda *motifs* and interlacing frets, was published three years before the architect of Somerset House and the Pagoda, orangery and pavilions at Kew Gardens issued his famous treatise on *Designs of Chinese Buildings, Furniture, Dresses, Machines and Utensils*. Chippendale's "Gothic" designs merely lifted a few ornamental devices from late mediaeval ecclesiastical architecture and applied them, rather unhappily, as decoration to articles that were severely classical in conception and proportions. He may have been guided by the attempt made by Batty Langley, an architect, to rationalise the forms of Gothic architecture, for, like hundreds of other furniture-makers, he must have possessed the book Langley published in 1747, entitled: *Gothic Architecture, Improved by Rules and Proportions, In many Grand Designs of Columns, Doors, Windows, Chimney-pieces, Arcades, Colonades, Porticos, Umbrellos, Temples and Pavillions, etc., with Plans, Elevations and Profiles, Geometrically Expressed*. That was the trouble about "Gothic" Chippendale furniture: its form was "geometrically expressed," and it was as stiff and uninteresting as much of the "Chinese" furniture was ornate and undisciplined.

The names of Chippendale, Hepplewhite and Sheraton dominate the history of English furniture-making; but there were many other craftsmen designers of ability, who enjoyed equal or perhaps greater eminence in their own day, also scores of lesser known men whose productions are only rarely identified. For example, it is known that a cabinet-maker named Hugh Granger had a place of business "at the Carved Angel in Aldermanbury" during the reigns of William and Mary, Queen Anne and George I. John C. Rogers records that Granger produced "some excellent work veneered

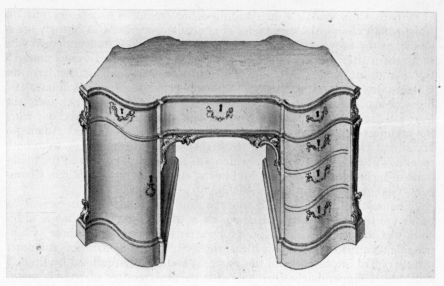

WRITING DESK
Design by Chippendale from the Society of Upholsterers' Journal

in walnut, a few pieces of which are possible of identification by reason of having his printed label pasted on a drawer." (*Furniture and Furnishing*, Chapter V, page 53.) Among Chippendale's contemporaries were Robert Manwaring, William Ince, Thomas Mayhew, Thomas Shearer, William Vile, William Hallett, John Cobb and the famous George Hepplewhite. Some of them were young men, still in the early stage of their careers, when Chippendale was fully established as a great fashionable maker. All these men were craftsmen-designers, working principally in mahogany, sometimes employing teams of other highly skilled men—chair-makers, upholsterers, cabinet-makers and carvers. William Vile held the Royal Warrant as cabinet-maker to the Crown during the early years of George III's reign, and made furniture for St. James's Palace; he was in partnership with John Cobb. Their place of business was on the corner of St. Martin's Lane and Long Acre. An amply documented account of their work, with some reference also to William Hallet who appears to have been in some kind of partnership with Cobb after the death of Vile, is given in that scholarly book by Mr. R. W. Symonds, *Masterpieces of English Furniture and Clocks*.

Robert Manwaring designed furniture in the Chippendale manner. Like Chippendale he made various experiments in the Chinese and Gothic styles, and produced some "rustic" designs, which anticipated the romantic complexities of Victorian taste. He was without the surety of touch that distinguished Chippendale's work; the proportions of his furniture varied;

DESIGN FOR A HARPSICHORD BY ROBERT ADAM

Executed in London with different coloured woods for the Empress of Russia, 1774

sometimes a notable refinement of form was apparent, but often the things he made were crude and clumsy. He published various works, including *The Cabinet and Chair Makers' Real Friend and Companion, or the Whole System of Chairmaking Made Plain and Easy*, in 1765, and a year later, *The Chairmakers' Guide*.

William Ince was also influenced by Chippendale's work, and produced somewhat lighter variations of it; but, like Manwaring, he lacked the innate sense of proportion that informed even the most fantastic of Chippendale's designs. Ince was in partnership with Thomas Mayhew, and together they published a book with plates illustrating over 300 designs of various articles, such as "hall chairs, lanthorns, staircase lights, side-boards, claw tables, tea-kettle stands, bookcases, secretaires, library steps, writing-tables, music desks, canopy beds, French bed-chairs, dressing tables, book and china shelves," etc. This book was entitled, *The Universal System of Household Furniture*, and was undated, though it was probably published about 1762. The use of the word *System* in the title of such works is perhaps significant: it suggested ability to depict an accepted code of design in operation; it may also have indicated a hope that the respect accorded to books on architectural design would also be extended to what were really undisguised advertisements for the wares of a tradesman. Many of these trade books were simply planned as catalogues. Some were the result of co-operative enterprise by various branches of the furniture trade. *Household Furniture in the Genteel Taste*, by the "Society of Upholsterers" was published in 1765, and ran into a second edition. In 1788 "The London Society of Cabinet Makers" published *The Cabinet Maker's London Book of Prices and Designs of Cabinet Work*, and to this book Thomas Shearer contributed many plates, which form an incomplete but valuable record of his work. Most of these plates were republished separately under the title of *Designs for Household Furniture*, and they disclose Shearer's gift for simplifying and refining the lines of furniture, thus endowing it with a greater elegance than it had hitherto attained. He was not a chair-maker; and it was by his cabinet-work, and in particular, his sideboards that he made the most conspicuous improvements to contemporary design. He inlaid his carefully selected mahogany with lines of satinwood and other decorative and exotic woods. But Shearer and George Hepplewhite belong to the latter half of the eighteenth century; their work distinguishes the transitional period from the fundamental firmness and clarity of Chippendale's designs—which were never debased in form however wildly ornamental they might be— to the delicately shaped, almost frail furniture that expressed the classical taste of the brothers Adam and the elegantly decorative satinwood and painted furniture designed by Thomas Sheraton. Before glancing at the development of furniture making in the closing decades of the century, it is necessary to examine the direct influence of the architect in the early and mid-Georgian periods.

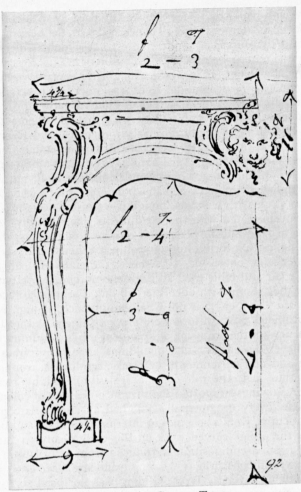

SKETCH FOR A CARVED TABLE
Pen drawing by Matthias Lock, c. 1740-1765

Many architects wrote books and published drawings of designs, though few of them indulged in the Gothic antics of Batty Langley. For example, a collection of copper-plate engravings was published in 1739, by William Jones, an architect, under the title of: *The Gentlemen's or Builders' Companion, Containing a Variety of usefull Designs for Doors, Gateways, Peers, Pavilions, Temples, Chimney-pieces, Slab Tables, Pier Glasses, or Tabernacle Frames, Ceiling Pieces, &c.* But apart from such specialised copy books there were comprehensive works, like Isaac Ware's *The Complete Body of*

95

Architecture; and books by James Gibbs, Abraham Swan, Thomas Johnson, Matthias Lock, and James Paine, all concerned with delineating, amplifying and indicating the universal application of those "noble rules" first made available by the enterprise of Lord Burlington. That noble scholar was the patron of William Kent (1685-1748), a singularly versatile architect with a gluttonous appetite for decoration. Kent was described by Horace Walpole as a "painter, architect, and the father of modern gardening," and on another occasion, in comparing his work with that of other architects, the same critic said: ". . . as Vanbrugh dealt in quarries, and Kent in lumber, Adam, our most admired, is all gingerbread, filigraine, and fan-painting." (Letter to Sir Horace Mann, April 22nd, 1775.) Kent's best-known works of architecture are the Horse Guards and Holkham Hall; but although he was an accomplished architect, he had a ponderous touch when he designed furniture. He dealt with wood as though it were stone; his massive walnut book-cases and bureaux, with their pediments, their heavily carved swags and festoons of fruit and flowers, their enriched mouldings; the scalloped edges—nulling, as that form of decoration was called—of desks and tables, the knees of chairs, encrusted with shells; the claw-and-ball and shaggy hoof feet of chair and table legs; all drew the unremitting attention of the eye, because they shone with burnished gilding. Perhaps Horace Walpole's use of the word "lumber" was not wholly unjustified, though Kent's magnificent adornments to furniture were always subject to the discipline of architectural design; the profusion of ornament might be almost oppressive, but it was never disorderly. The mouldings of mirror frames with their classical egg-and-dart enrichment; the masks, scrollwork, trophies and ubiquitous acanthus leaf; the gilt console tables, formed by a carved eagle whose outspread wings supported a gilt frame and a slab of coloured marble —every article, every ornamental *motif*, had an appropriate place in the studied grandeur of Kent's schemes of interior decoration and furnishing.

Much of the ornate carved work on this early Georgian furniture was executed in gesso, a composition introduced from Italy late in the seventeenth century, and consisting of whitening and size, used as a thick coating on wood, built up layer by layer. Gilding was not used so frequently in conjunction with mahogany; masses of gold and walnut might be happily associated, but the ruddy hue and beautiful figuring of mahogany were better emphasised by a reticent use of gilding—a member picked out here and there on a moulding, or a little pale gold in the hollows of fluting or on the glazing bars of bookcases. By the second half of the eighteenth century, Kent and his works were forgotten. The designs of Robert Adam (1728-1792) exerted the next great architectural influence on furniture, and it was their almost excessive refinement that provoked Walpole's remark about "gingerbread, filigraine, and fan-painting."

Robert was the most famous of the four brothers Adam: James, John and William were associated with him in business, and they were architects

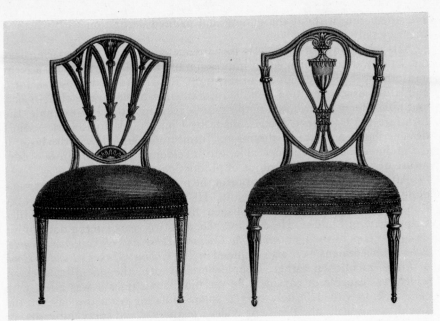

and speculative builders on a grand scale. Robert Adam designed houses complete with their contents; every detail of furnishing and interior decoration was pre-determined on the drawing board. Everything matched; there was a close, though slightly frigid alliance between ceilings, mantelpieces, lamps, chairs, tables, carpets, door handles and fingerplates, grates, wine coolers, sideboards, beds and chandeliers. All were impressed by the coldly correct taste of a profound student of Roman remains; for Robert had studied in Italy, and visiting Dalmatia during 1757, he had surveyed the ruins of Diocletian's palace. In 1764 he published a restoration of the entire building. His vast architectural erudition formed the basis of all his subsequent work. Where William Kent would have used flamboyant carving, Adam employed painted decoration—garlands, wreaths, ribbons, and the figures of fauns and nymphs—for the adornment of his furniture. Such artists as Pergolesi, Cipriani, Zucchi and his wife, Angelica Kauffmann, worked for him. He was always prepared to sacrifice the natural beauty of wood in order to secure, by extraneous means, some delicately ornamental effect. Much of the furniture he designed was made in mahogany, though many of his chairs and settees had gilded frames. Side-tables and sideboards, commodes, vase stands and torchères were frequently painted and gilded. There is a severity of line about Adam furniture which would be austere

97

and unpleasing without the gilding and painted decoration with which it was generally enlivened.

His mahogany furniture was less attenuated, though the tapering legs on chairs and tables created an impression of great slenderness. Like Kent and other architect-designers of furniture, Robert Adam imposed a form and left its exact execution to skilled workmen: cabinet-maker, chair-maker and upholsterer contributed nothing but executant skill. For example, the furniture for Harewood House, made by Chippendale to Robert Adam's design, shows no trace of the master furniture-maker's ideas: the taste of the architect might be impeccable, but it seldom inspired progress in furniture design or in the technique of production.

After Chippendale, perhaps one of the most influential of the craftsmen-designers was George Hepplewhite. He was apprenticed to Gillow at Lancaster, and eventually established himself in business at St. Giles Cripplegate in London. He died in 1786, and two years later, a book of his designs was published, entitled *The Cabinet Maker and Upholsterer's Guide.* A few of his designs were also included in *The Cabinet Maker's London Book of Prices,* mentioned earlier. Hepplewhite invented the shield back chair, which was capable of considerable variation; sometimes it was filled with canework or with delicately curved splats radiating from the base of the shield; occasionally the Prince of Wales's feathers would spray outwards, or ostrich plumes would be used, or urns with swags depending from them, and all manner of delicately interlacing ornamental lines. Bow-fronted chests, dressing chests, beds with turned and fluted pillars, serpentine- or bow-fronted sideboards, wardrobes, tallboys, and bureau-bookcases were designed by Hepplewhite, and were generally made in mahogany, discreetly ornamented by bands of inlay or carving in light relief. There was nothing rigid about this furniture: it was rich and bold and vigorous, as though the man who conceived it rejoiced in his power to use wood so aptly, and to give his customers such commodious and handsome things. Withal it possessed an agreeable formality, and the slightly paralysed elegance that stiffened many of Adam's designs never afflicted Hepplewhite's furniture. In common with all the best English work, it illustrated the craftsman-designer's abiding respect for the material he handled with such facility.

The next great name associated with English furniture design is that of Thomas Sheraton. He began life as a journeyman cabinet-maker, but he did not establish himself in business as a maker like Chippendale or Hepplewhite. He was born in 1751 at Stockton-on-Tees, and little is heard about him before 1790, when he was in London. It is difficult to attribute any actual furniture to him; but his influence upon design was extensive and continuous, and was spread by means of his published books. His earliest works, issued at Stockton, were religious writings; but in 1791, Bensley, of Bolt Court, Fleet Street, began to publish in parts Sheraton's most popular work, *The Cabinet-Maker and Upholsterer's Drawing Book.* This became

DESIGN FOR A CUPBOARD
AND DESK DESIGNED FOR CARLTON HOUSE
Coloured drawings from a book of sketches made for Gillow's, 1787
By courtesy of the Management of Waring & Gillow, Ltd. London

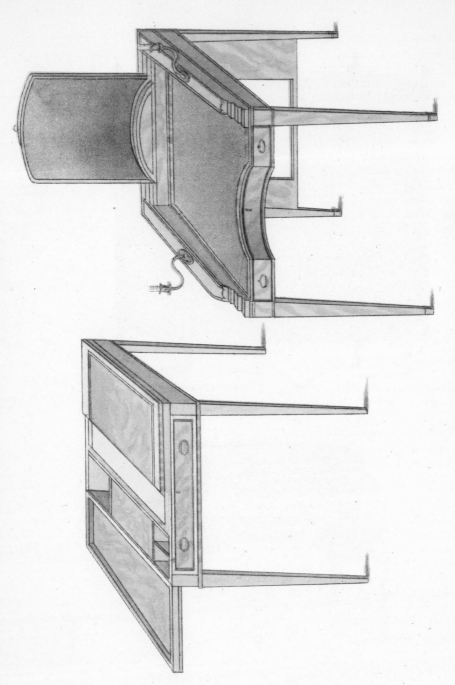

DRESSING TABLE AND FOLDING TABLE

Coloured drawings from a book of sketches made for Gillow's, 1787

By courtesy of the Management of Waring & Gillow, Ltd. London

a best seller, going into a second edition in 1793, and a third in 1802. During that year and the following, Sheraton published a new book, *The Cabinet Dictionary*, and in 1804, the *Cabinet-Maker, Upholsterer and General Artist's Encyclopaedia* was issued in parts. Six years after his death, a volume of eighty-four plates of designs for household furniture was published, most of them taken from his earlier books.

Although Sheraton was almost exclusively a drawing-board designer, his apprenticeship to cabinet-making preserved his knowledge of what could and could not be done with wood. He used mahogany and satinwood, and his furniture was decorated with painted work, and inlaid lines of box-wood and ebony. He earnestly pursued novelty in design, and was complacently patronising about earlier makers. Of Hepplewhite's *Guide* (1788) he said: "Notwithstanding the late date of Hepplewhite's book, if we compare some of the designs, particularly the chairs, with the newest taste, we shall find that this work has already caught the decline, and perhaps in a little time will suddenly die of the disorder. This instance may serve to convince us of that fate which all books of the same kind will ever be subject to. Yet it must be owned, that books of this sort will have their usefulness for a time; and when through change of fashions they are become obsolete, they serve to show the taste of former ages."

Sheraton was unaware that his own work had "already caught the decline," and was destined to lead makers into decadent complexities. Intricacy and ingenuity appealed to him: with great agility of invention, he depicted a variety of involved dressing-tables and washstands, and dual purpose objects, such as tables that with a little manipulation became library steps: indeed, some of these devices almost anticipated the ideas of Lewis Carroll's White Knight. But it is not by such mechanical tricks that Sheraton's work is remembered; he designed many gracious and lovely pieces of furniture, which preserved the stateliness of eighteenth century taste, but lightened it with a new, decorative freshness. Sideboards, bookcases, writing tables, dressing tables, china cabinets, and such small articles as toilet mirrors and fire screens, all bear witness to the genius of this strange, industrious and earnest man, whose life was so remote and detached from the fashionable world to which his work was wholly dedicated. His use of figured mahogany veneers, the edging of drawers and cupboards with bands of satinwood, the inlaying of coloured woods, and his confident borrowing from the ornamental treasury of Rome, Greece and ancient Egypt, gave a new lease of life to the taste for classical forms.

It is true that many of his chairs were spidery in appearance; their lines were refined almost to the vanishing point; they were not so much chairs as frail clasps of painted and gilded wood, worn by modish ladies and gentlemen when seated. Occasionally, all his English common sense and feeling for good proportion deserted him, and he would design such abominations as the Nelson chairs, which were involved assemblies of anchors and cables, tridents and dolphins. The taste of the French Empire affected his work, and he used bronze and brass mountings sometimes with an unbecoming lavishness; and in one of his designs for a canopy bed, an assortment of writhing eagles are used to support elaborate draperies. His pencil began to take charge of him, luring him to commit to paper things he would never have attempted to make with his hands, had he stuck to his workshop. His inspiration died on the drawing board, though its death was unperceived by his imitators; for lesser men copied his designs, choosing for reproduction and inept variation the models that gave the greatest impression of richness. That was the standard by which taste was to be formed in the nineteenth century. The clumsy and complex furniture that delighted the Victorians is foreshadowed at the end of the long Georgian period. There were of course many skilled and able makers of furniture in London in the early years of the nineteenth century; Sheraton mentions over two hundred and fifty "master cabinet-makers, upholsterers, and chair makers," in *The Cabinet Dictionary*. (Of these, the business founded by Thomas Seddon in the latter part of the eighteenth century survived as Seddon, Sons & Shackleton, and some authorities suggest that many of Sheraton's designs were made by this firm.)

STATE DRAWING ROOM
Coloured aquatint from George Smith's *A Collection of Designs for Household Furniture*, 1808

SISTERS' CYLINDER BOOKCASE
Thomas Sheraton's design from *The Cabinet Dictionary*, 1803

There was one final phase of classical taste, unctuously described in George Smith's *Cabinet-Maker's and Upholsterer's Guide* (1826): "But the period for the introduction of not only a chaste style in architecture, but likewise of ornament (and which extended itself to our domestic movables), was reserved for the late Mr. James Wyatt, whose classic designs will carry his name to posterity with unimpaired approbation. Here it would appear almost unnecessary for invention to have gone further, but perfection, it appears, was reserved for the present period, in relation to ornament and domestic embellishment. In the year 1804, Monsieur Denon's grand publication, detailing the antiquities of Egypt, became public. The novelty displayed throughout these fine specimens of art, calling to recollection so distant a portion of ancient history, gave rise and life to a taste for this description of embellishment."

Another foreign influence had arrived: the ideas of the ancient world, edited by the able French designers who ministered to the mounting vulgarity of their Emperor's taste, were to inspire English architects to use Greek, Roman and Egyptian decoration inside and outside their houses. Thomas Hope's *Household Furniture and Interior Decoration* showed how well this could be done. It was published in 1807, and Hope's designs for furniture started the style that was known as English Empire, which flourished agreeably during the Regency. In that period mahogany and rosewood

103

chairs and tables and desks were enriched with gilding or inlaid with thin lines of brass in geometrical patterns, such as the Greek key. Chairs borrowed their form from designs produced in the Periclean age. Strong and supple curves in back and legs absolved them from rigidity. Circular tables supported on a faceted central column, which was planted in a three or four footed base, provided new comfort in dining rooms, and their polished tops displayed large expanses of beautifully figured wood. Much of this English Empire furniture was painted black and relieved with gilding. It was the last time a foreign fashion in furniture was absorbed and skilfully anglicised: it was the swan song of good taste in furnishing. For a few decades in the country, craftsmen still continued to produce their versions of Chippendale, Hepplewhite and Sheraton chairs, making simple furniture by hand, choosing wood to give the best service, unaware that their standards of workmanship were already out of date, or that the shapes of the things they made belonged to a civilisation that was passing away. The golden age of design was over. The commercial machine age had begun.

THE REVIVAL OF FURNITURE DESIGN

Furniture design which had in former periods been influenced by fashion and architectural taste, was now controlled by traders whose standards were purely commercial. The furniture trade catered for a public that liked thick, lavish ornament and admired solidity of form, which suggested respectability, or an excessive and wiry complexity, which was mistaken for refinement. Mechanical production, never allowed to do its best, was used chiefly to make shoddy versions of current vulgarities in furnishing, to satisfy the cheap end of the market. The rumbling thunder of Cobbett's protests against such things died away; and everybody was delighted with everything in the home, until a rebellious poet, who was also an artist-craftsman of immense versatility and stupendous energy, started a doubt that founded a fashion. His name was William Morris. He rejected the contemporary world, would have nothing to do with the machine, and he attempted to rescue the rapidly perishing crafts from extinction. His influence grew slowly throughout the latter part of the nineteenth century. Dismissed at first as an "arty" crank, he became a leader of taste; and he inspired other gifted men to study and practise the crafts.

Unfortunately, the chief effect of his influence was to turn taste back to the past. When discriminating people became aware of the ugliness of contemporary furniture they began to acquire things made in former ages; so the dealer in antiques began to flourish as he had never flourished before. A few artist-craftsmen followed Morris, and began to make furniture of original design, and of these Ernest Gimson and Sidney Barnsley were the most outstanding. They picked up the lost threads of English tradition,

A CABINET IN ENGLISH WALNUT
Designed by Ernest Gimson

which fashion had unravelled at the Restoration; they used the woods of the countryside, English oak and walnut, elm and yew, and Gimson settled down to work in Gloucestershire, making fine and usually very expensive things and acting, unconsciously, as a research worker in design. Both had been trained as architects, and were closely familiar with all the crafts concerned with building, some of which they practised.

Gimson was himself a great executant craftsman, and the cabinets, sideboards and chests he made were often beautifully inlaid with ebony, bone, mother-of-pearl, and such woods as holly and cherry. He made rush-seated chairs with bobbin-turned spindles, ladder-backs and a new type of back consisting of three horizontal and two vertical members, within the outer frame. Such craftsmen did not fit into economic life. From the time Gimson came to London from Leicester, in 1886, when he was twenty-one, to his death in Gloucestershire in 1919, his work and his ideas about furniture-making and building were uninfluenced by the possibilities and limitations of commerce or industry. He made what he liked, and there were enough rich people alive with good taste to want what he made.

Another furniture designer, who inherited an old-established business, and was boldly experimental inside the furniture trade, was Sir Ambrose Heal. He too owed a debt to William Morris; but as the work of Gimson and Barnsley had continuity with that of the mid-seventeenth century craftsmen, so did Heal's work have continuity with the early nineteenth century. If taste had not declined in the Victorian period, some designer like Ambrose Heal might have succeeded Sheraton; for his work follows on naturally and easily after Sheraton's designs, though it is wholly original in conception, making no concessions to classical taste. After the first world war, a designer and maker of original furniture named Gordon Russell followed the example of Gimson, and began to produce work in oak, cherry, yew and other country woods. His furniture also had an affinity with the mid-seventeenth century, and was unmistakably English in character.

Such men, all of them directly or indirectly inspired by William Morris, have preserved and extended in the twentieth century the vast heritage of British skill in furniture-making. The furniture manufacturing trade has not yet accomplished an agreeable transition from personal craftsmanship to machine-production, but it is outgrowing the imitative propensity that has for so long obliterated all hope of original experiment in design, and as fresh industrial techniques arise, and new synthetic materials are perfected, it may even outgrow the use of wood. Then will the ancient partnership of woodman and craftsman be dissolved, though the memory of the skill it has generated and sustained for so many centuries may long endure.

ENGLISH GLASS

BY

W. B. HONEY

INTRODUCTION:

THE ORIGIN AND NATURE OF GLASS

GLASS is nowadays so familiar that many people take it for granted, without ever considering how it is made, or what part it has played in the history of human customs or as the medium of a branch of creative art. Yet, next to pottery, it ranks as chief among the "arts of fire," and even more than pottery stands for the miraculous transformation of common materials by the action of fire into something wonderful. Mere sand and ashes become a brilliant crystalline substance capable of a thousand delightful uses.

Glass may, in fact, be regarded as an artificial form of the mineral known as rock crystal. Not only is it closely akin in chemical composition, but the appearance of crystal has commonly been the ideal of the maker of glass, who has more than once in its history borrowed the name for his productions. Moreover the names of glass and crystal, and the comparison with ice which both words suggest, are appropriate in a less obvious way; the shaping of glass depends on its fluidity and plasticity when hot, making it subject to the will of the craftsman, whose rhythmical movements are recorded, as it were frozen, in its cooled form. Glass has, of course, its own special order of beauty in colour and in the play of light within its substance; and other ideals than a clear brilliance have sometimes been sought, with beautiful results. But a "water-white" crystal clearness has been the quality most often sought by the glass-maker, and no glass has reached this ideal with greater success than the English-invented "glass-of-lead," sometimes known as "lead crystal."

The origin of glass lies so far back in the pre-history of the Eastern Mediterranean that scholars are still unable to say how and where and precisely when it was first made. As a material for objects of use and ornament it was not suddenly invented in the form in which we now know it. It was a gradual discovery and for at least two thousand years was used in the making of decorative small objects, before the invention of the blowing-tube brought the now-familiar forms of useful glassware.

The story of the invention of glass in Syria as told by Pliny is not now accepted, and it seems probable that the earliest material of the character of glass was first used not alone but in the form of a blue glaze with which in pre-dynastic Egypt, perhaps as early as 4000 B.C., beads of stone were coated. Such a blue glaze, coloured with a copper compound, was probably discovered by accident and used to fabricate beads in imitation of turquoise and other greatly prized blue and green stones. The earliest glass vessels, again Egyptian and dating from about the 15th century B.C., were made by an adaptation of this bead-covering technique; threads of hot ductile glass were wound upon a core of clay and sand which was afterwards removed. Small vessels and decorative objects continued to be made by this process and by moulding and modelling, until just before the beginning of the Christian era, when a revolutionary change in practice was brought about by the invention, apparently in Syria, of the glass-blowing-tube. No technical change of comparable importance took place thenceforward until the introduction in the 19th century of machinery for bottle-making and the "pressing" of glass in moulds, and the large-scale manufacture of glass in sheets.

THE TECHNIQUE OF GLASS-MAKING

GLASS is essentially an artificial compound produced by the fusion of silica in the form of sand, flint or quartz, with the aid of an alkaline flux, normally either potash or soda. These are the essential ingredients, but to make a tough and durable glass small quantities of other substances, such as lime or one of the oxides of lead, are in practice required. Quartz and rock crystal, which the glassmakers have so often striven to imitate, are themselves almost pure silica. Pure silica may in fact be melted to form a glass, but the very high temperature required rules this out for all but small laboratory vessels required to resist great heat. The soda alkali was in the past usually obtained from the ash of certain marine plants, while the potash was produced by burning bracken or beechwood. At the present day the potash is prepared from saltpetre and from the commercial potassium

NAILSEA JUG
Late eighteenth or early nineteenth century

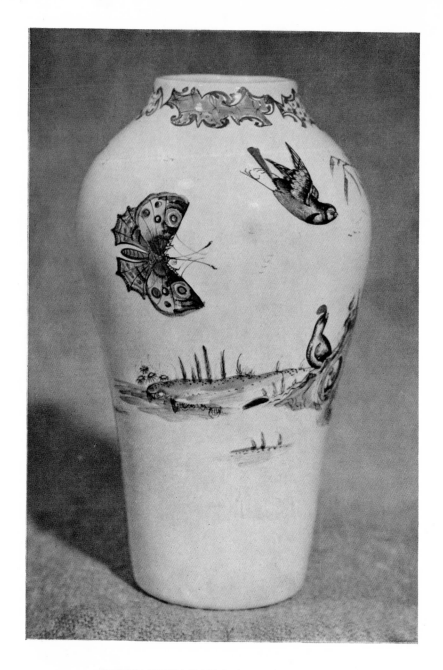

BRISTOL WHITE-GLASS ENAMEL-PAINTED VASE
Mid-eighteenth century

carbonate known as "pearl ash," while the soda is made from common salt. Lime was added in various forms, such as chalk or limestone. An oxide of lead was used as an ingredient from early times, especially in coloured glass, whose brilliance it enhanced; lead also facilitated the working of glass by increasing its fusibility. Lead glass was in fact specifically mentioned in a text of the 12th century as the material of imitation gems. But a workable glass containing lead in considerable quantity and capable of being formed into vessels was not made before about 1675, when the experiments of Ravenscroft produced the English lead glass, whose remarkable qualities will be described in due course. In both "paste" gems and the English "glass metal" (as it is called), glass-of-lead is distinguished by its brilliancy.

Glass is naturally seldom free from colour. The common presence of traces of iron as an impurity in sand usually gives it a greenish tone, and to obtain a crystal "whiteness" use is made of a decolourising agent in the form of an oxide of manganese, once known as "glass-maker's soap." "Common" or bottle-glass was not so treated.

Deliberate colouring is produced by the addition of metallic oxides such as iron for green, copper for turquoise blue or green, cobalt for blue, and manganese for amethyst pink or purple. All these have been in use for a very long time. The ruby-red of medieval stained glass was also obtained from copper, but another ruby-red and a pink, from gold, were 17th-century discoveries. A silver compound to give a yellow surface-stain had been for long employed by the makers of medieval and later window-glass, when fresh use was made of it in the 19th century. A dense opaque milk white was given by an oxide of tin; this was used also in the glaze or "enamel" of maiolica and delftware and other sorts of pottery, whence it is sometimes misleadingly called "enamel glass"; semi-opaque and opalescent "milk-and-water" glass was produced by an arsenic compound or by the use of calcined bones. Modern chemistry has added new colours too numerous to mention here.

These ingredients have generally been in practice mixed with a proportion of old broken glass (called "cullet"), partly to help the fusing, but also for the sake of economy, since the waste from the glass-factory itself could be utilised in this way, while at certain periods in England, on account of Excise Duties, it was possible to buy broken glass at a cost much less than that of the ingredients required to make it afresh.

For the melting together of the ingredients a dome-shaped fire-clay pot or crucible two or three feet high was for long the normal container. The making by hand, drying and firing of these pots was a highly skilled operation. They were ranged above a furnace heated by wood or coal. In early times vast quantities of wood fuel were consumed by the glass-makers, who were compelled to move from place to place in the forests as their supplies gave out. English glass-makers were the first to employ pit-coal, in the early part of the 17th century, and its use soon spread to other countries. Oil, gas and electricity have frequently been employed since the 19th century.

In a glass-house run on traditional lines using hand labour, such as that of Messrs. James Powell & Sons, formerly of Whitefriars in London and now of Wealdstone, Middlesex, the glass-pots are arranged in a ring round the furnace. Through an opening in the shoulder the molten glass is taken up by the workman. When melted, glass is more or less fluid, and very sticky, adhering to an iron tube or rod thrust into it. It is also very ductile, and may be drawn out, without breaking, into threads of great length. When a lump of molten glass has been "gathered" at the end of the iron tube and shaped into a globular or cylindrical mass by rolling on an iron table (called a "marver"), it may be blown into a bubble, and to this property was due the revolutionary change of practice already referred to. The bubble may be elongated by swinging, pressed or rolled, cut with shears and otherwise manipulated or transferred to an iron rod (called a "pontil" or "puntee") for inversion and further working. The plasticity of the glass during the shaping is maintained by repeated re-heating in the mouth of the furnace, which also restores the brilliant fused surface-condition known as fire polish. By constant rotation of the tube or rod the shapes are kept symmetrical about a central line like a pot thrown on the wheel or a piece of turnery. The working of glass by these hand processes, which call for great dexterity and a peculiar gift of rhythmical movement, has changed but little since Roman times. The same simple tools, and above all the chair in which the principal workman sits, with long flat parallel arms on which the rod is rotated by rolling, have continued in use until the present day.

The glass bubble can also be blown into a mould of baked clay, stone or metal. This process, which was perhaps the earliest of all forms of blowing, eventually led to the application of machine power to glass-manufacture. Complicated apparatus for mechanically blowing bottles in metal moulds was perfected in America towards the end of the 19th century, and the process has been extended to the making of other sorts of vessel of bottle type, such as electric-light bulbs. As many as fifteen thousand bottles a day may be turned out by one of the larger machines. Some modern bottle-making machinery makes use of "pressing" as well as of mechanical blowing.

In the "pressing" of glass, another 19th-century invention, comparable with the "jolleying" of the potter, a quantity of molten glass is placed in a mould giving the outside shape of the vessel, and a plunger is thrust into it to give the inside shape, forcing the glass upwards and outwards to fill the mould. Pressing was used at first as a means of imitating cut glass, but can equally well be applied to the mass-production of well-designed modern shapes.

All manufactured glass, whether made by hand or by machinery, requires to be toughened by annealing, a process by which it is placed in a heated chamber (called a "*lehr*" or "leer") and gradually cooled. This removes internal strains and stresses produced by its shaping and uneven cooling, which otherwise would leave it brittle and unserviceable. The behaviour of the glass toys known as "Prince Rupert's drops" is a demonstration of the

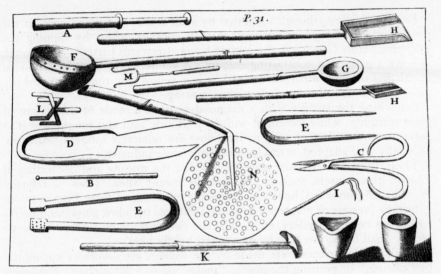

GLASS-MAKER'S TOOLS
Engraving from Haudicquer de Blancourt's *The Art of Glass*, 1699

properties of glass that has not been annealed. They are pear-shaped beads with a "tail," made by dropping molten glass into water, and their internal state of strain is such that they collapse into powder when the tail is broken off.

The most characteristic sorts of glass decoration are those which exploit its peculiar plasticity and ductility when hot. The rhythmical shaping of handles, the drawing out and tooling of stems into wings and discs and "knops" (or swellings), the waving of mouths and feet, and the application of threads tooled or melted in, are such types of decoration. Differing composition and consistency in the molten glass may suggest variety of treatment; one sort (such as the Venetian) may be fluid and encourage rapid elaborate manipulation, while others (such as the English lead-glass) are stiffer and call for more simple treatment.

Other types of decoration are shared with other materials. Thus the engraving and cutting of glass on the lapidary's wheel are grinding processes used originally on crystal and other stones. The wheel consists of an iron or copper disc, large or small, fed with emery and water, on to which the glass surface to be engraved is pressed. The engraving of glass has been condemned by (amongst others) John Ruskin, on the ground that it "conceals its ductility and confuses it with crystal"; but these critics have overlooked the special light-transmitting qualities of different sorts of glass. On the other hand painting in vitreous fusible enamels fired in a muffle-kiln is a process shared with porcelain and indeed has often been adopted in conscious rivalry with it.

Peculiar to glass, though suggested by such stones as layered onyx, is the process of "flashing" or "casing" it with another colour by dipping the gathering before blowing it, the coating being afterwards partially cut through to leave a pattern of contrasting colours. A similar result may be produced by cutting through a surface stained "silver yellow" by the process already mentioned as familiar in window-glass-making.

Scratching the surface with a diamond-point is a mode of decoration of great antiquity, while etching it with hydrofluoric acid and roughening it in patterns with a blast of sand or iron dust are relatively modern processes, especially well adapted to mechanised large-scale industry.

These, then, are the chief processes used in the making and decorating of English glass vessels, such as are generally meant when "glass" is referred to. The English word, however, covers the meanings of three French words —*verrerie* (vessels or glassware in general), *vitrail* (window glass), and *verroterie* (glass beads, jewellery, etc.). The last two of these lie outside the scope of this small book, but may be mentioned briefly here.

Small window panes were made by the Roman glass-workers apparently by "casting," or pouring the molten "metal" on to a flat surface. But larger pieces were made in medieval times and later by two adaptations of the blowing-process. By what was called the "crown" or "Normandy" process a bubble was opened while still on the rod. This, rapidly rotated, caused the bubble (continually reheated in the mouth of the furnace) to spread by centrifugal force into a nearly flat disc as much as four feet in diameter, with a thick boss or "bull's eye" in the middle. From this disc flat diamond-shaped or rectangular pieces were cut. By the "broad" or "Lorraine" process the ends were cut off an elongated bubble, and the resulting cylinder was cut longitudinally with shears and opened out and flattened. "Crown" glass shows a slight concavity and a faint rippling in concentric circles; in "broad" glass the ripples are straight.

Machinery was in the 19th century applied to the cylinder-process. An iron ring dipped into a tank of molten glass was drawn upwards to form a cylinder as much as fifty feet high; this was afterwards opened and flattened. Sheets up to six feet in width and of almost unlimited length are also produced by drawing out the glass on an iron bar dipped along its length in the molten "metal"; the sheet so produced is then passed between rollers, cooling as it proceeds. "Plate glass" was originally made by pouring ("casting") the molten "metal" on to an iron table where it was rolled and finally ground and polished with abrasives to a perfectly flat surface on both sides. Modern machinery enables polished plate to be made by passing the sheet between rollers, producing flatter surfaces requiring less grinding.

Glass jewellery (*verroterie*) is generally made of an easily fusible lead-glass, capable of being worked with simple tools in the heat of a lamp. Glass rods and tubes are thus fashioned by hand into toy figures, flowers and other decorative small objects.

TUDOR MEDICINE-BOTTLES

ROMAN AND MEDIEVAL GLASS
IN ENGLAND

WHEN Britain became part of the Roman Empire much glass was imported into the country, not only from Egypt and from Syria, where a great industry had grown up with the invention of glass-blowing, but also from the neighbouring province of Gaul. There Syrian emigrants had started numerous glass-houses which were already flourishing in the 2nd and 3rd centuries. Whether glass was also made in Britain, as well as imported, is still a matter of dispute. Even if it was made here, as seems probable, it could not be described as British glass; it would have followed the fashions prevailing in other parts of the Roman Empire. Nevertheless the tradition of Roman glass was the inevitable inspiration of many sorts of English, as of most other later European glass. Within two or three centuries after the invention of glass-blowing, the artisans of the Roman Empire had mastered almost every glass-technique subsequently in use. It is in fact tempting to say that Roman glass was the best ever made. In command of colour (doubtless inherited from the Egyptians), in the invention of austere and measured Classical forms, as well as of wild fantastic improvisations, and even in the use of engraving and cutting, alike in objects of luxury and articles of use, the Roman glass-maker was supreme.

With the decline of the Empire and the eventual withdrawal of the Romans from Britain, such glass as continued to be made in the North lost its Classical character; but several interesting types, such as some so-called "trunk-beakers" with claw-like appendages and some beautiful elongated cone-shaped cups, survive to represent the period of the Invasions and Migrations and the "Anglo-Saxon" period in England. There is no proof, however, or even probability, that any of these "Frankish" or "Teutonic" glasses were made in England, though many have been found here. By the 7th and 8th centuries, at all events, it would seem that no glass was being made in Britain, since there is a record of Abbots of Wearmouth and Jarrow then asking for glass-makers to be sent to England from Gaul and the Rhineland.

On the Continent the Roman art survived and the Roman tradition is still recognisable in the cups and small bottles roughly made of imperfect greenish metal, which continued to be produced throughout the medieval period. These form a link between Roman glass and the Northern European glass which in the 15th century came to vigorous life again and produced many masterpieces. At the same time, another and much more influential renascence of glass-making was in progress in Italy, particularly at Venice.

The medieval Northern glass is variously known by the German name *Waldglas* (forest glass), having been made in the forests, the ash of the beech-wood used for firing serving as the source of potash alkali, and as *verre de fougère* in France, from the use of bracken ash for the same purpose. It was never colourless, but had a greenish tinge from the presence of iron in the sand used; and the fully developed Northern glass-metal of the 15th century and later was of a most attractive sea-green colour, no doubt produced deliberately. The *Waldglas* was made at many places in France, Belgium and Germany.

How soon emigrants took the craft to England cannot be stated with certainty, but records make it clear that already in the 13th century, glass-makers from Normandy were settled in what was then the forest region of the Weald of Kent, Surrey and Sussex. They were chiefly makers by the "crown" process of coloured window-glass, of which this was, of course, a period of the highest achievement. By the 16th century glass-makers from Lorraine had begun to compete with the Normans in the Weald. All used great quantities of wood as fuel, moving from place to place as their supplies were exhausted. In this use of wood they were rivals of the important Sussex iron-founders, and eventually some of the Lorraine families, as well as some of the Normans, moved to Hampshire (Buckholt), and on to Gloucestershire (Newent, Forest of Dean, Woodchester) and to North Staffordshire (Bishop's Wood, Blore Park). Members of the same Lorraine families of Ensell (Hennezel) and Tyzack (Thisac) are recorded from the early part of the 17th century onwards at Old Swinford and elsewhere in the Stourbridge area, which was to become and still is one of the most important glass-making regions in England. These men from Lorraine were again chiefly makers of window-glass, using the "broad" process, but made vessels in *Waldglas* also. These are known from fragments found in excavations on the sites of glass-houses, and included many small phials or medicine-bottles of tapering conical or cylindrical form. Beaker-shaped drinking-glasses, often ribbed and standing on a spreading foot, are also found, as well as stemmed goblets already showing the Venetian influence which was soon to be paramount. The degree to which the Roman tradition was maintained in these vessels is shown by the fact that they are often mistaken for Roman work and have frequently been exhibited as such in English provincial museums.

GLASS
MADE IN ENGLAND
IN THE VENETIAN STYLE

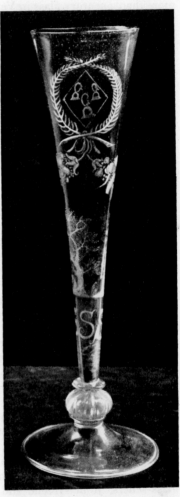

THE rise of the Venetian industry dates from the 15th century, when the making of an almost colourless glass, called "*cristallo*" after the natural stone, brought a new fame to its productions, which had previously been limited to beads and common glass in the medieval styles. Venice (or more accurately Murano) glass thenceforward set the European fashion among the well-to-do for nearly two hundred years. In every country of Europe Venetian glass stood for the new Renaissance styles, as against the medieval or Gothic taste; the latter, however, survived in a modified form, in Germany and elsewhere, as late as the 17th century. Much glass was exported from Venice, but more was made by emigrant Italian workmen who settled in other countries far and wide. Everywhere, with the spread of luxury, glass, and not only Venice glass, became fashionable. For England an Elizabethan writing in 1586 testified to the preference given to glass over even silver and gold, telling how "our gentilitie as lothing those mettals (because of the plentie) do now generallie choose rather the Venice glasses . . . such is the nature of man . . . that it most coveteth things difficult to be atteyned . . . and as this is seen in the gentilitie, so in the wealthie communaltie the like desire of glasse is not neglected . . .

THE CHESTERFIELD "FLUTE-GLASS"
c. 1663

117

the poorest also will have glasse if they may; but sith the Venician is some-what too deare for them, they content themselves with such as are made at home of ferne and burned stone." (This was, of course, the period of the Spanish-American silver and the raiding of the galleons.)

Emigrant Venetian glass-workers reached England at least as early as 1549, but most of them, temperamental as Italians and glass-blowers commonly are, did not stay. In 1570, however, more Italians were engaged to work at a glass-house in Crutched Friars in London, and from this time onwards for more than a century glass in Venetian style continued to be made in England. In 1575, after the Crutched Friars house had been burnt down, the first considerable figure in the history of glass-making in England, the Venetian Jacopo Verzelini (or Jacob Versaline, as he came to be called, b. 1523, d. 1606), obtained from Queen Elizabeth a privilege for twenty-one years to make Venice glasses in London and teach the craft to Englishmen. His glass-house was in Broad Street, in the city of London.

In 1592, Verzelini's privilege was taken over by Sir Jerome Bowes, who was a company-promoter and not a practical glass-maker at all, and for many years after this the industry in England was controlled by profit-seeking would-be monopolists importing Venice glass and employing Italians, until eventually, after the Restoration (in 1673 to be precise), the London Glass-Sellers' Company took up the matter and were instrumental in creating an independent art of English glass. The outstanding figure in the period of the monopolists was Sir Robert Mansell, a retired admiral, who by 1618 had bought out all his rivals; and the most noteworthy technical change was the use towards 1610–1615 of pit coal as fuel in place of wood.

The identification of the glass made in the various European countries *à la façon de Venise*, as it is often called, has always been difficult, and of the great number of 16th- and 17th-century specimens attributed to Venice many still unidentified must have been made abroad. The glasses of the kind made in England are no exception, and the matter is complicated by the fact that the Italians generally reached this country by way of the Netherlands, where Antwerp was the most active centre of Italian glass-making outside Italy. The glasses made in England would thus tend to form a subdivision of the Nether-lands class of Venetian-style glasses. Excavations made in 1874 on the site of Verzelini's Broad Street glass-house produced inconclusive results. Unlike broken pottery and kiln wasters, broken and defective glasses have intrinsic value as cullet for remelting, and are seldom as abundant on a glass-house site as the sherds found where a pottery has been.

The shapes of the glasses are, moreover, no certain guide, since it is known that specific orders were sent to Venice, and some drawings actually survive, with the instructions sent to the glass-maker Morelli by a London firm of glass-sellers, John Greene and Michael Measey, between 1667 and 1673. These, of course, come late in the period here in question, but they are evidence of the custom prevailing.

WINEGLASS PAINTED BY WILLIAM BEILBY
Mid-eighteenth century

COUNTRY-MARKET JUGS

Late eighteenth or early nineteenth century

Certain rare glasses in Venetian style, dated and inscribed with English names and mottoes, have for long been the only work positively ascribed to Verzelini. They are wide goblets with hollow knopped stems, and are mostly engraved with the diamond point. The earliest recorded is dated 1577. One such glass bears the names of "John" and "Jone" "Dier" (1581). Two others (1583 and 1586) bear the motto of the Pewterers' Company of London—"In God is all my trust." With the engraving on these surviving glasses, the antiquary Albert Hartshorne with considerable probability associated the recorded name of one Anthony de Lysle, an engraver of pewter, who came from France, where he presumably engraved another goblet, now in the Musée de Cluny, Paris, of precisely the same character as in those with English inscriptions; this bears a decoration of *fleur-de-lys* and the date 1578. Very closely similar in style of engraving is a cylindrical glass of German form in the Victoria and Albert Museum, inscribed with the name of William Smith (b. 1530, d. 1618), together with his arms and those of his wife Veronica Altensteig of Nuremberg, where he was living in 1582, the date on the glass. It seems probable therefore that the glasses engraved by this wandering artist were of various origins.

With these so-called Verzelini glasses are associated another, of the usual form but purple in colour, and another dated 1590 and bearing the gilt (not engraved) arms of the Vintners' Company of London and the name "Wenijfrid Geares."

Apart from these rare inscribed specimens, the productions of Verzelini and his Italian successors are probably to be found among the many glasses with hollow stems, either with moulded or gadrooned knops or of elongated baluster form. The former include a glass in the Victoria and Albert Museum dated 1602, diamond-engraved in the de Lysle manner, bearing the name of Barbara Potter. Of the latter type, which shows a kinship in the form of stem with the silver cups of Charles I's reign, fragments have been found in London excavations, and many complete specimens survive in this country.

The middle part of the 17th century, the period of the monopolists, is poorly represented by actual glasses to be claimed as made in England. Mansell employed a succession of Italians, one of whom, Paolo Mazzola, was recorded elsewhere as a maker of *verres ornés*. These were presumably winged or "serpent-glasses" of a well-known type; the stem of such a glass appears in fact to have been found in the Broad Street excavations. The more extravagant of these, however, are probably Netherlandish work, though certain light-winged glasses, not uncommon in this country, were perhaps made here.

For the third quarter of the 17th century a confusion with the Netherlandish glass is more than ever likely. A tall "flute glass" of a favourite Dutch form, once in the possession of an Earl of Chesterfield, bears diamond-engravings of the Royal Arms of England, together with those of Scudamore and the date 1663, and has on that account been confidently classed as English work. A similar "flute" in the Royal Albert Memorial Museum, Exeter, is

VERZELINI GLASS, 1583
Hamilton Clements Collection

122

engraved with a portrait bust of Charles II, and the inscription "God bless King Charles the Second." But this glass is precisely similar in shape and style of engraving to another, in the Wilfred Buckley Collection at the Victoria and Albert Museum, with a portrait of the young William of Orange and the inscription "Vive le Prince." It is at least possible that all these flute glasses were made and decorated in Holland. It has been argued that political relations between England and Holland at that time were unfavourable for this. In precisely this period, however, there is record of a Dutch dealer in London who may well have acted as intermediary.

Another famous glass with a long English tradition is a large straight-sided goblet formerly in the Joseph Bles Collection. This bears a portrait of Charles within a wreath of oak leaves on a formal tree inscribed "Royal Oak" (in memory of the Battle of Worcester when Charles hid in an oak tree), flanked by portraits of the same King and of Catherine of Braganza; it bears also on the back the Royal Arms of England and the date 1663. But this, with its cylindrical bowl and hollow knop, closely resembles another goblet in the Wilfred Buckley Collection, diamond-engraved with a figure-subject and an inscription in Dutch; and like the "Chesterfield flute" and its kindred this "Royal Oak Goblet" seems unlikely to have been made or even decorated in England.

THE CLASSICS
OF ENGLISH GLASS

THE revolution in English glass-making that came in the last quarter of the 17th century was part of a general movement in northern Europe inspired by a determination to be independent of the difficult Italians. In England, too, the Restoration brought a new spirit of scientific enquiry, of which one of the first results was the foundation in 1662 of the Royal Society, and in the same year the standard Italian book on glass-making—the *Arte Vetraria* of Antonio Neri—was translated into English by Christopher Merret. The desire for independence had also an economic aspect, in a growing demand for national self-sufficiency in industry and trade, parallel with the Mercantilism of Colbert in France.

In 1673 the London Glass-Sellers' Company took the step of engaging a chemist named George Ravenscroft (b. 1618, d. 1681) to undertake glass-researches for them, with the help of an Italian named Da Costa; in that year he was granted a patent for seven years for the invention of "a new sort of crystalline glass resembling rock-crystal." The Company kept up two glass-houses, one at the Savoy in London, the other, used chiefly for experiment, at Henley-on-Thames, and here from 1674 onwards Ravenscroft worked. It was evidently the Company's intention to provide an English substitute for the Venetian *cristallo*, made of English materials only.. The early adoption of the term "flint-glass" for Ravenscroft's productions may indicate that a new source of silica had been found in the English flints, replacing the imported Venetian pebbles; for the alkali, potash was substituted for the Venetian soda. The relative infusibility of the flints may have made it necessary to increase the proportion of an unfamiliar alkali, and excess of this brought a fault in the form of "crisselling"—a network or clouding of fine interior cracks. This is a well-known and progressive disease or decay of glass, always due to excess of alkali, leading eventually to complete disintegration. Some other fluxing agent was evidently called for, and this was found in an oxide of lead. Lead had, of course, been used in glass-making long before this, but the lead-glass compositions previously known had been unsuited to the making of vessels. Neri, in his book, had praised it, "as to colour the finest and noblest glass," while his translator and editor Merret added "'tis a thing unpractised in our furnaces, and the reason is because of the exceeding brittleness thereof." But Ravenscroft eventually arrived at a satisfactory composition, and in 1676 it was reported that "the defect in the flint glass (which was formerly observed to crissel and decay)" had been remedied. In the same year it was arranged that the Company's glasses should bear a seal, and Ravenscroft was allowed to use a raven's head as his device for this purpose. From this year, then, 1676, dates the beginning of a truly English art of glass.

Physically the new glass was much heavier, volume for volume, than the Venetian; it was also softer, and fused at a lower temperature. But it was apparently never as fluid as the Venetian, and was less apt for blowing thin and working into elaborate forms. It had an oil-like brilliance and a peculiar darkness in the shadows. More important still, perhaps, in view of its subsequent history, it shared with the earlier lead-glass "paste" a remarkable light-dispersing property, giving it exceptional interior fire. This quality in the English glass, which was naturally more conspicuous in thick-walled vessels and in those cut into facets, approaches that of the diamond, surpassing rock-crystal and all other sorts of glass.

Purple, green and opaque-white glass were also made in forms suggesting that they are of Ravenscroft's period; but they were of little importance compared with his crystal "glass-of-lead."

The new glass satisfied the English taste so well that by the end of the 17th century nearly a hundred glass-houses were making it. Sand was soon substituted for flints, but the name "flint glass" continued, and still continues, to be used for the English lead-glass.

Apart from the glasses with Ravenscroft's own seal and their kindred, and a few others with seals conjecturally attributed to other houses, it is seldom possible to ascribe specimens of old English glass to makers or even places. The customary attributions, based often enough on the unsupported conjectures of an older generation of antiquaries, have far outrun the evidence.

RAVENSCROFT EWER, *c.* 1675
Cecil Higgins Collection

BOWL AND COVER IN BAROQUE STYLE
Late seventeenth century

126

There are numerous records of glass-makers, but few surviving glasses to serve as documents for the identification of their productions. Traditional ascriptions are often of very doubtful value. The attribution to Norwich, for example, of certain horizontally ribbed glasses is unsupported by evidence; there is in fact no certain record of a glass-house in that city. Again, the practice of calling almost all milk-white and fine blue glass "Bristol" is also certainly unjustified, as is the contention that all Waterford glass has a blue tinge.

London evidently remained the fashion-leading centre, dictating the forms of wine-glasses and their decoration. At Henley, from 1676 onwards, Ravenscroft was succeeded by one Hawley Bishop, who also took over the Company's Savoy house on Ravenscroft's death in 1681. Other London manufacturers flourished in this period, particularly at Southwark. There continued to be important manufactures at Stourbridge (where the local fireclay was found to be especially valuable for the glass-pots), and at Newcastle-on-Tyne and South Shields in the North, as well as at Bristol and in Ireland.

BALUSTER WINE-GLASS
Early eighteenth century

127

GROUP OF GLASSES
Early eighteenth century

The glasses made under Ravenscroft's direction are recognisable by his seal (but less than a dozen of these are known to survive), and by a price-list issued by him in 1677. They range from mugs in forms recalling the Rhenish and Fulham stoneware with which the Glass-Sellers' Company was also concerned, to very large ewers and goblets. Perhaps the most remarkable of all these primitives of English glass are two inverted helmet- or bell-shaped ewers, very boldly ribbed, with massive twisted handles. One of these, now in the Cecil Higgins Collection, bears the seal; the other, in the Wilfred Buckley Collection in the Victoria and Albert Museum, lacks it, but is much crisselled and may be slightly earlier. Some sealed goblets of German *Roemer* form, decorated with raspberry-like impressed pads called "prunts," are perhaps evidence of a desire to break away from Venetian forms; though the *Roemer* was for long the accepted form of glass for Rhenish wine. On the other hand a sealed bowl and certain covered goblets are decorated in a variant of the Venetian style, with lobed "gadrooning" at the base, and extravagant loops, wings and finials. This was doubtless the "extraordinary work" mentioned in Ravenscroft's list. Decoration of "trailed" threads pincered into a network is presumably the decoration described by him as "nipt diamond waies." There are specimens of the sort in the Victoria and Albert

128

GROUP OF GLASSES
Second quarter of the eighteenth century

Museum with stems enclosing coins (as was frequently the custom from this time onwards) of 1680 and 1684; but such work continued to be done on occasion until well into the following century. The Master's chair of the Glass-sellers' Company, made in 1704, is in fact carved on the back with a representation of two vessels of the kind.

The style of these primitives is a curious hybrid, a product of the expiring Venetian fashions and the new English glass. It is nevertheless a genuine expression of the English baroque, with all the flourish characteristic of the art of Charles II's reign. It is the analogue in glass of the elaborately wrought furniture and silver of the time.

Before long, simpler and less grandiloquent forms began to prevail, and the half-century from about 1690 onwards saw what was probably the finest of all English glass-making. Some of the best work was done less in decorative vases and goblets than in wine-glasses for actual use, a department in which Greene's designs for Venetian glass (1666–1673), already mentioned, went some way towards the creation of an English style. Greene's short-stemmed glasses with "wrought buttons" or moulded knops gave place in the latter part of the 17th century to still plainer forms with longer stems, at first hollow but soon made solid, in conformity with the character of the lead

129

metal. The plain forms of the contemporary silver, encouraged by the softer "Britannia standard" which was obligatory from 1697 to 1718, and particularly that of the reign of Queen Anne (1702–1714), may well have influenced the style of the glass. The taste shown was shared by the other arts of the time— by the architecture, silver and furniture of the period of William and Mary, Anne and the first two Georges. In glass as in architecture it was a taste marked by a love of simplicity and fine proportions rather than ornament.

The typical creation of the period was the wine-glass with solid "baluster" stem formed of discs and knops. These stems are of immense variety, showing an admirable judgement in the assembling of the globular, cylindrical, urn-shaped, and true-baluster knops, and in their proportioning to the size and shape of bowl and foot. The baluster stems were sometimes made to enclose a bubble of air, and a decoration of such "beads" was for long popular. A well-placed ribbing of bowls and feet, with gadrooning and reeding ("incising") sometimes twisted spirally, were other favourite forms of simple decoration. The characteristic 17th-century "trailing" and nipping of threads of glass also survived for a long time.

German influence, due to the importation of glasses under the Treaty of Utrecht (1713) and the accession of the Hanoverian George I in the following year, brought a new type of shouldered stem into fashion, side by side with the baluster. This was of West-German origin, but is erroneously known among English collectors as the "Silesian" stem. In its later forms it is often polygonal and twisted spirally, and is sometimes inverted.

The bowls of the wine-glasses were at first straight-sided funnels, their height not less than that of the stems. In the reign of George I bowls tended to develop a waist and "flare" or curve outwards, and the relative height of the stem was gradually increased.

Besides the wine-glasses and goblets, which were sometimes very large, many smaller vessels were made in beautiful forms. There were short-stemmed glasses for strong ale, sweetmeat-glasses with wide shallow bowls on tall stems, and above all many small glasses believed to have been used for jellies, custards and sillabub. These beautiful vessels were of plain, or ribbed, or boldly faceted forms, with single or double handles, and appear to have been generally served on plain glass salvers with baluster or "Silesian" stems to match. All these types remained current throughout the first half of the 18th century and even later.

The glass candlesticks of the period were also of great beauty, with baluster stems showing the same fine taste in the assembling of knops, air-beaded or plain, or "Silesian" or spirally reeded stems, harmoniously composed with domed, ribbed or "terraced" feet. They are often difficult to date—the beaded knops of the baluster style being sometimes found used in conjunction with the "enamel-twist" stems of the following period.

Throughout the baluster period the heavy lead glass was used lavishly; the bases of wine-glasses were made thick and solid, while edges and feet were

GROUP OF CUT GLASS
Middle and late eighteenth century

often folded over, giving added strength. The total impression is one of harmony and repose.

The taste of the succeeding period was inclined to prefer lighter glasses and more decoration. To some extent this change was due to the rococo style then making itself felt in the decorative arts, but it was also in part the result of a gradually increased Excise Duty on glass, imposed to help to provide funds for the wars with France. It was levied (1745–46 onwards) by weight of materials used, and for nearly a hundred years the burden of the Excise affected the forms and character of English glass.

BRISTOL BLUE-GLASS BOX
c. 1750–1775

THE ROCOCO PERIOD
AND THE VOGUE OF DECORATION

THE fashion that favoured lighter glasses was partly due to reaction against the rigid symmetry and occasional heaviness of the baroque style. The rococo brought a new lightness into English decoration. At the same time the Excise Duty in effect encouraged the glass-makers to produce wares whose price represented the work expended on their decoration rather than the amount of glass used in making them; and since the duty was levied by weight the proportion of lead also tended to be lessened, and from the middle of the 18th century onwards the oil-like metal of the baluster period was gradually replaced by a somewhat lighter and more "watery" glass material containing much less lead.

The wine-glasses were of relatively few shapes. Some of these, too, strictly speaking belong to the end of the previous period. Some slender baluster forms with air-beaded stems persisted at least until 1765, in glasses made at Newcastle and elsewhere. The waisted thistle-shaped bowl and the ogee and double ogee had first appeared in the reign of George I but still continued to be made. What are called drawn stems also remained popular. These had a long ancestry, going back indeed to Venetian origins. In this type of wine-glass the stem was not made separately and stuck on, but drawn out from the trumpet-shaped bowl in one piece. It enjoyed renewed popularity as a large glass in the first half of the 18th century, but soon succumbed to the general fashion for lightness. It came again in a shorter form in the 1780's and survived into the 19th century in rough tavern glasses. Straight slender cylindrical stems came into fashion with straight-sided bucket-shaped bowls, though knops were sometimes still used, as already mentioned. These appeared as cusped swellings when submitted to the facet-cutting also fashionable in stems of the middle of the century.

It is for its decoration, however, that the mid-18th-century glass is chiefly valued. The principal methods of decorating the finished glass were by cutting and engraving it on the lapidary's wheel, by scratching it with a diamond-point, and by painting it in enamel colours. But first to be described, since it belongs to the making of the glasses themselves, is the extremely popular decoration of the stems by air-, "incised," enamel-, and coloured "twists." The first of these was developed from the air-bubble or "bead" often enclosed in the knops of the baluster and at the base of the bowl of the drawn-stem glasses. It was made by elongating and·twisting a gathering of hot glass containing one or more of these air bubbles. Glasses with air-twists were apparently sometimes called "wormed glasses." The "incised twist" or "wrythen stem" was produced by elongating and twisting a moulded gathering. The "enamel" (opaque white) and coloured (green, red, blue, crimson, etc.) twists were manipulated in the same way as the air bubbles to form threads or flat ribbons of spiral form, sometimes intertwined. Rods of white or coloured glass, arranged round a cylindrical mould, were picked up on a lump of molten glass, which after being covered with clear glass by dipping was drawn out into a rod. This was twisted and if necessary combined with other rods by a repetition of the process, which was essentially the same as an ancient Roman and Venetian technique.

Diamond-point engraving (or scratching) is found on English glasses of various dates, some of which have already been described. But the rococo period produced some especially noteworthy examples. The decoration does not in fact belong strictly speaking to glass-making at all; it could be practised after dinner by an amateur, while the finer examples were evidently the work

of professional engravers on pewter and silver. Among the last-mentioned are the occasional inscriptions in beautiful flourished lettering; a fine baluster-stemmed glass in the Wilfred Buckley Collection is an early example, inscribed "God Bless Queen Ann."

But the most famous of all 18th-century English diamond-engraved specimens are those bearing the cipher of the Old Pretender ("J.R.8") in monogram, with two or three verses of a Jacobite hymn, precursor of the British National Anthem, ending with the word "Amen." They are of hotly disputed date. Most of them are of drawn stem or baluster type, dating from any time between 1720 and 1750, but at least one is an air-twist glass of a type made at Newcastle from about 1745 onwards. Several bear dates between 1716 and 1749, some of which must be commemorative, or else later additions, since the hymn refers to the Young Pretender (as the "Prince of Wales"), who was not born until 1720. References to the birth in 1725 of Prince Henry, second son of the Old Pretender, are not necessarily contemporary with that event, while "the increase of the Royal familie" may not imply, as has been supposed, a date before the death in 1735 of the Pretender's wife, but may refer to the celibacy of Prince Henry, who became a cardinal in 1747. It had thus appeared probable that the glasses were later than had been supposed, when the recent discovery of a fragmentary specimen at Dunvegan Castle, Skye, provided unexpected confirmation. This bears a diamond-engraved inscription in the same hand as the hymn, dated 1747 and referring to a recorded associate of Prince Charles Edward. It suggests a date round about 1745–48 for all the "Amen glasses." The use of the Scottish title James VIII has suggested that the engraving was done in Scotland.

The Jacobite glasses are of no particular importance in the history of English glass-making as such, but association with the cult has given them an interest for collectors. They are found with wheel-engraved and facet-cut decoration and with enamelling, as well as with diamond-point work, and examples of these will be mentioned in due course. The cryptic legends and emblems they bear have been the subject of bitter dispute; it is sometimes even uncertain whether they refer to the Jacobite or to the rival Williamite cause. A large glass belonging to Mr. C. M. Fleury, diamond-engraved with St. George and the Dragon (?) and the date 1761, and inscribed "The Glorious Memory," was claimed by a leading Jacobite authority as a "disguised Jacobite glass." But this seems unlikely since another large glass engraved by the same hand is dedicated to Oliver Cromwell. These two specimens bear the signature of George Chapman, an engraver of whom nothing further is known; but the sensitive engraving of flowers on these two glasses entitles them to rank as the finest English work in the technique. The lateness of the dates suggests that they were engraved some considerable time after their making—a possibility always to be borne in mind where decorated glasses are concerned. English glasses were also much used abroad, in Holland, for engraving on the wheel and for the characteristic Dutch stippled work in diamond-point, and mistaken conclusions may well be drawn on this account also.

The art of cutting and engraving glass was at this time chiefly a German and Bohemian accomplishment, and in those countries had produced some of its finest masterpieces long before the end of the 17th century. But in England there was no sign of its adoption before the beginning of the following century at the earliest. The first record of the appearance of German cut glass in England is of a sale in 1709, when "a great disturbance" was made by "the Glass Sellers of London whereby the auction could not be carried on." When eventually cutting and engraving were accepted as modes of decoration, they showed a distinct style suggesting an origin to some extent apart. English taste was conservative, it is true, but it may well have been affected by an amply justified preference for plain glasses in the beautiful new English metal. At all events little surviving English cut or engraved glass can be ascribed to dates before the fourth decade of the 18th century. Yet in spite of the absence of specimens there is some evidence of earlier work. In 1719 a London glass-seller, John Akerman, was recorded as employing a Bohemian cutter (believed to be one Haedy), and it is thought that certain "scaloped" and "corner'd brim" glasses seen in London by Lady Grisell Baillie in 1722 and 1727 were his productions. Jerom Johnson, another dealer, advertised in 1739 "all manner of cut glass" including "scallop'd Dessert Glasses in the newest fashion." Two explanations suggest themselves for the scarcity of surviving actual specimens. Either the references were chiefly to imported German glass; or, as is more probable, most of the earlier English specimens were destroyed when no longer in the fashion, for use as "cullet." Such destruction was especially liable to happen in the period from 1745 onwards when the cost of the materials for new glass was so greatly increased by the duty.

Most of the surviving early specimens with cut decoration are in fact sweetmeat-glasses ("dessert glasses") of the "corner'd brim" or "scallop'd"

BRISTOL SCENT-BOTTLES
c. 1750–1800

135

type. They show a style of cutting less influenced by German models than by the art of the English "glass-grinder," whose trade it was to grind mirror-plates and bevel and "scallop" their edges into scrolled, wavy, and faceted forms. Shallow slicing and simple faceting were thus the rule on these early cut glasses. The faceting of stems was perhaps imitated from the German, but in effect showed a characteristic and charming English plainness. Cutting throughout the rococo period remained relatively shallow. Triangular, four-sided and crescent-shaped slices, often in groups with notches at the inter-sections, formed pyramids and diamonds in very low relief; bands of broad fluting and above all a pattern of intersecting concavities ("hollow diamonds") like the faceting of stems were popular motives. In this way the cutting gave a heightened play of reflections, but did not greatly diminish transpar-ency. Candlesticks and tapersticks, which in this period naturally tended to become lighter, were often richly decorated with cutting. "Diamond-cut scalloped candlesticks" were advertised in 1742. To this period probably belong some of the well-known four-sided spirit-bottles, found in sets in rosewood travelling-cases. Many bottles of the kind are Bohemian glass made for the Dutch market; but "triangular bottles, stopped" in an advertisement of Thomas Betts (1756) suggests that some, at least, were made in England. Ten years later "Ladies' Dressing-boxes and Sweet-water bottles for the Ladies' Toilets" were advertised at Bath, as "from the stock-in-trade of a German who was the first that brought the art of Cutting and Engraving of Glass from Germany"; this is sometimes thought to have been Haedy, the Bohemian cutter already mentioned as employed by John Akerman as early as 1719. The greatest development of this English cut glass came later and will be further described presently.

Wheel-engraved decoration was obviously inspired by the German, but shows much less accomplishment. Fine and elaborate specimens are almost always suspected of being Dutch or German work, though perhaps done in England by immigrant craftsmen; armorial glasses of the kind are not un-common. But the native English style is seen in unpretentious borders of scrollwork and formal flowers. The first unmistakable advertisements of these date from 1735, and by 1742 "flowered glasses" were being commonly sold. The engraving is at its best in such simple motives as baskets of flowers, vine branches on wine glasses, hops and barley on glasses for ale, and apple-trees on cider glasses. But more ambitious pictorial subjects are not uncommon. Convivial scenes (inscribed "Keep it up") and hunting-subjects are often crude but charming. Landscapes with ruins, *chinoiseries* and naturalistic flowers, take up the subjects painted on the contemporary English porcelain. Seldom of great artistic merit are the engraved Jacobite glasses made for a couple of decades after the rising of 1745, with emblems and mottoes such as "*Fiat*," "*Radiat*" and "*Audentior Ibo*," the rose with two buds, the sunflower, the butterflies and bees, and the stricken oak and sapling. Rough portraits of the Pretender are also found. On the rival Williamite

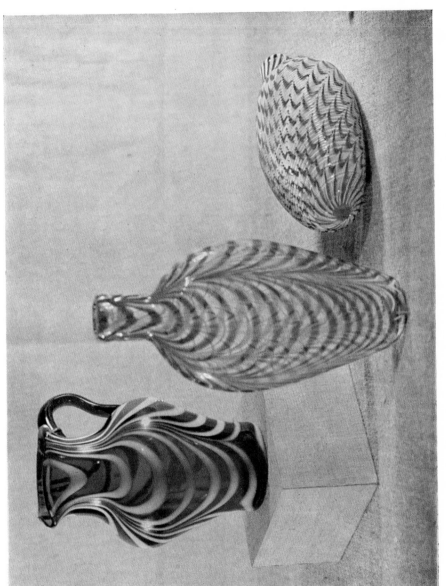

NAILSEA JUG AND FLASKS

Late eighteenth and first half of the nineteenth century

EARLY VICTORIAN GLASS FOUNTAIN WITH BIRDS

glasses are the orange-tree and equestrian portraits of William III with inscriptions such as "*The Immortal Memory*." Other glasses equally crude in engraving record the emotions of the Seven Years War (1756-63), when portraits of Frederick the Great and figures of Britannia were popular; other glasses of the time depict ships, with inscriptions such as "*Success to the British Fleet* 1759," while "*Success to the Eagle Frigate*" on another glass refers to the raiding of French shipping by the Bristol privateers.

Perhaps the most attractively simple of all the engraved decoration is that on decanters; beautifully lettered "labels" indicate the destined contents. An advertisement of 1755 speaks of "new fashioned Decanters with inscriptions engraved on them, viz., Port, Claret, Mountain, etc., etc., decorated with Vine-leaves, Grapes, etc." Decanters began to be more commonly made in clear glass in this period, taking the place of the dark-green bottle-glass decanters to be described presently as belonging to a different strand in the English tradition. The globular shape of the rare earliest type was obviously suggested by the decanter bottles, and has a rim for tying down a cork. Later specimens with glass stoppers are commoner from about 1750 onwards. At first of club shape with prominent shoulder and spire stopper, they became more slender towards 1760 and were often provided with flat stoppers in the form of a vertical disc. Gently tapering forms remained in fashion until the last years of the 18th century.

Painting in enamel colours, though common in earlier Islamic and Continental (especially Venetian and German) glass, was apparently not attempted in England until the 18th century. But soon after 1750 two sorts of enamel-decoration were practised with great success. The most original work was done by a family named Beilby, of Newcastle-on-Tyne, in particular by William (b. 1740, d. 1819) and Mary (b. 1749, d. 1797), brother and sister of that Ralph Beilby, heraldic engraver, to whom Thomas Bewick was apprenticed in 1767. The earliest recorded Beilby glasses commemorate the birth of the Prince of Wales (afterwards George IV) and are presumed to date from 1762. They continue until about 1778, when William and Mary Beilby left Newcastle for Scotland. The signed glasses bear no initial and it is difficult to distinguish the work of brother and sister. The enamelling is exquisite in colour, a cool bluish white and a soft turquoise predominating. The vine-branches, rococo scrolls and trellis and waving foliage on the earlier tall knopped glasses were painted with an exceedingly free and sensitive touch; this is presumed to be early work of William Beilby. Perhaps the finest of all Beilby glasses is a bowl—the only one recorded—given to the Victoria and Albert Museum by the Rev. G. B. Riddell, in whose family it had been preserved. This is signed and dated 1765, and painted with arms, foliage and a group of trophies, and with rococo shell scrollwork and trellis pattern, all touched in with the utmost delicacy and feeling. Later work on air-twist and opaque-white-twist glasses was not always so good; the subjects included birds, rural pastimes, portraits of the Young Pretender, and electioneering

GROUP OF ENGRAVED GLASSES
Middle of the eighteenth century

appeals. The glasses used by the Beilby family give, incidentally, a fairly sure indication of the local Newcastle types.

The second important type of enamel-painting was on opaque white glass, and a conscious rivalry with porcelain is apparent; though the popularity of the material may have been due in part to its omission from the terms of the Excise Act. Its reputed association with Bristol is of long standing, though the final proof that it was made there is still lacking. There were makers of "enamel glass," as it was called, in London and elsewhere, as well as at Bristol, and examples in "Ravenscroft" forms have already been mentioned. But the supposed Bristol type of white glass is different from these and of a very distinct and beautifully "solid" milk-white colour. Not all of it was painted; plain vases and bottles exist with no more decoration than well-judged vertical ribbing. Many of the forms fairly closely follow Chinese porcelain models; trumpet-mouthed waisted beakers and oviform and baluster-shaped vases were made in sets or *garnitures*. Cornucopia-shaped flower-holders appear to copy Worcester porcelain. Candlesticks of admirably proportioned profiles, finely reeded, and four-sided tea-caddies were also characteristic. Much of the supposed Bristol painting is of delightful pseudo-Chinese figures, with lively diaper borders, in fresh colours among which red and

GROUP OF CUT GLASSES
Late eighteenth and early nineteenth centuries

green predominate. This work is by one easily recognisable hand, formerly believed to be that of Michael Edkins, a Bristol artist who is recorded to have painted "enamel glass" for Bristol manufacturers. But the argument for this was based on the false identification of a Worcester teapot with this painting as early Bristol porcelain. Painting by the same hand is also found on Staffordshire salt-glazed wares. Enamelling in the style of the Chinese *famille rose* is associated with the *chinoiserie* subjects, again as on salt-glazed ware. Some painting of naturalistic birds and tight bunches of flowers in porcelain style by a different hand, on candlesticks and tea-caddies, was "authenticated" as his work by Edkins' grandson. Some other sorts of opaque-white glass, as well as much opal or "milk-and-water" glass were certainly made at Newcastle.

White glass was also used for *vinaigrettes* and scent-bottles, *étuis*, snuff-boxes and the like, and these pretty toys are also customarily called Bristol. But the painting on them—of pastoral figures, stars and diapers, flowers and exotic birds—is distinct from that just described and often recalls that on the enamelled metal boxes made in the Birmingham and South Staffordshire region, where the glass also may have been made. But London remained the fashion-leading centre and it is probable that some, at least, of the enamelled glass boxes, which were commonly cut all over with facets, were made there and decorated by London jewellers.

Blue glass (as well as purple and emerald green) was also used for the scent-bottles, and these again are called Bristol, though there is no proof of their making in that city, beyond a record that Michael Edkins enamelled "cans," beakers, and other objects (though not scent-bottles) of blue glass. That blue glass was, in fact, made at Bristol at a later period is shown by the mark of Isaac Jacobs on certain finger-bowls with gilt key-fret border of about 1795. His predecessor, Lazarus Jacobs, employed Michael Edkins between 1785 and 1787, and the gilt "labels" on decanters and other inscriptions on blue glass may well be Edkins' work. But much coloured glass was certainly made elsewhere, particularly in this period, when the stress on decoration brought by the Excise doubtless encouraged the makers to use it.

THE NEO-CLASSICAL PERIOD

IN the last quarter of the 18th century the rising vogue of cut glass and its increasing elaborateness called for substantial vessels, which owing to the Excise were costly to make. In 1777, 1781, and 1787, increased duties placed a still heavier burden on the English glass-industry, and there began an exodus of English glass-makers to Ireland, where there was no duty at all, which brought a somewhat questionable fame to Irish glass-making. At Waterford a new establishment was started in 1783 by George and William Penrose, merchants, with the help of a Stourbridge glass-maker named John Hill. At Dublin a London glass-cutter named Ayckbowm turned manufacturer in 1799, while in 1771 a Bristol glass-man named Benjamin Edwards set up an establishment at Dromore, Co. Tyrone, moving it five years later to Belfast. Designers and workmen were very often English and it is almost impossible in most cases to separate the productions of the two countries.

The glass in the Anglo-Irish style, as it may be called, dating from about 1780 to 1825 (when an Excise Duty was first imposed on Irish glass), is chiefly remarkable for Classical shapes inclining to heaviness. This was the period of reaction against the frivolous rococo of the mid-18th century, with its fantastic departures from symmetry, in favour of a new Classical Roman severity. Deep cutting was favoured and commonly covered the whole surface of the piece. Parallel or intersecting deep grooves gave ridges and "raised diamonds" in high relief, and these were often further cut with crisscross or stars, giving the so-called "strawberry diamonds" or "hobnail" cutting. To these new resources were added the fluting and slicing and circular concavities of the previous period. Heavy decanters and urn-shaped wine-coolers and vases are typical; boat-shaped salad bowls on insignificant moulded feet are characteristic "Irish" productions. But the only fully authenticated Irish pieces are some rather trivial finger-bowls and decanters with indefinite

. moulded fluting at the base, bearing the names of Irish manufacturers in relief on the bottom.

Some imposing cut-glass chandeliers began to be made about 1760 or earlier. A specimen in the Victoria and Albert Museum which came from a Waterford church has diamond-cut curved branches proceeding from a stem made up of globes and balls of ogee outline; but this was evidently an importation from London, where a large trade in such things was done by one William Parker of Fleet Street. Some famous chandeliers in the Assembly Rooms at Bath were made by him and bear his name. In the Regency period a favourite form of chandelier was formed by chains of small pendant drops.

In contrast to the heavy "Irish" types stands the more peculiarly English glass of the last quarter of the 18th century. Slender forms in the Classical taste and shallow cutting accord well with the mounts in silver and Sheffield plate with which they are often associated. Excellent use was made of well-placed narrow horizontal bands of low-relief diamonds in combination with shallow fluting. Wine-glasses tended to have short stems with fluting or faceting about the base of the bowl, which was often of ogee form, and square cut or moulded feet.

VASE
Late eighteenth century

143

This phase of English glass-making corresponds to the period of Wedgwood's predominance in English pottery; forms show the same Classical influences, and engraving when used at all was largely confined to the same formal motives. In the early part of the 19th century, the fashion for cameo reliefs exploited by Wedgwood extended to glass, and in 1819, to be precise, a successful manufacturer named Apsley Pellatt actually patented a process for making "silvered" and "encrusted" cameos in glass; this he had apparently learnt from the French, who were doing similar work much earlier.

By the 19th century, the English cut glass had secured a great market on the Continent. The brilliance of its lead-metal gave it an advantage over the Bohemian; and in this form English glass has continued to be preferred. This has often been regretted, the prickly monstrosities of the 1840's (for example) being poor representatives of English taste.

BOTTLES AND JUGS
AND THE GLASS MADE FOR COUNTRY MARKETS

DURING the whole period of the Venetian fashions and of the development and triumph of English crystal, common green glass continued to be made in forms that unmistakably show a Roman ancestry. Though disregarded by collectors, this bottle-glass, with its natural colouring of brownish green, is in some ways more admirable than the refined and colourless product of Ravenscroft's researches. It is well seen in the wine-bottles of the type known as decanter-bottles, but perhaps better described as serving-bottles, in which wine was brought from the cask to the table. These were made from the middle of the 17th century to about 1750, in a well-established sequence of forms, leading up to the long-necked cylindrical modern wine-bottle

DECANTER-BOTTLE
With medallion stamped : *T. Ridge* 1720

MODERN CARBOY
Green bottle-glass

suitable for storage in a bin. The practice of stamping a name and date on a pad of glass on the shoulder enables the evolution of shapes to be traced. The bottles were at first bulbous, with long neck and broad base with deep "kick"; from about 1680 to about 1735 the neck was shorter. Such bottles have continued to this day to be made for commercial and industrial purposes, their most distinguished direct descendants being the narrow-necked pear-shaped carboys, two or three feet high, used for the transport and storage of acids; these are objects of great beauty in form and material though disregarded by most people on account of their utilitarian purpose.

Bottle-glass was made at many places in London and the provinces, but an outstanding manufactory was at Nailsea, near Bristol, founded in 1788 by John Robert Lucas, a Bristol bottle-maker. Lucas sought to avoid paying some of the Excise Duty by making jugs and other vessels for domestic use in bottle-glass, which was taxed at a lower rate. These are usually of admirable form, their rich-greenish-brown material being diversified by irregular spotting and splashing of white; decoration was otherwise limited to a well-judged trailing of white threads round the neck and a crinkling of applied vertical bands. A second phase in the Nailsea production dates from the period of management of Robert Lucas Chance (1810–15), who in 1824 also took over a famous glass-house at Spon Lane, Birmingham, thus founding the still-existing firm of Chance Bros. In this period were made the typical Nailsea jugs, bowls and pocket-flasks decorated with loops of white or pink or blue or other contrasted colour. The new style is thought to have been due to French workers introduced by R. L. Chance. More sophisticated productions included glass walking-sticks and fantastically shaped tobacco-pipes for shop-windows, in the same pink-and-white style. The white and striped glass material was also used for the so-called rolling-pins, inscribed with mottoes such as "Be true to me," given by sailors to their wives.

The original Nailsea style was almost a branch of peasant art; and though inheriting the medieval and ultimately the Roman tradition, it was essentially English. The same native tradition was shared by other provincial glass-houses, in the Midlands, and especially in the North—in Yorkshire and at Newcastle and Sunderland. But it is usually impossible to assign a place of origin or even a date to the jugs, sugar-basins and simple vases made at these places, in green, blue, purple or opal-white glass. Some of them may date from the late 18th century, but most are later still, and the types continued to be made well into Victorian times. They were essentially country-market glasses, no doubt much sold at fairs and given as mementoes. All this simple coloured glass, which shows little refinement but excellent craftsmanship in shapes and handles, provided the models for several makes of early American glass. Much that is collected in America as Southern New Jersey, Pennsylvania, and Mid-Western work is scarcely distinguishable from this English provincial glass.

GLASS VASE AND BOWL DESIGNED BY KEITH MURRAY
Stevens & Williams, Limited, Brierley Hill, Stourbridge

LARGE GLASS VASE

James Powell & Sons, Limited, Whitefriars Glassworks, Wealdstone

VICTORIAN GLASS

THE Glass Excise came to an end in 1845 and the repeal was the signal for a great outburst of activity in glass-making, which had for some time previously been gathering force. The renowned Apsley Pellatt, already mentioned for his "encrusted cameos," was chiefly instrumental in a movement to revive past styles, while R. L. Chance of Birmingham was leader in a great advance in glass-technology. Colour in glass came into fashion again, inspired by the contemporary Bohemian renascence, but it was chiefly crude and harsh colour with a stress on strong reds and crimsons. All this activity found expression six years later in the Great Exhibition of 1851, which it should be remembered was held in the "Crystal Palace," then in Hyde Park, the first great building ever constructed chiefly of glass. The glassware exhibited was for the most part fantastically over-elaborate, showing an entirely mistaken belief in the value of applied ornament, and a misguided stress on size. Monstrous cut-glass fountains and chandeliers were made. Bohemian models were followed in "cased" or "flashed" glass, with coloured surface layer cut through to form a pattern. "Anglo-Venetian" glass, frosted or lavishly gilded, or of opal metal, was blown and manipulated into extravagant forms. So-called "Grecian," "Gothic," "Alhambra," and "Egyptian" work made a grotesque parody of former styles. Pressed glass, made in moulds after an American invention, figured largely at the Exhibition, and was used (as it still largely is) as a cheap means of roughly reproducing the appearance of cut glass.

Early Victorian glass, however, makes an appeal to one side of modern taste by its frequently amusing sentimentality; it is found to be so much old-fashioned nonsense, with period charm. Glass is of course a material that lends itself to fanciful play, and toys of many kinds may be fashioned from it. In the 18th century, we find glass swords being made, to be carried in processions, glass walking-sticks, practicable trumpets, and later on, exceedingly intricate models of ships. The fountain with long-tailed birds, here figured in colours, is a fitting companion to the wax fruits and stuffed owls similarly enclosed under domed glass shades in the early Victorian period. Its colour suggests that it too was made at Nailsea. The wonders of *millefiori* had been preached by Apsley Pellatt, and the Roman technique was now put to astonishing use in the making of paperweights in which the most prodigious "flowers" are seen growing at the bottom of a convex pool of clear glass.

After the orgy of the Exhibition, glass-making in common with other industrial arts set about to reform its ways, seeking with the help of the newly founded museums to achieve greater correctness in its imitation of past styles. Gothic now began to give place to Renaissance as the favourite style. In mid-Victorian times the Stourbridge School of Art helped the Stourbridge manufacturers to produce some faithful imitations of Roman cameo-glass, not without awareness of Chinese snuff-bottles. George and Thomas Woodall were noteworthy designers of this, and John Northwood is remembered for a reproduction of the most famous of all Roman cameo-glasses—the "Portland Vase." Painting on glass strove after a naturalism borrowed from porcelain, and particularly from Sèvres, and was much counterfeited in transfer-printing done by the newly invented process of colour-lithography. Towards 1875 a new influence came from Japan, then newly opened to Western trade; the asymmetrical foliate designs and diapers thus inspired eventually brought the style known as the *Art Nouveau*, at the end of the century. All the while cut glass in the Anglo-Irish styles, and pressed glass imitating it, continued to be made for both the English and the foreign markets, its "water-white" brilliance being still greatly admired. But until recent times no attempt was made to give it fresh treatment.

MODERN ENGLISH GLASS

SOON after the Exhibition, voices began to be raised in protest against the dishonesty of much of the "applied art" then fashionable, with its mechanically reproduced imitation of handwork, and its disregard of fitness for use. Ruskin with his theories and the practical sense of William Morris alike rose in protest, and in 1859 a landmark was reached when Morris commissioned Philip Webb to design for his use at the Red House, Bexley, some tumblers and wine-glasses, which were made for him by James Powell and Sons at the Whitefriars Glass-house in London. Fifteen years later, the same firm made other glasses for Morris to the design of another architect, T. G. (afterwards Sir Thomas) Jackson. From this time onwards the Whitefriars firm, under the direction of Harry J. Powell, began to recover the older and better tradition which prevailed in England before the fashion for extravagant cutting had obscured it. Not only finely manipulated glass in the

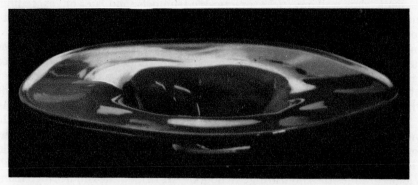

DISH DESIGNED AND MADE BY TOM HILL
James Powell & Sons, Limited, Whitefriars Glassworks

VASE DESIGNED BY CLYNE FARQUHARSON
John Walsh Walsh, Limited, Birmingham

English and Venetian manners, with trailed and tooled decoration, but austerely designed cut glass, simply faceted or fluted, was made at White-friars. In more recent times, the same firm (which in 1922 moved its premises to Wealdstone in Middlesex) has made much glass of fine quality to the design of Barnaby Powell, Tom Hill, James Hogan and others, depending for its appeal chiefly on skilful workmanship. No other modern glass surpasses Whitefriars in its exploitation, by subtle waving of surface and variation in thickness, of that interior play of light which is so essential a part of the beauty of glass; and no other firm has such lovely colour at command, in clear jewel-like blues and greens, amber and amethyst.

The cutting of glass, in spite of the bad example of the 19th century, may indeed be a veritable enhancement if used with imagination and restraint;

and some of the Stourbridge firms have lately broken away from their "traditional" prickly extravagance so far as to employ independent designers of original talent. The most successful of these was the architect Keith Murray, who designed for Messrs. Stevens and Williams of Brierley Hill, Stourbridge, a range of plain and decorated vases, and some table wares, showing a profound appreciation of the qualities of the material, especially when cut. This Brierley Hill glass is chiefly a crystal of ice-like purity, though some rare dusky greens are also of unique quality. The light-dispersing character of English lead-glass, with its mysterious play of reflections, has probably never been better revealed than in Keith Murray's great vases and bowls with their austere faceting and grooving and slicing in half-moons. His designs for engraving might seem to challenge comparison to their disadvantage with the super-subtle contemporary Swedish work, but the strength

DECANTER AND GLASSES
James Powell & Sons, Limited, Whitefriars Glassworks

DECANTER AND GLASSES
Thomas Webb & Corbett, Limited, Stourbridge

and directness of their firmly stylised plant-forms—the "Cactus," "Thistle-down" and others—make them in fact quite distinct. Other gifted designers, such as Graham Sutherland and Eric Ravilious for Stuart's, and Clyne Farquharson for John Walsh Walsh Ltd., of Birmingham, have done fine work occasionally, but none has shown quite the same mastery and understanding as Keith Murray during his short spell with the Brierley Hill firm.

But all such work as that just described, whether freely blown and wrought by a craftsman or ground down to an architect's paper plan, must at the present day rank as luxury art, aside from the main stream of development of glass-manufacture in England, where the machine has inevitably come to stay. However much we may crave it, hand-made glass is economically unreal, serving a luxury market and satisfying a self-conscious and sophisticated taste. In an age of mass-production and high wages handicraft is an anachronism, incapable of providing useful wares in such quantity as would make them available for all. However much we may regret the loss its coming implies we must recognise the machine as a potentially beneficent force in human society. Its association with a predatory commercialism is not necessary or inevitable, and in responsible hands it could bring amenities of many kinds into the lives of men and women at large. Already, in glass-manufacture, articles mass-produced by pressing are available at extremely low prices and only require the indispensable contribution of a designer of authentic talent to become works of art of a new order. Table-wares, containers for liquid merchandise, and a hundred articles of daily use are now made of glass largely by mechanical processes, and the principles that should govern their manufacture may well be regarded as more important at the present day than the merely decorative art of hand-made glass.

Many mass-produced vessels, undecorated and made for industrial, laboratory, and commercial uses, make no claim to be works of art but achieve that status largely through the unconscious artistry or sense of line and form of the engineer-designers responsible for them. And though few forms are absolutely determined by function there always seems to be a closer approach to what is felt to be the form dictated by the requirements of use. This is a matter of "period" taste common to handwork and machine-work alike.

Now the distinction between handwork and the art of the machine lies chiefly in the fact that the latter must lack the organic ("freehand") irregularity of the other. This is due to the nature of machine tools, which differ from the implements of the craftsman in that form is imparted to them with

OVEN-GLASS CASSEROLE
Phoenix Glassware Company, Birmingham

154

(as the word implies) mechanical regularity and perfection. The craftsman's design is worked out in the making, while machine work is comparable rather with the art of architecture, in which a studio-drawn design is carried out impersonally and the object may be multiplied endlessly without deviation. Thus in the mechanised making in glass of bottles and drinking-glasses, oven-ware, storage-jars and jam-pots, flasks and carboys, scent-bottles and other articles for the toilet-table, preference should be given to novel plain but well-proportioned and harmonious forms, with no decoration save slight relief frankly produced by the mould, together with such simple adjuncts to form as faceting, fluting and reeding, contrasts of texture, and the "waving" of surface produced by an indefinite faceting softened in the furnace. Colour too is all-important, but need not always be bright colour. Smoky tones and greenish tinges may have an equal charm, and here modern chemistry may offer much valuable help.

In this essentially modern art English firms such as the great house of Chance Bros. and the vast undertaking known as the United Glass-Bottle Manufacturers have had a rare opportunity which they have not failed to take. The admirable American-designed "Pyrex" oven-ware has its English rival in "Phoenix," while the English perfume-bottles have shown themselves fully equal in attractiveness to the best work of the French glass-houses in a department formerly regarded as exclusively theirs.

Modern English glass-technology, in which a leading place is taken by the great College at Sheffield, has also found many new uses for the material, uses which lie outside the scope of this book but call for a word in conclusion. In architecture above all glass has been more and more employed in recent times as a covering for walls and ceilings, either plain white or in opaque colours or black, or in the form of large sheets of polished plate with engraved, etched or sandblasted decoration on a scale never attempted before. Outdoing the builders of the Crystal Palace, which had a framework of iron, our glass-architects have constructed whole walls entirely of glass-bricks, opening up a range of new possibilities. In this the great firm of Pilkington Bros. of St. Helen's have been pioneers.

Yet such uses must always rank below the making of glass vessels. In these alone is the wonder of glass fully revealed, with its translucency and luminous colour, its crystalline brilliance and the soft mysterious play of light within its substance. For this beauty of material no glass has ever surpassed the English.

ENGLISH

POTTERY AND PORCELAIN

BY

CECILIA SEMPILL

INTRODUCTION

THE purpose of this book is not to discuss the merits of the finest examples of English Ceramics, or to compare them with the work of other countries ; rather its aim is to bring to the fore all that is individual in the work of English potters, and all that is peculiar to, and typical of, this country.

Pottery has always been a universal craft, closely allied to the lives of the people and very characteristic of different races. It is indigenous to this country and we have all the essentials here in profusion. The finest clays and ample firing have been generally available, so that the difficulties and expenses which would have been incurred had these to be imported, have not been there to limit the trade. Partly, perhaps, for this reason it has remained an intimate and personal industry, and even when its reputation became world-wide the personal thread never disappeared. This is in strong contrast to most continental pottery when the patronage of wealth so often completely overlaid the intimate peasant character of the ware and produced elaborate masterpieces of ceramic art. Certainly this patronage also produced some lovely work, but from the human point of view it is not nearly so interesting as that which has developed naturally from the day to day demands of ordinary people.

It is undeniably true that the prosperity and self-satisfaction of the nine-teenth century had a very unfortunate influence on all craft and industry of that time, and pottery and porcelain suffered with the rest. But one is tempted to observe that even in our worst periods there has been ex-hibited a humour, unconscious no doubt, but peculiarly native to this country. And through all the ages this humour recurs and gives the feeling that the English potter enjoyed his work, that he potted because he wanted to, because he loved his craft and not just because he had to earn money.

In emphasising the individual character of the work of our potters, it must not be assumed that they worked in a rarefied atmosphere, immune to outside influences. This was indeed far from being the case, but foreign influences were mostly soon absorbed and reproduced with a strong native character. A particularly interesting case of this kind is shown in the salt-glaze of the eighteenth century. This particular type of ware is generally supposed to have come to this country originally from Germany in the seventeenth century, but it was rapidly developed here on such lines that it far surpassed anything of the same kind on the Continent, and in fact the eighteenth century salt-glaze made in England is now often considered to be some of the most typical and beautiful ware this country has produced. Later the Chinese influence was very much in evidence here, as in other countries ; but once again it was given a very definite English twist, and though this influence was never so important as salt-glazing, it has left us with some very notable and lovely designs. It probably had a great influence on our own development in porcelain decoration, and brought out our best sense of colour. For in the early English porcelain the colours of the decoration are peculiarly and charmingly our own, even though the symbols are derivative ; and in their directness and simplicity they seem to have a very definite link with the water-colours of Cotman, who was so essentially an English painter.

JUG WITH VERTICAL SLIPWARE DECORATION
From the site of the Bodleian extension, Oxford.   Fourteenth century

159

BALUSTER JUGS
Green glaze with network pattern. Fourteenth century

FIRST DISTINCTIVE SHAPES

It is not until the thirteenth century that we begin to find really distinctive shapes in our native pottery. Before that time it would be easy to confuse the pots made here with those of many other countries, not excluding oriental work. This similarity was surely not due to influence from other lands, but much more likely it would seem that the early potters all the world over in their beginnings made the same shapes and used the same decorations because they were the easiest to do. Just as amateur draughtsmen usually find it more easy to draw faces looking to the left, so it is likely that the unskilled potters found certain shapes came more easily to their hands.

With the thirteenth century, though not many examples exist, we find very definite and characteristic slender jugs, undecorated except for a green or yellow glaze. In the fourteenth and fifteenth centuries these develop into fine sturdy shapes with applied decorations in the form of rosettes and diaper patterns in different coloured clays. The decorations are often extraordinarily rich in effect, and the scale and placing of the designs shows a remarkable sculptural sense. Some of the under-glaze paintings in simple brush-work sweeps, are masterly in their restraint and decoration ; but it is in the shapes of the vessels themselves that the real character is found. They are robust, generous and hearty and seem to be typical of Chaucer's England.

With the sixteenth century we have the so-called "Cistercian" ware in which we see the beginnings of slipware, which was later so richly developed. The Cistercian ware is notable for its curiously metallic black glaze, and the workings towards slipware in the simple patches of different coloured clay applied under the glaze. Tankards, mugs and tygs (tall, somewhat trumpet-shaped mugs with several handles) are the usual shapes, and they are called "Cistercian" from the fact that most, though not all specimens, have been found on abbey sites. The monks were fine potters in those days, and there are also some good examples of their tiles still in existence. These are often heraldic in decorative form and a favourite method was to inlay the pattern in different coloured clay by an impressed method, probably done with wood blocks.

CISTERCIAN WARE BEAKER WITH TWO HANDLES
Dark brown lead glaze. Sixteenth or seventeenth century

161

STAFFORDSHIRE SLIPWARE
Mug with initials R.W.
Dated 1695

SLIPWARE

The slipware of the seventeenth and eighteenth centuries is of immense importance in the study of English ceramics. This method of work reached a height of skill and excellence in this country which it never attained elsewhere. Most of the specimens still existing are obviously the show pieces of the potters, made for some special occasion, such as a wedding perhaps or christening, as an outlet to compensate for the duller everyday work. Little of the ordinary utility ware is left, though we have reason to know that this too was of a high standard in simple design, though it had comparatively little decoration. The show pieces were things of sheer delight, and in them we see all the humour and imagination of the potter who loved his work. There is a fantastic freedom of imagination which reminds one of the gargoyles and pew seats of the

STAFFORDSHIRE SLIPWARE
Mug excavated at Burslem probably made by J. or R. Simpson, c. 1690
Tankard of *sgraffito* slipware, c. 1725

medieval sculptor, and indeed it is likely that these latter were in the same way an outlet for the sculptor as the posset-pots and loving cups were for the potter.

As W. B. Honey so rightly says, the technique of this ware is very similar to that used in decorating an iced cake. Different coloured slips were trailed on the pot in scrolls, arabesques, dots, "stitching" and all manner of ways in most intricate and subtle designs, and afterwards glazed. There certainly is an almost edible quality about some of the most richly decorated pieces, though again the simpler ones, notably the dishes of the Tofts, which usually have some central figure surrounded by more formal patterns, are masterly in execution and sureness of design which though unsophisticated are utterly convincing and satisfying. Many different coloured slips were used, and though the more usual are red, white, black and different shades of brown, there is also occasionally a very attractive olive green. The use of counterchange in colours was highly ingenious, and remarkable skill is shown in the handling of the patterns.

The names most prominently associated with this work are those of George Richardson and Nicholas Hubble, and also of course the Toft brothers. The first two worked at Wrotham in Kent, and until Dr. Glaisher made extensive researches in this neighbourhood the names of the Wrotham potters were all unknown and "Wrotham wares" covered this particular class of work, which ranged from approximately 1612 to 1721. Wrotham ware is on the whole less skilful than the Staffordshire slipware, and the total effect is more cakelike and less pictorial. Certain "stitching," probably meant to resemble stump-work, is peculiar to this district and applied rosettes and pads of clay cut into flower and star forms are much used. The Staffordshire slip-workers used a greater variety of coloured clays and were apt to be more pictorial in their designs, particularly on the large dishes usually associated with Thomas and Ralph Toft. These last potters reached the highest peak of slipware, and some of the pieces attributed to them show an incredible skill in the handling of this very difficult process of decoration, quite apart from a fine sense of design. There is a freedom of line in the Staffordshire work which is very distinctive from the Wrotham wares.

Another group of the same type of work is generally known as "Metropolitan" ware from the fact that the pieces have generally been found in or near London. The decoration is much more simple than that of either Wrotham or Staffordshire, and pious texts are usually combined with simple flower designs. It was made roughly during the middle part of the seventeenth century, but seems to have finished with the great fire of 1666.

In Staffordshire particularly there were various other methods of using slip apart from the icing-sugar technique, and "feathering" and "combing" were particularly effective. Both these were very similar in method and result to the marbled papers used in book-binding and some of the pieces are extraordinarily lovely. "Agate" ware, yet another process used about this time, was a mixing of different coloured clays in the body of the pot so that the effect was not unlike those lumps of plasticine which are composed of the odds and ends of various coloured sticks. On the whole not very attractive, though some of the bolder pieces have charm. Finally there was the incised method, when the design was scratched through the outer slip to a contrasting body; or in some cases large areas of outer slip were cut away to leave as it were a stencilled pattern underneath. Altogether it was an exciting period for the potters, and their work was full of imagination and invention.

FULHAM STONEWARE AND LAMBETH ENAMELLED EARTHENWARE
Seventeenth and eighteenth century

MAIOLICA AND DELFT WARE

We must now turn to an important type of work which overlapped the slipware period. This is tin-enamelled or maiolica and delft ware and as the names imply these were of Italian and Dutch origin, though the best of this class of work was essentially English in character, and the names maiolica and delft are now only used to distinguish between polychrome and monochrome tin-enamelled decoration respectively.

Tin-enamelling is roughly a process of lead-glazing low-fired earthenware, with the lead-glaze whitened and made opaque by oxide of tin. This is then painted before firing, and though the range of colours is somewhat limited, it is brilliant compared with anything used in this country before.

The earliest examples of this ware are curiously enough more unlike their foreign counterparts than much which came later, and the sturdy silver mounted jugs (the silver mounts dated about the middle of the sixteenth century) enamelled in deep blue or splashed in purple, brown or yellow, are very typical of this country. Later the maiolica potters who settled in Lambeth and those parts worked in a much more Italian manner, and it was not until nearly a century later that the enamelled ware of our potters showed its true development on lines independent of foreign influences.

At first both colours and designs were very derivative and the English potters were evidently feeling their way with a dazzlingly bright new range of colours hitherto unknown to them. Even so the shapes of the pieces were distinctive and personal, and the barrel-shaped mugs, two handled and lidded posset-pots, and narrow necked pot-bellied wine bottles were peculiar to this country.

Perhaps the best known maiolica wares, which are associated with Lambeth, are those usually decorated with stylised flowers and pictures of the Fall, the latter drawn with much unsophisticated humour. The later Bristol wares, which seem to reach the highest point in this class and period of work, include portraits and hunting scenes on these typical large dishes or chargers, and better still there are from the same town lovely posset-pots, bowls and tiles decorated in monochrome, usually blue or purple.

But perhaps the loveliest of all this ware as made in England is found in the so-called Bristol Delft, which combines the technique of tin-enamelling with strong Chinese influence on the design. Perhaps it is more accurate to say Chinese inspiration, for the designs though certainly inspired by the orientals would never have been executed by them. Once again we have an unmistakably English approach to the subject, and the freedom of thought and drawing quite apart from the use of colour, are all our own, as may be seen particularly in the first half of the eighteenth century. Here we have dishes, punch bowls and table-ware decorated with the most charmingly romantic landscapes in which stroll, as it were, oriental or Gainsborough-like figures. Amongst the little houses, trees and lakes, boats and people come and go, sometimes in blue or purple alone, and sometimes in the most surprisingly bright colours with a particularly noticeable clear red.

The Liverpool-Delft ware was on the whole not nearly so interesting, though, in passing, mention must be made of the very typical punch-bowls from these parts, mostly made in the eighteenth century, with topical inscriptions and coats of arms. At Liverpool they also used transfer-printing on tiles, which though not very pleasing in effect is historically not unimportant. Much Liverpool ware is of disputed origin; the best is apt to be claimed as Bristol, and on the whole this seems likely to be true.

Mention must be made of that charming group of wine bottles which come into the Delft class. These mostly date from the middle of the seventeenth century and are usually only decorated with the name of the wine and possibly the date, and an arabesque or flourish usually in blue or purple. The lettering is completely adequate as decoration, and these bottles are amongst some of the most delightful and typical English tin-enamelled ware.

ENAMELLED EARTHENWARE PAINTED IN BLUE
WITH PORTRAITS OF TWO CHILDREN
Inscribed on the back—E. A. Taylor
Bristol. Middle of the eighteenth century

THE BEGINNINGS OF STONEWARE

John Dwight of Fulham (1637 to 1703) is one of the important single figures in the history of ceramics in this country ; not on account of the beauty of his productions, for though there are many excellent pieces which come under his name it is now generally agreed that these were made by others working under his direction. The fame of Dwight rests on the fact that it was he who first introduced stoneware into this country. In 1671 he took out his first patent for stoneware, which up till then seems not to have been made in England at all. From the Dwight works in Fulham now comes an entirely new class of work which was later to be developed into one of the finest and most individual classes of English pottery. Stoneware is merely pottery fired at a very high temperature, which makes it extremely hard and impervious to liquids. But its true beauty and usefulness was found when it was salt-glazed (through salt being thrown into the kiln at the height of the firing) which added a very hard film of glaze to the objects in the kiln.

Very little remains that can be attributed with certainty to Dwight, though the most important and interesting pieces without doubt came from his works. These are of course the salt-glaze busts and figures which show a perfection of technique for ceramic statuary. One of the reasons why so few pieces remain is due to the fact that each bust or figure was the actual work of the artist and was not duplicated in any way. The very hardness of this ware was particularly suitable for the clear cut forms of sculpture, and the thin salt-glaze gave a most attractive liveliness to the surface. Most of these figures are of a white or slightly buff colour (also an innovation of Dwight's) though there are one or two examples in dark brown, which is the colour with which salt-glaze is usually associated nowadays. The most charming figure of all is that inscribed "Lydia Dwight dyed March 3rd 1673," a half-length recumbent figure of a child modelled with touching simplicity and feeling. However, it is not to be assumed that even this was the work of Dwight himself, though it undoubtedly came from his factory. The name of the sculptor is not known with any certainty, but the present opinion seems to be that it may have been the young and then unknown Grinling Gibbons.

In 1693 Dwight brought a lawsuit against John and David Elers and others for infringement of patents in connection with his processes, and this is another important landmark in this story. The Elers brothers who were of Dutch-German origin, started their lives as silversmiths and then later learned the art of stoneware in Cologne. Having sound business instincts, and seeing the great possibilities of this ware, they came to England and settled first in London, where they started to work. Later they moved to Staffordshire where ample clay and firing were ready to hand, which made it a more suitable centre for pottery. Their appearance

By courtesy of the City Museums, Stoke-on-Trent

SLIPWARE DISH BY THOMAS TOFT, C. 1675
The design shows, though incorrectly, the Royal Arms of England
The initials C.R. stand for Charles II

By courtesy of the Syndics of the Fitzwilliam Museum, Cambridge

STAFFORDSHIRE TEAPOT DECORATED WITH APPLIED RELIEFS, C. 1755

From the Glaisher collection

'ELERS' WARE
The cup probably by Elers, c. 1695. The teapot c. 1750

in Staffordshire was to prove of the utmost importance, for they not only introduced salt-glaze to that district but also taught the advantages of refining and mixing the clay body, and then the thinness and precision which could be obtained by turning. They in no way competed with Dwight in the making of busts and figures, but where they most successfully encroached on his ground was in the matter of what was known as Dwight's "red porcelain," which was in fact a fine red stoneware, unglazed and of hard texture. This was made to imitate the so-called Chinese red porcelain, which at that time was being imported into this country, and as used by the Elers brothers for tea-pots and the like, it had an immediate success.

The shapes of the tea-pots and mugs attributed to these brothers often show the influence of their silversmith training, but a new lightness and thinness was also brought into the working of clay which was a very important step forward. The hard, tough body could be turned with precision on the lathe, and its same toughness made it very suitable for the applied decorations of sprigs and sprays of flowers and occasionally heads and figures which are so characteristic of the Dwight-Elers work. Staffordshire had now indeed come to the threshold of a new era which was to lead to a lasting world-wide reputation.

STAFFORDSHIRE SALT-GLAZE PEW-GROUP
White with brown decoration. Early eighteenth century

THE RISE OF STAFFORDSHIRE FAME

With the Elers brothers an entirely new field had opened, which could compete in quality with the imported Chinese wares in such demand owing to the rising popularity of tea-drinking. The potters were inspired to experiment and work for a suddenly growing market, and salt-glaze was an exciting new process. Always now the working was towards something akin to porcelain, not only in texture but also in colour, and the next step naturally became white stoneware, the Staffordshire salt-glaze which in its class is unsurpassed to-day.

Before the true white-bodied stoneware appeared, the ordinary clay was surface-washed with a white Devonshire clay (which was non-plastic and so not suitable for making bodies) in a manner similar to the process of tin-enamelling. This innovation is usually ascribed to Astbury (died 1743) though there are varying opinions on this point, as also on the question of who first introduced calcined flint into the clay itself so as to give a white body. This too is now generally thought to have been Astbury's innovation, and by 1730 white stoneware had really come to stay. Shortly after this the use of porous moulds for casting (a method imported from France) caused the Staffordshire wares to take another bound forward and opened up yet another line of development. By this process it was possible to make much thinner and lighter bodies than before, and at the same time much more complicated shapes, such as

STAFFORDSHIRE SALT-GLAZED STONEWARE
Middle of the eighteenth century

could not have been thrown on a wheel or turned on a lathe. Added to this it was also possible to reproduce exact copies of certain shapes in large quantities and with rapidity, so that they could be sold at a price which was within the reach of most people and far below that of imported wares.

The commercialisation of the Potteries was at hand; all the ingredients were there, and at this point Josiah Wedgwood came on the scene and by his masterly direction established the fame of the Potteries, not only at home but abroad. But here we must go back a little, for the rise of Wedgwood marks the end of the salt-glaze period, and this period produced some of the most beautiful and most typical work of English potters, and cannot be dismissed without further comment.

Nottingham salt-glaze, which flourished from the beginning of the eighteenth century until nearly the end, stands in a class by itself. It is curiously uninfluenced by Staffordshire, and has a sculptural simplicity about its shapes which are all its own. Most of the pieces are of a warm brown colour, and the decorations are usually incised formal flower patterns or even more usually simple cross-hatchings and patterns not unlike the pargettings of the old Essex plaster walls; dates are often included and all this is placed with the utmost restraint and in no way confuses the noble and dignified shapes; two-handled loving cups, bowls and mugs, were all made with a lightness which again distinguishes it from other salt-glaze of that time.

STAFFORDSHIRE ENAMELLED SALTGLAZED STONEWARE. MIDDLE OF THE EIGHTEENTH CENTURY
Toy teapot with red rose design on a black ground

On returning to Staffordshire we find that Astbury's white washes and white clay bodies had inspired a use of colour which had not been employed on stoneware before. The white grounds lent themselves to painted decoration which gave further opportunities to compete with the gaily decorated imported porcelains.

One of the first uses of white salt-glaze was in contrast with coloured clays, and so we have an interesting development from the earlier slipware. Now we find sprigging, vining, rosettes and stamped reliefs in white on coloured bodies, and the results are often very charming indeed. Astbury's name is associated with much of this work, but Thomas Whieldon (1719 to 1795) developed his ideas further. Whieldon made great use of "agate" ware for bodies, which though technically interesting were not always very beautiful. But we find his most attractive development in his lead-glaze ware on which he combines a number of fine coloured glazes with moulded and applied reliefs in "vineing" and stylised flower spriggings. The colours of this typical Whieldon-ware (most often in teapot form) are strong and rich and mark an important advance in coloured decoration. Whieldon also made some birds and figures very charmingly decorated and glazed in these same colours.

But of all Staffordshire figures the most interesting and most typical of this time, or perhaps any time, were the famous pew-groups of the first half of the eighteenth century. There are not a great number of them in all, and it is thought that they may all have been the work of Aaron Wood, a famous block-cutter of that time, who started work as an apprentice to Thomas Wedgwood in 1731. These stylised figures have all the charm and humour of the Toft brothers' slip-ware, and the childlike simplicity of approach has a directness which is completely satisfying for the material used. These groups are usually in white salt-glaze picked

174

out most amusingly in brown slip. Seated figures of couples smirk at each other in their pews or gaze ahead with embarrassed aloofness. The dresses of the period are rendered with intriguing details of buttons, bows and curling wigs. There is a superlative group of the Fall in the Glaisher collection, and the whole story may clearly be read in the expressions of Adam and Eve. Though the figures are naïve, the design of the tree and its decorative composition with the whole group is masterly.

The Whieldon-type figures (mid-eighteenth century) are of course coloured, and though they too have a childlike charm they are certainly more sophisticated than the pew-groups, and seem to have a slightly oriental character. The coloured groups attributed to Ralph Wood (second half of the eighteenth century) and much sought after to-day are more mature still, and though they have humour it is not as spontaneous as that of the earlier pew-groups. The colours however are lovely and very individual, though the figures themselves are often copied from French groups or even engravings. This same Ralph Wood was of course primarily famous for his Toby jugs ; but these too are now thought to have been inspired, or even originally modelled, by a Frenchman. The salt-glaze stoneware enamelled in colours, again in emulation of the imported oriental porcelain, once more takes a bound forward and some pieces now clearly show their workings towards the first English porcelain designs. William Duesbury, who later made porcelain at Derby, was previous to that known to have decorated salt-glaze ware for Staffordshire. There are some good pieces (again mainly tea and punchpots) attributed to him and his workers, dating between 1750 and 1760, in which the oriental flowers and figures are given a new and personal life and vitality.

Shortly after this, transfer printing began to be used with salt-glaze. In its initial stages it was very charming, and the colours were used sparingly and effectively, and the transfers themselves were placed with a sure sense of design. It was later of course that this type of decoration became so debased, when it was plastered on at random by people who had no eye for design and only had an urge for more and more ornament.

STAFFORDSHIRE 'WHIELDON' WARE TEAPOT
Agateware c. 1750

DETAIL FROM A CATALOGUE ISSUED BY JOSIAH WEDGWOOD
IN THE EARLY NINETEENTH CENTURY
Plate engraved by William Blake

JOSIAH WEDGWOOD
AND THE SOPHISTICATION OF POTTERY

As has been noted before, the rise of Wedgwood marks the decline of salt-glaze, for Josiah Wedgwood's cream earthenware was from every point of view a better commercial proposition than the white salt-glaze, and Wedgwood was certainly a very good business man quite apart from his other qualities.

It is fashionable nowadays to deplore the commercialisation of the Potteries as being the death of true ceramic art in this country, but this is a very short-sighted view of the true case. Sophistication, commercialisation, industrialisation had to come, as inevitably as middle age must follow youth unless the youth dies young. And as this development was inevitable so were we lucky to have it brought about primarily by a man of such high standards as Josiah Wedgwood. The texture and quality of his cream earthenware from about 1760 until the present day has been unsurpassed, or for that matter, unequalled ; and his simpler shapes from then until now have always shown an appreciation of what the ordinary people needed, and they were given it in the very best forms. Wedgwood's work has been much obscured by the exotic demands of the mid-Victorian era, but even when his firm was turning out the most extravagantly vulgar of their pieces (and they were never as vulgar as those of other potters) at the same time it will be found there was also a steady flow of excellent, simple tableware, of first-class design and quality, to fulfil the everyday needs of ordinary people.

At the end of the eighteenth century there was great demand and scope for new tableware. The white salt-glaze which had been so successful had its drawbacks. It was very brittle, and its great hardness wore away silver spoons and forks. The new cream earthenware had not these disadvantages, and it had a smoother surface which was more suitable for table use. Its success was immediate and its influence wide-spread,

Dairy Ware

1109

Cream Vase

1110

Butter kit

1113

1116

1119

1121

ARTICLES FOR USE IN THE DAIRY
From Josiah Wedgwood's first Shape Book

not only in this country but on the Continent where it achieved a great reputation.

But there was also another way in which Wedgwood made a profound mark on the Potteries, and that was in the improved transport facilities which came about largely through his far-sighted and businesslike vision. He it was who agitated until the canal connecting the Trent and Mersey was built, and on July 26th, 1766, he actually cut the first sod of this himself. This means of short-circuiting the transport of clay from Devon and Cornwall, and salt and flints from other parts of the country, reduced the charges per mile to less than one-seventh of what they had previously been.

It may be of interest to mention here also Josiah Wedgwood's connection with James Watt, and his pioneer work in the use of steam power in the Pottery Industry. The first mention of any engine in those parts was that of John Turner of Stoke who employed an engine of sorts, but not a steam engine, to pump water. Spode seems to have bought this later and also used it for pumping. After some experimenting in 1782 and 1784 Wedgwood ordered in 1793 a 10 horsepower steam engine from Watt, to be used for the following purposes : 1. To grind flints. 2. To grind enamel colours. 3. To operate a sagger crusher. 4. To temper or mix clays. This engine was still working up till 1912, when it was demolished and sold for scrap, but it had been the beginnings of all power production in the Potteries.

Leaving the business side of Wedgwood's genius and returning to the wares he produced, we find that as a potter he was infinitely skilful though as an artist he was more persevering than inspired. He produced the most excellently made and designed utility articles, and it is interesting to note that he took great trouble over these simple designs, employing first-class men. (We even find that his successors commissioned William Blake to draw and engrave the illustrations for the catalogue of shapes in 1815.) He perfected such well known wares as Black Basalt (black unglazed stoneware of extreme hardness and fineness of grain) and Jasper Ware, (a new white body of great hardness, which could be polished on a lapidary's wheel and stained in various colours with metallic oxides). These two wares were largely used for decorative pieces, vases, urns and the like and the famous plaques, cameos and decorative mounts, which were classical in design : sometimes very charming but more often rather dully derivative. The table-ware and intimate little pieces such as buttons, snuff-boxes and beads, were far more interesting and personal.

On the other hand the decoration of his cream earthenware, or Queensware as it is called, even though it was also classical in feeling, showed much more imagination and artistic sense, and many of the early border designs are quite lovely in every way. There was great charm too in his perforated ware, which was later to be developed and copied so success-

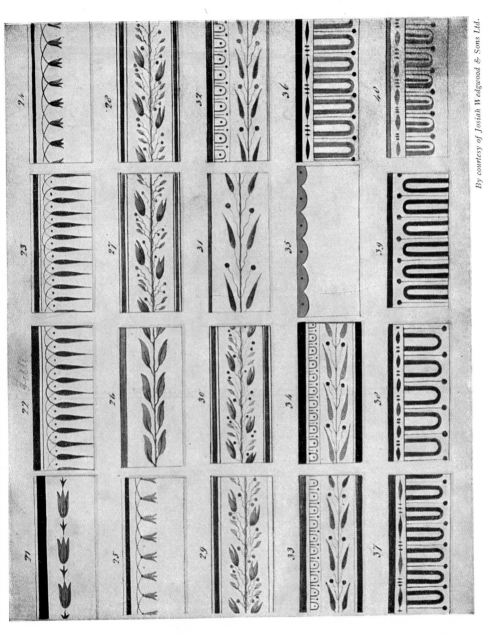

PATTERNS FOR TABLEWARE

Designs from the first pattern book of Josiah Wedgwood begun shortly after 1759

WORCESTER TEAPOT AND BOWL, C. 1765-1770

1238

Asses milk vessel

1240

Inhaling Pot

ARTICLES FOR USE IN THE SICK-ROOM
From Josiah Wedgwood's first Shape Book

fully at Leeds. It was inevitable that a man of Wedgwood's inventive genius should have many imitators, but not many of them even approached the very high standard of his productions in the perfection of finish on which he insisted, and certainly none was successful in such a variety of techniques in which he excelled. William Adams, John Turner and Henry Palmer were some of those who made jasper, basalt and marbled wares after Wedgwood's patterns. Often they made blatant copies, though sometimes, as in the case of Turner, the designs were more original than the models. The first Josiah Spode naturally owed much to Wedgwood also, but he broke out in an entirely new line in "blue-printed" earthenware. It was in 1770 that he began making printed cream ware, and by 1790 this was the most popular ware produced in the Potteries, and decorated tableware was within the reach of ordinary people. The first printed ware produced by Spode was on glaze in black with the colour (cobalt blue) filled in by hand. Later he learnt from Turner of Worcester the art of under-glaze printing from coloured transfers, not so unattractive when the colour was confined to blue only, as with Spode's ware. He made an enormous fortune from this type of work, and created a fashion for blue and white which dominated the last half of the eighteenth century.

Leeds also took up many of Wedgwood's innovations, but it is principally on that pottery's developments of the pierced cream-coloured ware that its reputation rests. Lovely and delicate tableware came from there from 1774 onwards, and the finely pierced borders and centre pieces are worthy successors to the first of this type of work made by Wedgwood. Between 1760 and 1780 there was also produced some very charming enamelled cream earthenware, notably that in red and black only, which is now almost always attributed to Leeds though Staffordshire claims some too.

At the end of the century much Staffordshire ware was sent to Liverpool to be painted, and it is often very hard to tell which are local productions. Much of this was made for the American market at this time, particularly jugs and mugs with rustic scenes and inscriptions. With the close of the eighteenth century and the development of porcelain, there is an end to the vigorous growth of true pottery in this country. It is true, as has been observed before, that there has always persisted a vein of excellent productions for those who looked for them or needed them, in mass-produced earthenware of such factories as Wedgwood's. But the peasant pottery which was so typically English was swamped by the new fashions and new demands for cheaper, 'prettier' and brighter tableware, which also insisted on a white body; and we find for a time that the naïveté and charm which seemed to leave earthenware with the industrialisation of the Potteries, passes to the new discovery of porcelain, until it, too, becomes sophisticated and in its cleverness loses its charm.

STAFFORDSHIRE CREAM-JUG IN BLUE JASPER WARE WITH CAMEO RELIEF IN WHITE
Made by John Turner. Late eighteenth century

Before we go on to the nineteenth century it seems more fitting now to go back a little time to the beginnings of English porcelain.

Porcelain had been made in Europe long before the English potters discovered the secret. It was known in Italy as early as the end of the sixteenth century, but the earliest dated piece known to have been made in England is a Chelsea jug of 1745 (now in the British Museum) though the Bow factory came into existence just before that.

Most English porcelain is what is known as "soft paste" and is, as its name implies, softer and more opaque than true, or "hard paste" porcelain as made in the Far East. Hard paste was only made at Bristol, Plymouth and New Hall. English eighteenth century porcelain is very "peasant" in comparison with contemporary work on the Continent, which was at that time greatly patronised by the nobility and so more sophisticated and elaborate. This continental work was much imitated in England, but in such a fresh and naïve way that it took on a new life. Over-glaze painting is the most usual decoration of English porcelain, and printing on porcelain (used most extensively at Worcester) was an English invention perhaps of more interest than merit. The colours used in painting, particularly in early work, were particularly fresh and clean, notably in yellows, emerald green and an excellent purple. The feeling for figures and groups which developed about this time gave great scope for this new material ; and the lively colours, and the fashion for tea-drinking called for new and lighter tableware which could be supplied by porcelain.

Bow is generally accepted as being the earliest porcelain factory set up in this country, and its manager for some time was Thomas Frye, who in 1744 took out a patent for making porcelain in which he used an imported clay from America called unaker. A second patent of his in 1748 mentions the inclusion of what seems most likely to have been calcined bones, and some fifty years later Josiah Spode perfected the use of this bone-ash which came into general use and is still one of the usual ingredients of English porcelain to-day.

In 1768 William Cookworthy of Plymouth took out a patent for making true hard-paste porcelain, but it was an expensive commercial proposition and could not compete with other wares of that date. Cookworthy moved his works to Bristol in 1770 and in 1781 sold his patent rights. Hard paste was made in small quantities for a short time after this at New Hall (Staffordshire) but by 1820 it was no longer made in England.

The Bow factory made much tableware for general use, but it is in fact for its figures that it is probably best known. The earliest Bow pieces, which include figures in plain white porcelain, are of somewhat uneven textured paste with a thick greenish-yellow glaze, and where colours are used they are apt to be rather crude. From about 1755 onwards however, some really lovely work came from this factory. The paste and glaze had improved and extremely skilled modellers and enamellers were employed. A certain Frenchman called Tebo (or Thibaud) who at one time worked for Wedgwood, is known to have worked as a repairer in the Bow factory, and is also thought to be the modeller of some of the early groups marked To. A certain John Bacon was also thought to have been one of their modellers, and J. T. Smith in *Nollekins & his Times* quotes a conversation between Nollekins and Panton Betew in which the former declared that Moser, Keeper of the Royal Academy, modelled also for this factory.

Concerning the enamelling of these pieces there is much speculation and controversy, but it is interesting to find that William Duesbury, who was known as a salt-glaze enameller, also worked independently decorating Chelsea, Bow and other ware. It is not known for certain if he enamelled, or merely decorated in unfired colours, but certain pieces seem to be very typical of his work. Later he bought up the Longton Hall works and started the Derby factory in 1756.

Whoever modelled or enamelled these charming Bow figures, the fact remains that they are some of the best that were ever made in porcelain in this country. They are on the whole simpler and cleaner in form than the Chelsea groups and there is an unusual use of colours, often discordantly lovely, which is very typical. The birds are quite fantastic in their colourings, but the light-hearted invention has all the attractiveness of a fairy tale.

The figure groups were often copies of those from Meissen, but they were simplified and endowed with a new life and character. The tableware on the other hand was more imitative of Oriental decorations, not so well assimilated or translated, though some of the printed decoration and underglaze blue painting is fresh and sprightly. The printed designs are usually of French or Italian influence. There are some lovely plates painted with fruits and flowers, very similar to some from the Chelsea factory, and possibly even done by the same hand.

The later work of this factory showed a great falling off in quality of material and design, and in 1776 it was closed down.

The Chelsea factory is known to have existed in 1745, though it is uncertain how long before that it had been started. It is believed that two Frenchmen called Charles Gouyn and Nicolas Sprimont were the original owners of the works, and certainly the porcelain they made was of the French type of soft paste of a very translucent, creamy quality. Sprimont was a silversmith, which probably accounts for the fact that some of the earliest shapes were derived from silver work. This earliest work is marked with an incised triangle, and the famous "goat and bee" pieces belong to this period.

LOWESTOFT MUG WITH SCALE BORDER, DECORATED WITH FLOWERS
From the collection of Mr. G. F. Hotblack

BOW, POSSIBLY WORCESTER, FIGURE OF A LADY IN A BLUE HAT WITH
YELLOW JACKET AND SKIRT STRIPED IN BLUE AND PUCE, C. 1765
From the collection of Mr. G. F. Hotblack

About 1750 a denser paste was used and a colder glaze, and the anchor mark first appears, in relief on an oval medallion. Figures and birds began to be made in large quantities, much influenced by Meissen though not direct copies of these subjects. The colours were much more naturalistic than those of Bow. Between 1750 and 1760 some good work came from this factory, both in groups and figures and in table ware. The former are justifiably well-known, though the uncoloured groups are not as generally familiar as the coloured, which is a pity as they show off the thick cool glaze to perfection.

When colour was used it was with immense taste and skill, and the interpretation was essentially English and often more lovely than the originals. The colours of flowers and birds were clean, lively and un-expected, but they never seemed out of place as so often is the case with later paintings on porcelain.

Nicolas Sprimont was evidently a man of great taste, for he seems to have taken over the factory entirely about 1750 and under his rule the highest peak of its manufacture was reached. About 1754 we have the first mention of the "Toys" comprising snuff boxes, trinkets, smelling bottles, seals, etc., which achieved a European reputation. These lovely little objects certainly are the essence of all the charm and humour of the best of our porcelain, and are quite unlike anything made elsewhere.

The tablewares of this date are characterised by decoration in the form of scatterings of birds, flowers and insects in an irregular and light-hearted manner, and are typical of the popular idea of Chelsea china. At the same time were made those plates with large botanical paintings of flowers and fruits with butterflies and insects amongst them. These are some of the loveliest productions of this factory, with their bright, sharp colourings, improbable and yet convincing. This type of decoration was much imitated later, but became more and more naturalistic until the porcelain itself was completely forgotten and by the last half of the nineteenth century it degenerated into the too realistic representation of inconsequent vegetation.

The first anchor mark (relief) was followed by the red (enamelled) anchor which shows perhaps the best period, and the one to which the finest of the botanical designs belongs. Little gilding was used during this period, but from about 1759 it was used much more lavishly and from then onwards the mark was a gold anchor. The Chelsea gilding is very soft and warm in colour and by comparison makes the highly burnished work of later times seem vulgar. Very little blue and white was made at Chelsea, which is regrettable as the little that is known is very beautiful, both in colour and glaze. The designs were mostly derivative from the Chinese or Japanese.

Little is known about the artists who worked for Chelsea, though there is much speculation on the matter. J. T. Smith in *Nollekins & his*

Times makes Nollekins assert that his father (who was a painter) worked for this factory, and in the same paragraph Betew states that Sir James Thornhill and Paul Ferg did so also.

In 1770 the factory was bought up by Duesbury of Derby, and from then until 1784 is the Chelsea-Derby period.

The Derby factory seems to have been started about 1750. There is some uncertainty about the original owners of the works though Andrew Planché, John Heath and William Duesbury are mentioned in the early stages. Duesbury and Heath are known to have been the owners when Chelsea was bought up in 1770, and in 1779 Duesbury became sole manager.

The early Derby products are noticeable for the rather bluish glaze and general lightness of body. The figures, which were made in large numbers, are stiff and self-conscious beside those of Bow and Chelsea and though they have a certain charm they are not in the same class as the best groups from either of the other factories. Some of the early figures have been confused with those from Bow, but the colours, though similar, are apt to be blurred. The tableware was negligible in the early days, but later it was developed in a distinctive and formal manner, and after the amalgamation with Chelsea some really good work was produced.

The Chelsea-Derby tableware is some of the most perfect tea-table ware imaginable. It has all the delicacy and precision of fine craftsmanship, and the slight but fascinatingly satisfying decorations seem to symbolise all that the tea-table stood for in those leisured days. It is essentially English, and irresistibly conjures up pictures of Jane Austen and her friends, and the water colours of Thomas Girtin. The shapes of the teapots and cups show a real and practical appreciation of the art of tea drinking, and the wreaths, swags and delicate flower decorations only enhance the shapes themselves.

In 1784 the Chelsea works were closed down entirely but Derby continued until 1848, though its productions rapidly deteriorated in taste after the beginning of the nineteenth century. Mention must be made of the biscuit (unglazed) figures and groups which were made by this factory from about 1770 onwards. They are interesting as being the first of this type of figure to be made in England, in imitation of Sèvres. Unglazed porcelain has a sickly and smug quality which is not pleasant used in this way.

The Worcester factory was started in 1751 by a small company of men who set out to perfect a new porcelain formula incorporating the use of Cornish soapstone, which was first experimented with by William Cookworthy of Plymouth. It was probably due to this new body that early Worcester pieces are so much lighter and more clean-cut than most of their contemporaries. The early shapes are once again very reminiscent of silver work, and the glaze, which is of a fine even texture, is apt to be

CHELSEA FIGURE
Boy in red coat, yellow vest and turquoise breeches

spoilt by the addition of cobalt in order to conform to the popular taste which admired the bluish tinge of the imported oriental wares.

As usual, the earliest productions were some of the most individual and attractive, and the first pieces are particularly crisp and fresh. Blue and white was very popular, and by 1759 the factory was in full swing making some of its best wares. The tea-sets of this period are charming with delicate, arabesque-like borders and sprinklings of flowers and insects in the Meissen tradition, but with fresh inspiration. A particularly delightful type of work about this time is the monochrome painting of oriental landscapes in lilac, black or crimson.

Transfer printing was early practised at this factory (1757) and developed and used to a great extent, for the owners had a strong commercial sense. The designs were seldom original, but they were excellently placed in relation to the shapes of the wares, and the simple black, brown, purple and sometimes red printings have definite charm, particularly when regarded as the cheap, everyday ware for general use. Robert Hancock's name is associated with most of the early engravings for these printings.

The Japanese influence was very strong at Worcester even from the earliest days, but it was well assimilated and freshly interpreted, and in the tableware particularly there was done some very pleasant work of this type in the early years. Later this mode of decoration deteriorated even more rapidly than most. The shapes of the tablewares are restrained, elegant (in the best sense) and serviceable, and show a sound appreciation of their purpose.

About 1670, the coloured grounds for which Worcester achieved such a name, were perfected and much used. Technically they are excellent, but as a type of decoration they never seem to be part and parcel of the

STAFFORDSHIRE (NEW HALL) PORCELAIN
Late eighteenth and early nineteenth centuries

body itself, and one is haunted by the horrible developments of the nineteenth century which they foreshadow. Their gilding on the other hand was in excellent taste,.for those who like it. About 1780 the decline in taste really began, gently at first, but later in the wave of Victorian prosperity it rushed downwards.

This factory, alone of the early ones, has continued working until the present day, although inevitably its work deteriorated during the nineteenth century. But it still has a fine tradition of craftsmanship, and there is no reason why it should not produce some work of real interest in the future.

Thomas Turner of Worcester introduced the manufacture of porcelain to the works at Caughley in 1772, and from then until about 1814 porcelain was made, which is often extremely like some of the early Worcester. The Caughley body is less blue than Worcester, but in other ways is very like, and also contains soapstone.

Blue and gold was much used at this factory and some of the plain blue decoration of sprays and flowers is very charming in design and rich in colour.

Porcelain was made at Bristol as early as 1750, but the factory, owned by William Lowdin, was bought up by Worcester in 1752. The Lowdin Bristol and early Worcester pieces are not easily distinguishable, but on the whole the pieces now definitely attributed to Lowdin have a simpler and more naïve charm. The shapes were very derivative from silver-work as in early Worcester, but the paintings in colours were fresher and more interesting than the usual work from that factory.

In 1770 William Cookworthy set up his factory at Bristol for making hard-paste porcelain. This was taken over by Richard Champion in 1773 and in 1781 the patent rights were sold to a Staffordshire Company which started works at New Hall. Tebo (or Thibaud) who worked at Bow and Worcester, seems also to have worked at Bristol for Champion, and his hand is seen in the statuettes in the Meissen manner made at these works. The ordinary tableware, such as tea-sets, made by this factory were admirable and emphasise that individual and utilitarian tradition in manufacture which is always to be found somewhere. Gilding was omitted for cheapness, but the results were often more distinguished without it. Simple sprays of flowers are scattered over practical and pleasant shapes, with sometimes simple ribbon or wreath borders.

Liverpool porcelain manufacture began in 1756, and is generally regarded as another offshoot of Worcester, on account of the fact that one of its workers, Podmore, is said to have passed on the knowledge of the use of soapstone which he brought from Worcester. The porcelain is somewhat greyish in colour, but there are some excellent pieces, notably jugs and mugs, painted in blue with a freeness very reminiscent of the delftware painters. There are also some charming transfer-printed wares in the Worcester manner, notably mugs and punch-bowls.

William Littler at Longton Hall made the first porcelain in Staffordshire, and he is known to have been working there in 1752. His productions are noted for their raised leaf borders often painted in blue and for the rather heavy figure groups which are apt to be decorated with thick, not very attractive, colour and have the features picked out with theatrical harshness. The paste is glassy in character. It is known that Duesbury decorated ware for this factory, and it is believed that he bought up the works when they were closed down about 1760.

The small factory at Lowestoft, which made porcelain from 1757 until about 1803, has a reputation out of all proportion to its size or production, though none the less deserved. It had no pretensions to grandeur, and was almost entirely occupied with making utilitarian objects, which is probably the reason why its products seem to be such a personal expression of the people and their everyday life. Though the earliest pieces are nearly always decorated in underglaze blue with a strong Chinese influence in the designs, the character of the work is essentially peasant in its outlook, and this is more strongly noticeable in the later diaper-edge and flower sprinkled patterns more usually connected with this factory. It is interesting to note that this latter type of ware was actually copied in China, and later these flower painted pieces were also imitated in France. A number of mugs and inkstands are inscribed "A trifle from Lowestoft"

but otherwise the marks are vague and often merely imitated from other factories. The body is similar to Bow, but the glaze is much thinner; typical borders are diapered in strong pink and brownish-red. The tea-sets are particularly charming and express all the friendliness of country cottages and village maidens. One of their chief decorators is thought to have been a Frenchman called Rose, a refugee from the French Revolution. At one time this factory did a flourishing trade with Holland and its failure and subsequent closing down was said to be due in part to the heavy loss sustained by the works when Napoleon captured Holland and destroyed a valuable store of Lowestoft porcelain in Rotterdam. In any case, it was an expensive factory to run, being far from both clay and coal.

Hard paste was made for a short time in Staffordshire at New Hall from 1781 in diminishing quantities until about 1810 it was superseded by a bone porcelain and the factory was closed in 1825. The early hard paste New Hall has distinct charm and shows a boldness of design which is striking in comparison with other contemporary work. Lustre was often used with a freedom reminiscent of some of the Maiolica painting, and the birds which appear are of quite a different type from those usually depicted.

With the end of the century a new era began and it was to be a dark age for pottery and porcelain in England. With increasing prosperity the demand for purely decorative wares grew rapidly, and the richer and more complicated the decoration the more popular it became. In the old days, as in the time of the Toft brothers, decorative ware was only made in the leisure moments of the potters or to mark some special occasion, and the light-hearted enjoyment of the makers is clearly to be seen in these personal expressions of the people. Now the same type of object began to be made in vast quantities for those who only wanted some expression of their opulence, and by those who worked for the money to be made rather than for the enjoyment of their work. This distortion of outlook overtook all the arts of that time, but some trace of the popular tradition survived in pottery and porcelain among the cheapest and most utilitarian wares.

BIRD FOUNTAIN
Earthenware with Copper Lustre Motif
Early 19th century

TWO WEDGWOOD MUGS DESIGNED BY ERIC RAVILLIOUS
Wedgwood Commemoration Mug. Erruria 1730 : Barlaston 1940
Edward VIII Coronation Mug dated 1937

FLOWER POT BY NORAH BRADEN
Oil painting by Beryl Sinclair

With the beginning of the century we find that all the original porcelain factories, with the exception of Worcester, had either already closed down or were on the point of doing so. The early soft pastes of so much charm had been superseded by the bone-china which was perfected by the second Josiah Spode and came into general use, being sold in large quantities all over the world. The prosperity and commercialisation of the Potteries had a profound effect on the whole of Europe, and in fact the great Danish ceramic historian, Dr. Hannover, goes so far as to say that the development of all the ceramic arts of Europe was brought to a standstill by this great new English industry.

The mass produced bone-china was now so inexpensive that it virtually ousted pottery for general use, and when pottery was still made it usually strove to emulate porcelain shapes and colours with most unfortunate results.

It was left to Josiah Wedgwood to develop earthenware on suitable and sound lines, and to show that there was still a place for good design even in mass production. It is in the Wedgwood factory, more than any other, that we find the personal thread representing the needs and feelings of the people still persisting through this industrial revolution. It was Wedgwood who realised that, now the potter was no longer the artist but merely the mechanic or craftsman, it was necessary that the mechanic should have first class designs to guide him.

But before we review the work of the larger manufacturers of this century mention must be made of those smaller factories which came into being for a short time in the transition period. In 1796 a porcelain factory was set up at Pinxton in Derbyshire, and there was employed there one of the painters from the Derby works, William Billingsley, who subsequently founded the works at Nantgarw; therefore it is not surprising to find the work of these two factories very similar. The porcelain of both factories was very translucent, and the decorations were apt to be mainly imitative of Sèvres. The Pinxton works being the earlier of the two, its productions were inclined to be rather more unsophisticated and charming.

There had been a factory at Swansea since 1764, but it was only in 1814 that porcelain began to be made there, once more under Billingsley who was brought in by Dillwyn, the owner. The paste was again of the Nantgarw type, and much of the decoration was done in London.

Perhaps one of the greatest characteristics of the nineteenth century was the lack of assimilation of foreign influences. In earlier days we have noted how the continental and oriental designs were more the inspiration of the English potters than models for the mere copyist. Flowers and figures were translated into our own idiom and with our own ideas of colour to give new life, and one has the feeling that the potters and decorators had a full understanding and enjoyment of what they were doing. With the new outlook of the nineteenth century the continental and oriental designs were copied and elaborated because they were fashionable, and no longer were they the inspiration for designs of our own. This was of course mainly due to the fact that the potters were no longer artists, but commercial craftsmen who were caught up in the whirlwind of the new material age.

We find every sort of elaboration both of form and decoration ; and gilding, coloured grounds, embossments and fantastic shapes of all kinds flow in profusion from the Potteries. The craftsmanship is excellent but the taste is merely expensive. On the other hand, in the cheap transfer-decorated wares we often find some of the earlier naïveté and charm still lingering, for these cheap wares were made for the use of the people and not for the display of wealth.

Perhaps the two best known names which arose in the nineteenth century were those of Spode and Minton. As has been remarked before, the first Josiah Spode had come into notice at the end of the eighteenth century as a follower of Josiah Wedgwood and his cream-coloured earthenware, and later the second Josiah Spode sprang into fame by his perfecting of the bone-ware china. Some of the early Spode earthenware pieces are very similar to those of Wedgwood, and not only the shapes but also the decorations seem to have been copied freely. The early Spode porcelain was sometimes comparatively simple and pleasant in its decoration, but it soon took to the indiscriminate but fashionable use of gold and over-richness of pattern. Gilding in relief was particularly sumptuous in effect and is said to have been first done at this factory. Turquoise blue as a ground was also said to originate from here, and was much used at this time. A large amount of underglaze printing in blue (and later other colours) on both pottery and porcelain came from this factory as well as others, and in the first half of the century a large American market in this sort of ware developed. The favourite decorations were in the form of scenes of topical events and English landscapes. To this day much of this type of work is still exported to America, particularly for use in the larger universities and institutions there. The Minton factory achieved a world-wide reputation for fine jewelled tableware, and certainly the texture and finish of their work was excellent, though the patronage of wealth once again brought over-ornamentation and gilding.

Worcester, early in the century, produced some interesting and comparatively restrained Japanese designs, but later degenerated in the mid-Victorian period. They were particularly noted for their fine painting in imitation of Sèvres. From a technical point of view the work of this date was often very remarkable, but it was a mockery of the ceramic arts when plates and teapots began to be seen only as surfaces on which to paint realistic scenes of Windsor Castle, or still more realistic groups of expensive looking fruit. It was a tragic development, if one could so call it, from the charmingly stylised fruits and flowers painted a hundred years previously in the Chelsea works.

A more individual and therefore more interesting class of ware which flourished during the first quarter of the century was what is usually called Sunderland ware, made at Sunderland, Newcastle, and various places in the North. Lustre, particularly of a deep pink, was much used, in splashes and with crude dabs of enamel on topically printed earthenware mugs, jugs and bowls. As a contrast to the fine workmanship and sophisticated richness of the large Staffordshire firms of this date, this ware was crude in the extreme. But there is a wholesome vulgarity about it which is extremely attractive, and it has an intimacy with the ordinary people which is lacking in the more technically perfect but elaborately ostentatious productions of the larger factories.

Very little stoneware was made at this time that is worth mention; though in the early part of the century the Adams and Turner factories did produce some characteristic jugs decorated with embossed designs and dark brown enamelled necks. The Rockingham (Swinton) and Coalport works both produced notable examples of exuberant Victorian rococo. This was not without humour, though of the unconscious kind. Mention must be made here of Mason's "Ironstone" china which was patented early in the century and had a wide sale and popularity. Its chief virtue was its cheapness, and though it was also very durable this was a doubtful virtue owing to the usually hideous decoration. Blotting paper pink roses and brick red borders were typical of this ware.

The Great Exhibition of 1851 seemed to set the seal of approval on all the worst influences current at that time, and from then onwards there was an endless stream of grotesque "styles" in all the arts and crafts, and pottery did not escape. Indian, Greek and Moorish jostled each other in undigested confusion, and about 1860 the whole of Europe was swept by the vogue of Japanese art. Unfortunately, only the least worthy of Japanese art came to Europe : the overdecorated Satsuma ware, as well as special lines made for export. It was not until half a century later that our potters found and were influenced by the restrained and beautiful shapes which were representative of the best in Japanese art.

William de Morgan must be cited as an important single figure of this time, in that he headed a reaction against the complicated and vulgar designs of the second half of the century. He produced some good work in the Pre-Raphaelite manner, clean-coloured and clean-shaped, and he showed a bold and pleasant use of lustre. But his influence was limited and of short duration.

The century closed in a welter of sumptuous distortion which gradually simmered down to a return to nature (as it was then thought to be) in

LUSTRE VASE BY WILLIAM DE MORGAN

L'Art Nouveau which now appears as a period of sickly and boneless sentimentality.

Yet all this time good pottery, and to a lesser degree good porcelain, was still being made for those who had the eyes to find it. For instance, much of the cheap earthenware turned out by Wedgwood was not only of excellent quality but it was well designed; and in many Victorian servants' halls the tableware was still representative of the best of English pottery traditions, whereas above stairs the tables groaned under the fashionable nightmares of ceramic art.

PRESENT DAY REACTIONS AND INFLUENCES

The new period of enlightenment which has lately been noticeable in the Pottery Industry is largely due to two causes. Firstly, there has been a fashionable revival and appreciation of all things pertaining to the last half of the eighteenth century. Secondly, the so-called studio potters have had an influence far beyond the few intellectuals who applauded their beginnings some twenty-five years ago. Taking the first cause, it is noticeable that in architecture the best of the modern houses are more closely related to those of the late eighteenth and early nineteenth centuries than to anything since, and this has reacted in all domestic taste. In the pottery world factories have searched their museums for early designs which have been adapted for present day purposes, and there is a general desire for the simple and serviceable prettiness of those early shapes. The florid exuberance of Victorian, and the wilting shapelessness of the Edwardian tablewares look hopelessly out of place in the modern house. The first is vulgarly self-conscious, and the second is depressingly insignificant. The new simplicity of architecture has made people unconsciously more aware of the importance of shape and therefore less demanding for richness of decoration. The worst tendencies nowadays are perhaps more towards undigested intellectualism rather than towards some equally undigested foreign influence.

The studio potters are perhaps responsible for most of the intellectual yearnings, but they have also taught much sound sense which had been forgotten for a century. They spoke of the right use of clay ; of the reason for a pot and its fitness for its purpose; of the importance of shape apart from decoration ; of the function of decoration to emphasise and not obscure a shape. They reaffirmed that the designer must also be a worker in clay, and must have a practical knowledge and experience of the nature of his material. This is now at last being understood by the factories, who are beginning to see that in mass production it is as important for the designer to know and understand the machinery as it is for the individual potter to know and understand his clay. The studio potters went to the East again for their inspiration but unlike the Victorians they sought out the best of oriental examples, and rejected the meretricious ware made to catch the eye of the traveller only. Perhaps they sometimes erred in being over-intellectual and exact in their interpretations, but at least they avoided vulgar distortion and grasped the fundamentals of pottery design.

Such people as Bernard Leach, W. Staite Murray and Michael Cardew, later followed by Miss Pleydell Bouverie, Miss Norah Braden and John Cole, have played a very real part in what looks like being a revival of the true art of pottery in this country. Bernard Leach worked for many years in Japan and has produced at his pottery at St. Ives some excellent

work, noticeably stoneware. Michael Cardew has rediscovered English peasant pottery and has used slipware with particularly noticeable success in producing moderately priced and typically traditional oven and tableware.

Of necessity the work of the individual potters is much more expensive than that made by the large factories, but there is a very real place for both. It would seem that to-day the individual potter is more consciously a sculptor and an artist than of old, and his real triumphs are in the decorative pieces which have individual and personal beauty, and are the descendants of those show pieces of the Toft brothers and other workers of the seventeenth century.

But the advance of machinery cannot be ignored in any branch of industry, and just as furniture and textiles have become mass produced and sophisticated, so too must pottery do the same. The hand-made pots, together with hand-made furniture and textiles, can still be entirely lovely for those who have the leisure to make, or the money to acquire them, but there is no reason at all why beauty of a different kind should not spring from the machinery used for mass produced goods. The trouble comes when it is not understood that the beauty from machinery must be of an entirely different type from that of hand-made products. The one must not attempt to copy the other.

Some of the industrial potters in 1939 (at the beginning of the recent war) were not only reproducing old designs, but were also beginning to use young designers of distinction who worked in the factories and thoroughly absorbed the processes of manufacture and understood the qualities of the materials for which they designed. Amongst these we find the interesting work of Eric Ravilious for Wedgwood's, and also the

CIDER BOTTLE BY MICHAEL CARDEW

work of Graham Sutherland for William Brain. How different is the work of these men from that of the "designers" of the last century, who only saw a teapot as a good background for a realistic painting of a few plums or a plate as an opportunity to display an elegant sketch of a Stately Home of England.

But it is not only in decoration that the artist designer is making his mark on mass produced pottery, and we have for example in Keith Murray's beer mugs and jugs (designed for Wedgwood) simple undecorated shapes, which though essentially modern, have recaptured much of the understanding of clay which was so evident in the work of early English potters, and translated this knowledge into the idiom most suitable for mass production.

Salt-glaze, again, which was at one time the glory of English potting, has long fallen into disuse and until recently was principally to be found only in the manufacture of such articles as gingerbeer bottles and drain-

STONEWARE BOWLS MADE BY B. LEACH, NORAH BRADEN AND W. STAITE MURRAY

pipes. It is therefore interesting and inspiring to find such excellent work in this ware being produced by William Gordon at Chesterfield. The salt-glaze process is extremely inexpensive and economical in firing, and the wares so produced are very durable. The salt-glaze of the eighteenth century produced some of the loveliest and most typically English examples of ceramic art, but it was superseded by Wedgwood's cream earthenware which for domestic purposes had advantages over the salt-glaze. However, with greater knowledge and improved methods it now seems as though salt-glaze has special properties which may reinstate it as one of the most useful and charming types of ware. William Gordon's work shows a full appreciation of these special properties as well as a fine understanding of the salt-glaze tradition in this country, and it is to be hoped that he has opened up a new future for this typically English process of manufacture.

It is interesting and heartening to see to-day in the cheap stoneware jugs and kitchen pots made by Joseph Bourne of Denby, the direct descendants of those lovely jugs and pots made in the fourteenth and fifteenth centuries by our early potters. The texture and finish of Bourne's productions are indeed mechanically very different from those of the early potters, but the generosity and humour of the shapes, and the sound understanding of the purposes for which the vessels are made, are the same to-day as they were six hundred years ago.

CONCLUSION

We have now briefly traced the history of English pottery and porcelain through some six centuries, and coming to the present day it seems that we can end on a note of optimism for the future. This is an industry which has its natural roots in Britain, and since the earliest days the personal thread which has been particular to this country, has always persisted for those who cared to look for it. As each new process was perfected the inspiration then shifted to yet another channel, absorbing as it went the various foreign influences which crossed its path. With the nineteenth century it seemed as though for a time our national genius had been smothered by too much success and prosperity, but now it seems that new life has come to the Industry.

The studio potters have brought back to us the personal charm of the individual potter's craft, and have shown their awareness of the traditions of English ceramics in relation to foreign influences. They have absorbed those influences in the fullest sense and interpreted them in our native idiom. At the same time the industrial potters seem to be awakening to the fact that they must move forward again, and that future success now lies in ability to use the new machinery and processes as an inspiration to further effort and not to regard them as a quick and cheap way of reproducing the work of the past. It is too easy to criticise the present and mourn the passing of old methods and fashions. We must go forward or die, and provided we continue to build on the solid foundations of the past and keep in sight the needs of the people of this country, we cannot go far wrong ; and the future should hold much in store for this most indigenous of British industries.

SALTGLAZE WARE BY WILLIAM GORDON

BOW   CHELSEA

CHELSEA-DERBY   DERBY   LONGTON HALL

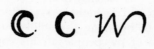

CAUGHLEY   WORCESTER

PLYMOUTH & BRISTOL   MINTON

SOME EXAMPLES OF THE EARLY MARKS ON ENGLISH PORCELAIN

It is impossible here to give a comprehensive list of English porcelain marks as these are so very numerous and various. All that has been attempted is to indicate the most obviously important, without going into the date variations of the factories. Certain marks, such as Lowestoft, Swansea, etc. are often self-evident by having the name in full, when the pieces from these factories are marked at all

BRITISH
CLOCKS AND CLOCKMAKERS

BY

KENNETH ULLYETT

PAST PRESENT AND FUTURE

For our Time is a very shadow that passeth away.

Quotation from the Book of Wisdom, ii. 5

WITH characteristic doggedness, British clock craftsmen for 350 years have striven to perfect that curious instrument the clock which measures something that does not exist: Time.

Past, present and future are intangible, but from the dawn of mankind the space of a man's day has been measured by the rising and setting of the sun. As the solar system cannot be carried around in the pocket, the early clockmaker devised the sand hour-glass and the clepsydrae (water-clocks) to measure the ebbing of time by the dripping away of water; then the "escapement" of some mechanical spring- or weight-driven machine was used to allow the mechanism to "escape" in synchronism with the setting of the sun, so to mark the hours. But what are the hours? Only since the fourteenth century has man divided the day and night into a total of twenty-four hours and in some parts of the globe they divided periods of night and day into a number of "temporal" hours, usually twelve. Often the length of an hour in the daytime was not the same as that of an hour at night, and both varied according to the seasons. In Japan temporal hours were the measure until 1870, and I treasure an old Japanese clock, the wheels of which are hand-filed out of solid steel discs, with a complicated system of weights necessitating a visit of the local Temple priests to the household every day to reset the mechanism for the appropriate temporal hours of the season.

Of course we were wise to abolish the temporal hours, but until we can devise something better than the relative and intangible Time, we can hardly hope for complete sanity! Even *Punch* on "Time" says: "The public . . . must treat Time as the fourth dimension—and like it. The boundary between past and present is not easy to define, human nature being inclined, for example, to classify a three-months-old unanswered letter as the 'present' and a day-old newspaper as the 'past'...."

And when we tinker with Time and put the clocks to B.S.T., offering up a prayer, perhaps, that no longer do we have to run our days according to *D.B.S.T.*, the foolishness of Time as a tape-measure of Eternity or of our lives (whichever may be the more important) is exposed by Sir Alan Herbert's jibe:

> Advance your clocks, good Briton. You will not change your ways
> Because the season changes, likewise the length of days.
> Advance your clocks, good Briton. You make me pretty sick:
> You will not get up earlier unless we play a trick.
> Advance your clocks, poor Briton: but sadly recognise—
> Here in the citadel of Truth, Big Ben is telling lies.

This peculiar non-existent and therefore intangible non-element Time is, however, the subject of our narrative, and the perfection of the measurement of this Time, which has no place in the domain of reality, has been the goal of a craft pilgrimage for British clockmakers.

I have said that they set out along this road towards the precise measurement of Time some 350 years ago, but the weight-driven clock, the use of which had spread across Europe from Italy in the very beginning of the fourteenth century, arrived in this country in about 1368, and that is truly where our British story must begin—not only the story of the Clock, but of the makers of such "orleges," "horyloges" or "horologues." Such delightful vague terminology arises from the Latin word *horologium,* and in the earliest records it is quite impossible to tell if our craftsmen in monasteries were makers of hour-glasses, water-clocks, sun-dials, horacudii (i.e. hour-striking clocks, without dials), or true timepieces bearing even the slightest resemblance to the clocks of to-day.

THIRTY-HOUR STRIKING AND ALARUM BRASS LANTERN CLOCK
Jeffrey Bayley.   Signed and dated 1653

THIRTY-HOUR STRIKING HANGING CLOCK IN INLAID MARQUETERIE CASE
Christopher Gould, *c.* 1690

> Wel sikerer was his crowyng in his logge,
> Than is a clokke, or an abbey orlogge

wrote Chaucer in 1386, and some thirty years later Caxton printed:

> And by this tyme the Horologue had fully performed
> half his nytes cours . . .

In the year 1449 Reginald Pecock, Bishop of Chichester, proclaimed "that men schulde make and use clockis forto knowe the houris of the dai and nyt," and since then the "abbey orlogges," the clepsydrae and clock chimes of the church, the castle, the manor house, the palace, and the home, have marked Britain with a pattern of Time, until to-day the chimes of Big Ben are broadcast on short waves around the globe as a sort of horological theme-song from the heart of the Empire.

Primitive and early medieval English clocks have made former castle, abbey and manor houses live in history long after their glory would otherwise have passed away. Dover Castle, Glastonbury Abbey, the Cathedrals at Exeter, Norwich, and Peterborough: these and many others have connections with horology which in some cases transcend their importance in the busy world of to-day, and such important things as a thriving clock industry or a fine new standard of British craftsmanship have risen from the fact that in medieval monasteries it was the sacristan's duty to adjust the "orloge" to strike at the hour and awake the monks for matins. That some of these early horologes were not weight-driven clocks but merely clepsydrae is a subject antiquaries love to debate, because even the chiming clocks were worked by water, as for example the attainment of a certain level by water dripping into a basin, which would then float a ball over the rim so that it dropped on a bell: but it is interesting to turn back to Dante's *Paradiso*, which must have been written before 1321 when he died, to find in Canto X: "Then as the horologe, that calleth us, what hour the spouse of God riseth to sing her matins . . . wherein one part drawing and thrusting other, giveth a chiming sound *(tin tin sonando)* of so sweet a note . . ." And in Canto XXIV: "And even as the wheels in harmony of clock-work so turn that the first, to whoso noteth it, seemeth still."

It seems to me that the Wicksteed translation is accurate enough to show a point of some significance, that the Italian *tin tin sonando* is imitative, and suggests a small bell of medium or high pitch, such as one associates with a chamber clock rather than the boom of an abbey bell. Machines for delivering a rapid succession of blows to a bell are depicted in many early manuscripts, and whether such mechanism was an integral part of a weight-driven clock in the fourteenth century, or whether it was separately set in motion by a clepsydra is a subject we can safely leave historians to haggle over; in any event, the critical point in the history of clocks is not the substitution of weights or spring-driven barrels for the floats of a clepsydra, but the introduction of the foliot bar or the pendulum as a mechanical "escapement" to allow the mechanical energy to "escape" away and thus enable the wheels second by second to record the passage of—of what? Shall we say of Time?

That the monks and the artificers in metal who cast the bells, built and repaired the organs and constructed the horologes were proud of their work goes without saying: that the benefits of good time-keeping were soon transferred from the cloisters to the layman's hearth, and that public clocks soon grew atop medieval religious buildings, was a tribute to the ingenuity of the intricate mechanism. The very first appearance of the word "clock" (accurately, *clok*) in English literature coincides with the construction of the first public timepiece in Britain, and is in a document published in the time of Edward III, the general sense of which is: A piece of land 72 feet long and 24 feet wide in "Seynt Martynplace" in Gloucester is granted to the burghers for the erection of a tower "in which certain bells shall always sound, the hours of the day and night being indicated by a clock, vulgarly called *(clok vulgarit' nuncupata)*, placed and hung in the tower ..."

The material used in the mechanism of such clocks was invariably iron. Most early sixteenth-century clocks, even house clocks, are of iron, but by about 1575 iron and brass were both used. Country clocks made as late as the seventeenth century are of all-iron construction, but in general it appears that the English makers and the Flemings favoured brass, while the South Germans and the Swiss prolonged what Percy Webster used to call the "Iron Age" of clocks. Apart from an initial slavish fashion in design and material, English craftsmen also at first borrowed from Continental clockmakers the diverting conceit of the automata and "jacks," or mechanical figures. It used to be held that we took the word from the French *Jacquemart*, which still survives as a French surname, derived from Jaccomar-chiadus, a man in a suit of armour, but it now appears more reasonable to suppose that our stolid English "Jack" took its use from the naming of any appliance that mechanically does a man's work. We have screw-jacks, and those quaint spring- or weight-driven roasting jacks which add to the interest of the English hearth, and we even see the word verbalised so that to-day we talk of a man "jacking" up his car. Look, for instance, at *Richard II*, Act V, scene v:

> but my time
> Runs posting on in Bolingbroke's proud joy,
> While I stand fooling here, his Jack o' the clock.

What a solid English use of the word is that: and if you like to go back a little there is a 1498 reference to the history of the Church of St. Lawrence, Reading: "Item: payed for the settyng of Jak with the hangyng of his bell and mendyng his hond, iiij *d*." Not an expensive repair.

INTERIOR DIAL OF WELLS CATHEDRAL CLOCK SHOWING JOUSTING KNIGHTS
Originally made before 1394 but frequently restored

But the first British clock-tenders, clockmakers and clock-devisers were
not well paid for their work. Ten shillings a year, for example, was the
stipend of the "clock custodian" (but it may have been a water-clock) at
Wells Cathedral in the 1400's: the exact wording of the Chapter Rolls is:
"*Item: in stipendium custodientis la clokk x.s per annum.*" Ten shillings

a year: and they say we have avoided financial inflation. But it was not intended that the clock-tenders should go hungry. There is some thought for human needs in the Exeter Records of 1318, by which the Bishop Peter Quivil provides grants to the bell-founder Roger de Ropford, Agnes his wife, and his son Walter: ". . . and the said Roger, Agnes and Walter and their heirs shall . . . as often as need be repair or cause to be repaired the musical instruments *(organa)* and clock *(orologium)*: while so employed all necessaries of food and drink shall be supplied to them."

Mechanical jacks on clocks never became truly anglicised, and after a time this foreign fashion was dropped. But we are left with the 4 ft. 7 in. high quarter-boys on the north face of the tower of Rye Church, with "Jack-Smite-the-Clock" at Southwold, the Blythburgh Man, the quaint little seventeenth-century jacks at Norwich, the giants atop the Thomas Harris clock in Fleet Street, London, the top-hatted man at Hagley Hall, and many similar jacks which strike the hours. Most of them do so in a way which could hardly have taxed the ingenuity of their makers, for usually the right arm alone moves, being pivoted as a simple lever at the shoulder. The figures at Southwold, Blythburgh and Wells also turn their heads, and Wells' internal popular Jack Blandifer, who sits high up on a perch inside the cathedral, has the additional accomplishment of kicking quarter-bells with his heels while using a hammer held in his hand. From Mr. Blandifer—reputed despite many coat-changes and repaintings—to be one of the earliest automata in Britain, we have a long procession of clock jacks, to the present-day Regent Street robots above Liberty's shop where St. George and the Dragon celebrate the passing of the hours thanks to the electro-mechanical apparatus, invented by F. Hope-Jones, which activates their daily tourneys to the delight of West-end shoppers.

It was during these early centuries that the craftsmanship of English workers in horology was established, but there was of course the transitional phase when timepieces were first built for other than clerical establishments, and when secular persons of exalted position were proud to possess chamber clocks ticking away their own private hours. Thus, Sir John Paston, in a letter written in the spring of 1469, says: "I praye you speke wt Harcourt off the Abbeye ffor a lytell clokke whyche I sent him . . . and as ffor mony for his labour, he hath another clok of myn whiche St. Thoms Lyndes, God have hys sowle, gave me."

Harrison Ainsworth saw the little gilt bracket clock which is said to have been given on her wedding morn to Anne Boleyn by Henry VIII, and noted that still visible on the copper-gilt weight cases were the initial letters of Henry and Anne with true lovers' knots above and below, and engraved "Dieu et mon droit . . . the most happye." "This love token of enduring affection remains the same after three centuries," commented Ainsworth, "but four years after it was given, the object of Henry's eternal love was

NICOLAUS KRATZER, ASTRONOMER TO HENRY VIII
Oil-painting by Hans Holbein, 1528

sacrificed on the scaffold. The clock still goes. It should have stopped for
ever when Anne Boleyn died."

Far from stopping, the clock lived on, gathering more interesting historical associations from century to century. Horace Walpole eventually bought
it, and because it "looked Gothic" he kept it in his sham collection at

215

WATCH IN CASE AND COVER OF SMOKE CRYSTAL WITHOUT FRAMES
AND WITH DIAL OF ENAMELLED GOLD
Michael Nouwen of London, 1609

Strawberry Hill, whence Queen Victoria bought it at the sale for just over £110. In the sale catalogue it was described in flowery auctionese as "a clock of silver, gilt, richly chased, engraved and ornamented with fleurs-de-lis," but this is pardonable salesmanship for the clock case is gilt on copper, and the weights are of lead cased in copper and gilt; the whole construction is such that South German influence is apparent though the actual workmanship may be London. In a Royal Household Book dated 1542 it appears that Henry had several such clocks: "Item: oone Clocke of iron with a case of glasse . . . Item: oone Clocke of copper and gilt, with a chyme to the same . . . Item: oone Clock of Iron with a Larum [*i.e. alarm*] to same. . . ." Henry was a pioneer among English chamber clock owners, as he was indeed a pioneer among other less praiseworthy fashions. I doubt if many of these clocks are of English manufacture. In the Privy Purse expenses of Henry VIII it is recorded that in July 1530 was paid "to a Frenchman called Drulardy for iij dyalls and a clokk for the King's Grace the sum of 15£." One Vincent Keney also received £19 16s. 8d. from the King "for xj clocks and dialls" in 1530: but it would be rash to

STRIKING CLOCK IN ENGRAVED SILVER-GILT CASE
Bartholomew Newsam, *c.* 1590

217

assume from this one record that Keney was the first English maker of chamber clocks for private use. Indeed I am forced to the conclusion that the first two English makers of such clocks who merit real attention, and whose work is extant to-day, are Bartholomew Newsam and N. Vallin who later became clockmaker to Queen Elizabeth.

Newsam appears to have been a master of his craft, and although some of his work, including one fine specimen in the British Museum, has a German flavour, he was the first of the English master makers of chamber clocks. That his work was at first influenced by European taste is not surprising, for he must have learned his craft at the hand of Kratzer, a Bavarian who resided for many years, it is said, at the Court of Henry VIII without being able to speak English, and of whom a letter was written to Cardinal Wolsey: "In these parts I met with a servant of the King's called Nicholas Craczer, a German, deviser of the King's horologues. . . ." But Newsam, before he died in 1593, created a new art form in the domestic clock, and his table clocks are a present-day delight to the eye. It was a Continental fashion to have platter-like clocks, their dials parallel with the table, and Newsam took the conventional table-clock design and gave it an English air. His work was appreciated in his day, and after a brief appointment to the Court of Queen Elizabeth he wrote petitioning Sir Philip Sidney to speak on his behalf. The petition was granted, and Newsam was granted the office of clockmaker to the Queen, for a period of three years until his death.

The evidence on N. Vallin is slender. There is a reference to one "N.V." in the Calendar of State Papers in the time of Queen Elizabeth, but this is more probably a reference to Nicholas Urseau, former clock-keeper and colleague of Kratzer "the Astronomer." In a private collection to-day, however, is a fine Elizabethan chiming clock with a carillon of thirteen bells, all of iron and brass, and beautifully fashioned, engraved at the base N. VALLIN, 1598. The clock is so far ahead of what used to be considered the technique of the late 1500's that some doubt had been thrown upon it, but now the discovery of a contemporary early English watch also signed "N. Vallin" appears to have removed all doubt. This Vallin chamber clock is of "lantern" construction, but being designed before the introduction of the oscillating pendulum the "escape" of the seconds is effected by the ticking backwards and forwards of a large balance wheel, in similar fashion to the 'scape wheel of a modern watch except of course for the absence of a "hair" spring. The balance wheel of the Vallin chamber clock is about five inches in diameter, and so heavy that it swings in its partial revolution once in two seconds.

Naturally people of refinement, or at least of wealth, were not content to leave the Time at home when they walked abroad, and it was not long before British pocket "horologes" were being made for those who could afford them. The average price of a British watch in the year 1600 was

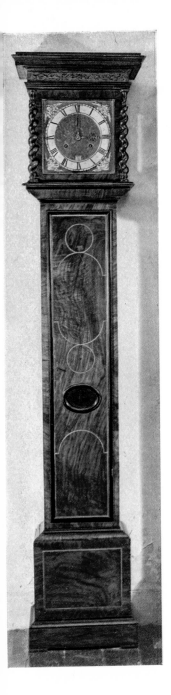

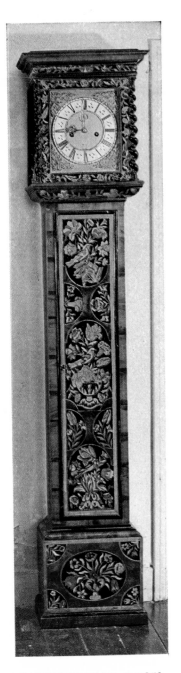

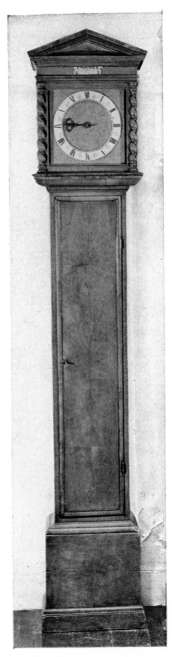

EARLY LONG-CASE CLOCKS

Thirty-hour, ten-inch dial clock.
Walnut veneer and inlaid boxwood
stringing
Thomas Tompion, *c.* 1675

Second-and-a-quarter clock in inlaid marqueterie case
Thomas Harris, *c.* 1690

Thirty-hour, portico-top clock in
walnut case
Henry Crump, *c.* 1670

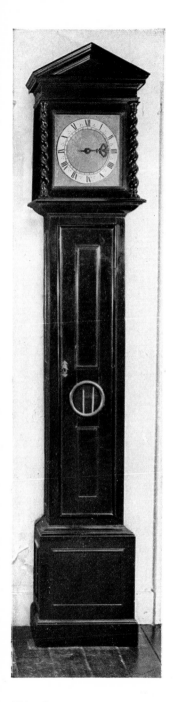

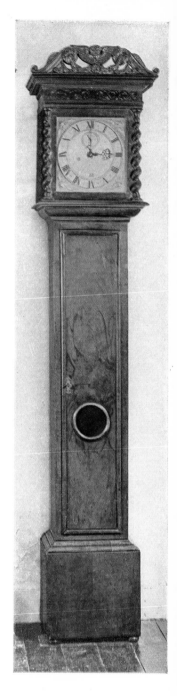

EARLY LONG-CASE CLOCKS

Thirty-hour striking clock with single hand and engraved dial plate. Ebony veneer on oak case
Early Daniel Quare, *c.* 1671

Ten-inch dial, striking and alarum clock in marqueterie case
Joseph Windmills, *c.* 1685

Long-case clock with skeleton silvered hour-ring cut away to show gilt dial. Walnut veneered case.
John Ebsworth, *c.* 1690

£20, which no doubt it would be fair to compare with £500 to-day. I have used the adjective "British" here advisedly, for one of this island nation's earliest watchmakers of particular renown was a Scot, David Ramsay. This Scot comes into the story in the way that Bonnie Prince Charlie came back into British history — from France. In the *Dictionary of National Biography* David Ramsay is listed as belonging to the Ramsays of Dalhousie, and David's son William recorded that "when James I succeeded to the Crown of England he sent into France for my Father, who was there, and made him page of the bedchamber and Keeper of his Majesty's Clocks and Watches." In 1622 David Ramsey [*sic*] is named as King's Clockmaker, and he was paid the then considerable sum of £232 15s. for repairing clocks at Theobalds and Westminster, and for making a chime of bells for a clock at Theobalds. His patron died three years later, but Ramsay kept his Court post, and there are many references in the State Papers of Charles I to Ramsay either by name, or as Page of the Bed-chamber. On the 13th July 1628, for example, a warrant was signed to pay him £415 for clocks delivered for the king's service. His early work is beautiful, and bears many signs of a distinct break-away from the South German tradition. The British Museum collection of watches includes a gold watch by Ramsay, the period being about 1600, and it is signed "David Ramsay, Scotus, me fecit." Such treasures were often mislaid for many generations, and within living memory the tapestry which had decorated the dining-room of Gawdy Hall was taken down for preservation, and in the wall mouldings behind the tapestry was found a small star-shaped watch, together with some silver apostle spoons and documents bearing silent witness to the dangerous days of Cromwell. The silver watch was made by Ramsay, and it may well have been one of the little pocket watches included in the trio which he made in the year 1612, when, so the records of the Keeper of the Privy Purse show, there were: "Watches, three, bought of Mr. Ramsay the Clockmaker lx li" (i.e. £60), and they are listed among the King's "Guyftes and Rewardes," so that one may well have found its way to the former owners of Gawdy Hall.

In *The Fortunes of Nigel* you will find that Scott introduces Ramsay as the keeper of a shop a few yards east of Temple Bar, and in a note to "Nigel," Ramsay is described as "Constructor of Horologes to his Most Sacred Majesty James I." It is strange that Scott should parade such a pedantic word as "horologe," for by now the word "clock" had even become common as an English surname, one of the most interesting curiosities of horology, surely. Even in Ramsay's time we find a reference in State Papers to one John Clock, of Staple Inn, Middlesex, who is to receive £20 lent by him to the King on Privy seal: and there is in 1618 a reference to one Petter [*sic*] Clocke, living in St. Olave's, Southwark.

Although the Dutch word *clok* had grown thus into common usage, British craftsmen were not a little concerned about the influx of foreign workmen to London, particularly, and very early in the seventeenth century there were fifteen clockmakers and two watchmakers in London, all of whom were foreigners. By *A true Certificat of the Names of the Straungers residing and dwellinge within the City of London* taken by the Privy Council in 1618, we find that in the ward of Farringdon Within was then living "Barnaby Martinot, clock-maker, born in Paris, a Roman Catholique." And in Portsoken Ward was living "John Goddard, clockmaker; lodger and servant with Isack Sunes in Houndsditch; born at Paris, Fraunce; heer 3 yeers; a papist; yet he hath taken the oath of allegiance to the king's supremacy, and doth acknowledg the king for his soveraigne dureing his abode in England."

The fact that these foreign workmen were willing, though "Catholiques," "papists," and "of the Romish church," to give an oath of allegiance to the king, so that they might peacefully ply their trade in the City of London, was a serious thorn in the side of the British craftsmen, who no doubt felt that the nation had little use now for foreign workmen or their ideas, and that the quality of the British work justified some State protection against this invasion. In the spring of 1622 a petition was drawn up complaining to the king of the "great number and deceitful tricks" of foreigners practising their trade, and begging that they might not be permitted to work except under English masters, and that no foreign clocks might be imported. A crisis had been reached in this early phase of the history of British clockmaking. Obviously something had to be done, and by a curious stroke it was the Scot, David Ramsay, who did it.

JEFFREY BAYLEY'S SIGNATURE

222

*One can buy ordinary watches in London at three guineas
in silver, and seven in gold, and upwards. Precision timekeepers are nowhere better or more perfectly made than in
London . . .*

Philipp Andreas Nemmich's account of a Journey to Britain, 1806

NOT all the glory of triumph in the sphere of Time measurement is
due to the clockmakers. The men whose work inspires these pages
almost preclude the idea of death, but their genius in fashioning
things with their hands, in filing beautiful clock parts from drawn steel and
cut brass was aided by the skill and ingenuity of many leaders of scientific
thought and learning. The Worshipful Company of British Clockmakers
was helped beyond all measure by Robert Hooke, by Sir Christopher Wren,
by Flamstead, William Derham, and even by Sir Isaac Newton, who when
lodging in an apothecary's house in Grantham, at the age of twelve, built
himself a water clock.

Although we talk to-day of clockmaking as an art, or as the progression
towards precision timekeeping of almost fantastic exactitude, according to
the branch of horological appreciation which we feel most deeply, the blunt
truth is that with very few exceptions clockmaking for over 500 years has
been a business, and not a dilettante devotion. Clockmakers are business-
men, in trade, and the only ideas they were able to absorb from the Hookes
and the Isaac Newtons were those which would facilitate construction
(very important in the era when it took months to make and assemble
a clock), or make their timekeepers more accurate than those of their
competitors.

So it was that the quarrel with the invading foreign workmen in the City
of London assumed proportions which, though unfortunately common to-day,
were of vital importance to the early seventeenth-century craftsmen who had
their apprentices to pay and their families to keep. The petition of 1622 had
set the ball rolling. Five years later there was a proposal put forward, no
doubt, by some French members of the Court who wanted a more plentiful
supply of watches and trinkets, to grant letters patent to French clockmakers to carry on their trade in London. It was this which really took
the London craftsmen by the ears. Before then, individual craftsmen had
usually kept their status by being associated with one or other of the
existing Companies—the Blacksmiths' as a rule. But the French competition
forced their hand, and in 1630 they went into conclave, drawing up a
petition as a result of which the new Clockmakers' Company came into
being, in August, 1631.

WATCH SHOWING THE SIGNS OF THE ZODIAC, MOON-PHASES AND DATE
Benjamin Hill, d. 1670

The Worshipful Company was incorporated by Royal Charter from Charles I as "The Master, Wardens and Fellowship of the Art of Clockmakers of the City of London." The company had power by their charter to make by-laws for the government of all craftsmen using the trade in London, or within a radius of ten miles, and for the regulation in general terms of the way in which the trade should be carried out *throughout the realm*.

Although the jurisdiction of the Clockmakers' Company was limited to the capital, the influence was very strong and spread more specially to Edinburgh, where the craft also very soon arrived at a high standard.

To prevent the public from being injured by persons "making, buying, selling, transporting and importing any bad, deceitful or insufficient clocks, watches, larums, sundials, boxes or cases for the said trade," powers were given to the Company by charter "to enter with a constable or other officer, any ships, vessels, warehouses, shops, or other places, where they shall suspect such bad and deceitful works to be made or kept, for the purpose of searching for them," and if entrance should be denied they might effect

it by force. The right of entry was constantly exercised until the end of the century. The town was divided into districts, periodic searches were made and many instances are recorded of deceitful works being found and broken up, or of masters taking on too many apprentices so that there would be a danger of "mass-production," and of a consequent reduction in quality standards.

The Scot, Ramsay, was elected first Master, and Henry Archer, John Wellowe and Sampson Shelton were the first wardens. The Company from their establishment in 1631, having no hall, held their meetings at some tavern in the City. In 1656, the famous clockmaker, Ahasuerus Fromanteel, and some thirty other members were forced to complain at this lack of dignity.

Many other famous Companies had their City halls, and many other Companies had also tried hard for livery and succeeded. The Clockmakers' Company had no hall, no livery. Fromanteel, who was in fact to engage himself in fairly constant bickering with the officials of the Company for many years, registered a complaint that "in spite of members having

to pay 4d. a quarter, the Companye's meetings are still held in Taverns." Fromanteel, of Dutch extraction, may have had therefore a personal reason for differing in many ways from the Company's rulings, and he also became restive under the somewhat inquisitorial proceedings of the Company's court of inquiry about his large number of apprentices and their antecedents. But any pressure which he put on the elders of the Company to build a hall fitting to the craft was unfortunately counteracted by the Fire. The Castle Tavern in Fleet Street, where the meetings were so often held, was afterwards rebuilt, and under the ownership of Sir John Tash, an Alderman of the City and a wealthy wine-merchant, it became for some years the home once again of the clockmakers. In 1671 the Company was granted the honour of carrying arms, and in view of the considerable number of women workers as silversmiths it is interesting to note that so early in the history of the Clockmakers' Company as 1715, sanction was given to female apprentices. For many years the Company petitioned for livery, but this was not granted until 1767, some fifty years after the death of most of the famous early craftsmen whose names appear in this present volume: and incidentally it is to be noted that although the Clockmakers are an integral part of the grand guild system which has helped to make British workmanship what it is to-day, quite a number of clockmakers (such as John and Joseph Knibb) must have evinced hostility to the, at times, autocratic methods of the Company, and never submitted themselves for Mastership. Even the great Thomas Tompion, buried in Westminster Abbey and recognised to-day as the Father of English clockmaking, was admitted a freeman by redemption in 1674, and served thirty years before deigning to accept the Mastership.

The granting of livery was a turning-point in the recognition of clockmaking as a true craft

BRASS TABLE CLOCK
Daniel Quare, 1648–1724

among the fine arts, and on the inauguration of Thomas Harley, brother of the Earl of Oxford, on Lord Mayor's Day, 9th November, 1767, a London news-letter records: "The Tin-Plate Workers' Company and the Clockmakers' Company joined the Lord Mayor's procession for the first time since they were made Livery-Companies, and made a genteel appearance."

Now it would be a pleasant tribute to the history of British clock and watchmaking if the stories could be told of all the important, interesting, inventive and creative craftsmen of this gallant Company, from its inception

ENGRAVED DIAL OF A STRIKING CLOCK
Edward East, 1610–1673

in 1631 to the present day. But unfortunately there are considerable gaps in the chronicles, partly through failure to keep records, partly through the change in clockmaking from craftsmanship to mass-production (an important source of omission, this, for the research of present-day collectors stops short at a period long before the Swiss clock and the American watch), and partly through the splitting up of the interests and energies of the old clockmakers themselves to other guilds and learned societies.

We may learn much more of George Graham, for instance, from the Proceedings of the Royal Society, of which he was a distinguished member, than from the minutes of the Clockmakers' Company: yet Graham was Tompion's companion and successor, and to-day they lie together in Westminster.

BRASS LANTERN CLOCK
John Hilderson, c. 1665

The biographical facts about the pioneer clockmakers can be seen in many works of reference, notably the late F. J. Britten's *Old Clocks and Watches*, which gives a list of some 12,000 makers. There is a short bibliography of other works at the end of this volume, and I acknowledge credit to nearly all of them for extracts given here—but especially to Britten's, which is the vade-mecum. *Who* they were is not nearly so important as *where* they were, and how they worked: and to those in search of a hobby I suggest the tracking-down of places of business of the clockmakers, and investigation of their early shops, forges and stock-rooms. In the country you may pleasurably search parish records and even advertise, as I have done, in county papers for family-trees and other documents about the makers. And in the City of London you can tread the ground where many famous clock-shops once stood, and where Edward East sold watches to Charles I, from his lodgings and clock-premises in Fleet Street; or where Henry Jones, East's apprentice, sold "ye first barometers whiche were yet made in England," from his shop by the Inner Temple Gate.

It can be a fascinating study, for although from 1660 to 1780 the "great" makers worked all within about five square miles, with the Royal Exchange as the focal point, their exact place of business was seldom given. Even as late, comparatively, as 1789, Thomas Earnshaw, one of the inventors of the chronometer, was told by Dr. Maskelyne, the Astronomer Royal, that an order for two marine watches had been lost to Earnshaw, because Maskelyne did not know where he worked. From my own collection of antique English clocks I have discovered that the maker often gave his place of business for the first few years, but later was content with the bold "London" or *Londini fecit* (made in London), leaving it to his patrons to say: "I bought my fob watch from Charles Gretton, over against Sergeants Inn Gate," or "My fine new gilt brass clock came from Richard Ames, near St. Andrews Church in Holborn." I have one of the first long-case clocks ever made by Daniel Quare, the great Quaker clock craftsman second in importance only to Tompion. That clock is signed *Daniel Quare in Martins Le Grand Londini fecit*, but many years before Quare became famous and made clocks for William III (you can see his handiwork to-day in Hampton Court) he was content to give his address merely as "London," though in fact he had moved to The King's Arms, Exchange Alley—near where the statue of Rowland Hill now stands. Even when the name and address were given, changes in geography or errors in engraving make it difficult to identify them. Thus John Hilderson's early clocks were signed "in Chessil-street," a thoroughfare which I have failed to find on the old London maps, and a Joseph Saer clock (*circa* 1687) in my collection, as well as a few others, are signed "Joseph Saer in purpoole Lane, Londini," which is a mis-engraving either for Penpoole or Purple. We may never know which.

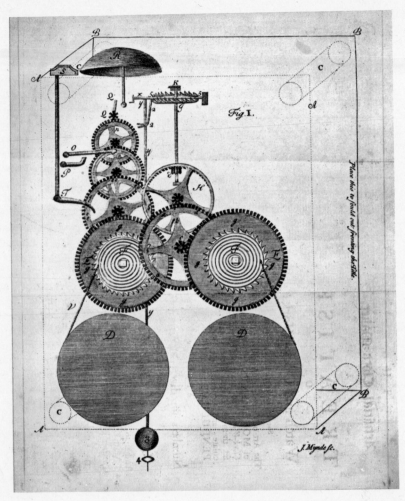

MOVEMENT OF A VERGE STRIKING CLOCK
Design engraved by J. Mynde from William Derham's *Artificial Clockmaker*, 1696

Sweeting's Alley, probably a corruption of Swithin's, was near Cornhill and the Royal Exchange, and for some hundred years was a favourite spot with the craft, but it perished in 1838 when the old Exchange buildings were destroyed by fire. Fleet Street, home of many fine clockmakers, remains unchanged, and the little turning off it, Water Lane (the scene of so much of Tompion's work) is now Whitefriars Street. Glass for the bezels and lenticles of many old seventeenth-century London clocks was made at the Whitefriars glassworks between this street and the Thames—

a glass foundry mentioned by Pepys and still producing British glass to-day, though on another site.

There are, as I have said, inevitable gaps in the chronicles of the clock craftsmen, and it would be too much to expect the story of some 300 years of quest for precision time-keeping to be told without some omissions in the telling. But as Robert Gould says in his *Antiquities of Freemasonry*, "Between the region of fancy and the province of authenticated history lies a borderland of tradition, full of difficulties which can neither be passed without notice nor ever perhaps finally explained. . . ." If we cannot always have authenticated history we will at least keep away from the region of fancy! The tales I tell here are culled from that amusing *Artificial Clockmaker*, first published in 1696 by William Derham, D.D., a Divine who came up from Worcester to become not only Canon of Windsor, but a recognised authority among clockmaking technicians ("Artificial," of course, is explained by the complete change of meaning of the word in the eighteenth century: in the preceding century the accent was on the "art"); from the Diary of Robert Hooke, the wild-eyed genius who was colleague and friend of Sir Christopher Wren, Sir Jonas Moore and Tompion; from old publications, broad-sheets and news-letters including *The London Gazette*, John Smith's *Horological Dialogues* of 1675, *The Commonwealth Mercury*, *The Affairs of the World* (1700), *A Pacquet from Wells* (1701), *The Daily Post*, *The Daily Advertiser*, the *London Magazine*, and from many similar records which combine to give a photographic impression of the rich, industrious life of the old makers. Some, like Tompion and Quare, were honoured to become Court clockmakers. Some, like Edmund Denison Beckett, designer of the movement of Big Ben's clock, were raised to the Peerage (he became Baron Grimthorpe), and some, like Christopher Gould, died bankrupt; just before he died, a petition was raised that he might be given the post of ale-taster, to save him from the debtors' prison. Of such varied stuff are the clockmakers made.

Edward East, first of the famous company of clockmakers after Newsam and Ramsay, has one of the most famous names in English horology, but the present evidence shows that there must have been two Edward Easts, probably father and son. An Edward East was established in Fleet Street in 1635. Lady Fanshawe tells in her memoirs how, when she came from France, she was sent to lodge with Mr. East the Watchmaker in 'Fleete Streete'. Before that he must have had watchmaking premises near the Mall, and his early silver-dial watches were given by the King as presents in seventeenth-century tennis tournaments. One of East's watches was always kept at the bedside of Charles I, who is said to have wound it himself and taken great pride in its alarm mechanism. The watch woke the King up on 30th January, 1649, the morning of his execution, and was given by Charles on the way to the scaffold to a courtier, Sir Thomas

Herbert, and for 200 years it stayed in the Herbert family.

Even thirty years after Charles's death, another Edward East was still famous as a clock and watchmaker. The son, if son it be, has left us many fine long-case clocks, the later specimens of which were made at "Ye Sun, outside Temple Bar," but most East workmanship is signed in the Latin fashion, "Eduardus East, Londini."

It is worth digressing here from chronological order to another famous maker, Henry Jones, for he was an apprentice of the East family. He tramped to London from Southampton and served his apprenticeship with East from the age of twenty-two. We have North's *Life* as evidence that "barometers were first made and sold by one Jones, a noted clockmaker, in the Inner Temple Gate, at the instance of Lord Keeper Guildford." That Jones also made many pocket watches is proved— as in the case of several other famous makers—by the considerable number of "Lost and Wanted" advertisements we find in the old records: yet to-day a Henry Jones watch is a comparative rarity, and we know him chiefly by his clocks. A typical advertisement is in the *London Gazette* for October, 1689, and reads: "Lost on the 21st Instant, between the Hay Market near Charing

TAVERN CLOCK IN TRUNK CASE, *c.* 1760
Mahogany case with applied decoration
carved and gilded

233

HOOD OF LONG-CASE CLOCK WITH LACQUERED
DECORATION
James Markwick, *c.* 1720

Cross and the Rummer in Queen Street, a round gold Pendulum Watch . . . it was made by one Henry Jones, Watchmaker in The Temple, the Out case had a Cypher pin'd on It, and the Shagreen much worn. . . ." Jones crops up in history again when he made the clock which Charles II gave to Mrs. Jane Lane in memory of her services after the Battle of Worcester.

A colleague of the Easts was John Hilderson, one of the several early makers who for some 300 years have remained almost in obscurity and who are historically speaking only now being discovered. The few clocks signed by him are of the same high quality as East's early work, and his zenith appears to be in the 1660–65 era. There is a Dutch tang about the name, and at least three of his clocks are strongly reminiscent of the Dutch craftsmanship which came to Britain during the early part of the seventeenth century, and which was soon absorbed by the better quality of the English work, transformed in the course of the quest for precision timekeeping, but which still kept its distinctive art form and, so some like to believe to-day, began a horological tradition.

But is this tradition Dutch any more than the Classic style of Wren is Dutch merely because Wren's best work was produced at a time when the Orange influence on London and society was at its height? The rise of the City merchants, the growth of the nation's total population to something like five millions, and the gradual establishment of a prosperous middle class, with the decline in the power of the Crown, meant that many thousands of potential purchasers awaited the trinkets, watches and proud household timepieces which the brethren of the Clockmakers' Company could produce. And of course they wanted these things in a style enabling them to ape their betters. The successful clothier could not bring a Wren cornice or architrave to every feature of his grand new town house, but he did like to see these Classic details reproduced in his furniture, and especially in his costly pieces, such as clocks. The prosperous wine merchant had, in the course of his trade, helped in the reaction against Puritanism, but nevertheless he did not think it odd that his clock cases should be in the Puritan style, ebony veneered on oak, of the type extensively made in Holland and England, but now labelled Dutch. Indeed the case-makers set a convention which was slow to change. As late as 1675 Sir Richard Legh (according to a record discovered by the horologist John James, and published in *The Antique Collector*) went to buy a new clock. "I went to the famous pendulum maker Knibb," he wrote, "and have agreed for one, he having none ready but one dull stager which was at £19. For £5 more I have agreed for one finer than my father's, and it is to be better finished with carved capitals gold, and gold pedistals with figures of boys and cherubims all brass gilt. I would have had it olivewood (the case I mean) but gold does not agree with the colour, so took their advice to have it black ebony which suits your cabinet better than walnut-tree wood, of which they are mostly made. . . ."

In clock design the so-called Dutch tradition includes mantel clocks with ebony veneer, a portico top supported on pillars in the beam-and-lintel fashion, a narrow hour ring, a spade hour hand. But the use of the Classic Orders has run through British architecture and British furniture since the days of Inigo Jones, when the Palladian style, named after the Italian architect Palladio, became the vogue, and the classic elements of the plinth, column and portico were worked willy-nilly into building and furnishing. If any proof were needed that the use of the Classic style in English clocks is not predominantly a Dutch characteristic, it is to be found, I think, in the excellence of the British workmanship and the stern adherence to Classic rules. The capitals of Ionic and Corinthian columns used in the casework of early Quare, Knibb, East, Hilderson and Henry Jones clocks were finely finished, and—more important—in the English clock case the proportions of the architrave and portico are strictly derived, as they should be, from the diameter of the column. The Dutch case-makers, in clocks earlier and later than the English, did not follow this

235

strict Classic tradition, and to our eye the cases appear ill-proportioned, with the architrave and frieze too top-heavy for the columns. Oddly enough, when the Classic revival came in Victorian days, and portico-and-pillar marble clocks were mass-produced in their thousands, it was the Dutch fashion which was followed, and not the English classic. There is evidence that Hooke, Wren and Tompion were in consultation, and that Tompion's grandest cases were strictly architectural. Even when Tompion designed a special clock for his friend "Beau" Nash, for the new Pump Room at Bath, completed 1706, he used a strongly architectural motif of a Doric column to harmonise with the column-motif of the Pump Room, and indeed the whole oak case is built behind a half-section of a column, down which the clockweight can fall, with the pendulum swinging behind. It is appropriate here to point out that our ancestors did not refer to "grandfather" clocks, but to "tall" or "long-case" or even "coffin" clocks. The so-called "bracket" clock of to-day was in its time a mantel clock. "Grandfather clock" did not inflict itself on us until some time after the 1880's, when that song "My Grandfather's Clock" swept England and America, and then of course it became something implying derision, and not a furnishing style of fashion!

It is in the era of the Fromanteels, a famous, thriving family of craftsmen who operated in London from about 1625, that the mingling of Dutch and English styles is seen to best advantage. An entry in his diary dated 1st November, 1660, from Evelyn reads: "I went with some of my relations to Court, to shew them his Maties cabinet and closset of rarities . . . amongst the clocks, one that shew'd the rising and setting of the Syn in ye Zodiaq, the Sunn represented by a face and rais of gold, upon an azure skie . . . rising and setting behind a landscape of hills, the work of our famous Fromantel. . . ." And on another occasion Evelyn refers to Fromanteel and "Zulichem" in one single entry, Zulichem being the district in Holland from which Christiaan Huygens originated, and the place-name being used as a surname in the fashion common in bygone times. "I return'd," he wrote, "by Fromanteel's, the famous clockmaker, to see some pendules, Monsieur Zulichem being with us." Despite the importance of the Fromanteels—Ahasuerus, Daniel, John, Abraham and their sons— and the prolificacy of their handiwork, few Fromanteel clocks have survived, so they are much sought after by collectors. A grievous loss in the bombing of the Dutch Church of Austin Friars, during London's long blitzkrieg, was the destruction of a fine long-case Fromanteel.

It seems certain that after Christiaan Huygens, Evelyn's "Monsieur Zulichem," first applied the pendulum to the timepiece, one of the Fromanteel family returned to Amsterdam to become apprenticed to one Samuel Coster, the first craftsman to construct a clock with the "Huygens" pendulum. Within six months the London Fromanteel family were advertising in *The Commonwealth Mercury* of 25th November, 1658: "There is lately

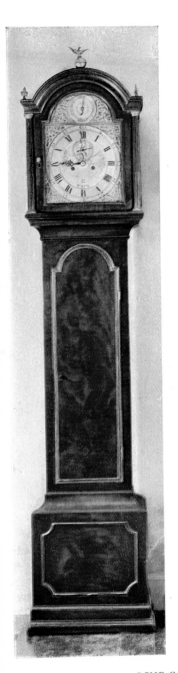

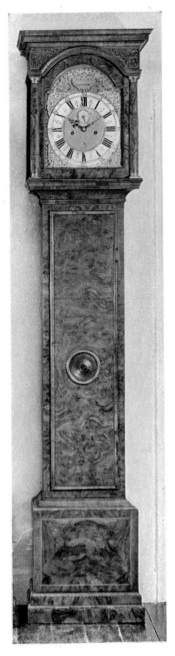

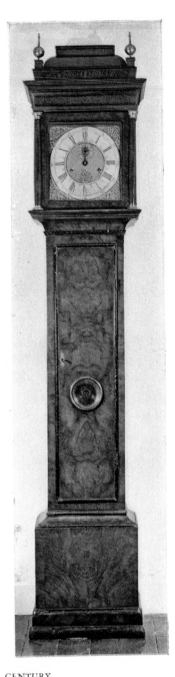

LONG-CASE CLOCKS OF THE EIGHTEENTH CENTURY

Twelve-inch arch dial clock in
Mahogany case
John Ross of Tain, c. 1780

Early arch dial clock. Walnut case
Joseph Windmills, c. 1710

Twelve-inch dial month clock
with semi-sonniary striking
Daniel Quare, c. 1720

ALARUM AND STRIKING MANTEL CLOCK IN EBONY-VENEERED CASE
Henry Jones, *c.* 1685

a way found out for making Clocks that go exact and keep equaller time then [*sic*] any now made without this Regulator (examined and approved before his Highness the Lord Protector, by such Doctors whose knowledge and learning is without exception) and are not subject to alter by change of weather as others are, and may be made to go a week, or a moneth, or a year, with once winding up, as well as those that are wound up every day, and keep time as well; and is very excellent for all House Clocks that go either with Springs or Waights: and also Steeple Clocks that are most subject to differ by change of weather. Made by Ahasuerus Fromanteel who made the first that were in ENGLAND. You may have them at his House on the Bank-side in Mosses-Alley, SOUTHWARK, and at the Sign of the Maremaid in Lothbury, near Bartholomew-Lane end, London."

Not all the fine makers began in London; some were attracted from their country workshops by the fame and fortunes to be made in London. Some, like John Knibb, couldn't bear to work there. The Knibbs were a prolific family of clockmakers, including Joseph, John, Edward, Peter and Samuel, but the two whose work remains probably most important to-day are the brothers Joseph and John. They were Oxford men and first set up business in the parish of St. Clements. At times they were at loggerheads with the guildsmen of Oxford, but in 1689 made their peace, and a year later Joseph Knibb moved to London, setting up in business it would appear at "the sign of the Dyal, near Serjeants-Inn." John remained behind, and in 1700 became Mayor of Oxford. Tiring of London life at the close of the seventeenth century, Joseph Knibb sold up his effects, after a life-time's clock and watchmaking, first at the "Dyal" and then at a more fashionable address, nearer Whitehall, in Suffolk Street, and he moved to Hanslope, a small village near Stony Stratford. He did not cease making fine clocks, however, and Knibb clocks signed "Joseph Knibb of Hanslop" are more rare to-day than those *"Londini fecit,"* and are much sought.

Public clocks by the pioneer makers have survived, though unfortunately there are now many with the hands of Esau and the works of Jacob. So early as 1630 Ahasuerus Fromanteel had been noted in the parish records of East Smithfield as a maker of steeple clocks. During the building of St. Paul's it was commonly said that Wren had asked Tompion to build a masterpiece of a clock for this masterpiece of a cathedral, and a newsletter of 1700 records that Tompion had contracted for £3,000 to erect such a clock, to run for a hundred years at one winding. Subsequently it was Langley Bradley, spoken of by Derham as "the judicious Workman of Fenchurch-street," who built the clock for Wren, and within a twelvemonth he must have had cause for regret.

St. Paul's clock, which ran until the movement was replaced by the present one in 1892, was built by Bradley for £308 9s. 10d., and the task was completed by 1708. But Bradley became involved in the disputes which involved Wren, Jennings, the chief carpenter, and the Dean himself, and so bitter were the wranglings that in 1713 a pamphlet was produced: "Fact Against Scandal: or a Collection of Testimonials, Affidavits and other Authentick Proofs in Vindication of Mr. Richard Jennings, Carpenter, Langley Bradley, Clock-Maker and Richard Phelps, Bell-Founder: To be referr'd to in an Answer which will speedily be publish'd to a late false and malicious Libel Entituled: Frauds and Abuses at St. Paul's."

From this document it appears that a minimum wage of 11s. a week was paid to the clock builders and carpenters, and that the chief retort of Bradley to those who said the clock was always wrong, and no true standard of time for the metropolis, was the meddling of people who were let into the tower to see the great bell, and who then tinkered with the works. "It is not the fault of the Clock," wrote Bradley, "but by its being made a Show of." And he was probably true at that, for subsequently he built clocks for Cripplegate Church and St. Clement Danes in the Strand, and there were no complaints. In the first St. Paul's clock there was no dial, the chimes being considered sufficient for a clerical building, and a clock-face incongruous. The Church of St. Vedast, Foster Lane, so cruelly damaged in the 1941 German raids, also originally had a turret movement which struck bells but did not show the time on a dial. Bradley's clock in St. Clements was subsequently modified to strike each hour twice. The main strike of the hour was given on the great 24-hundredweight bell, and then this was echoed by the small Sanctus bell in the tower—a fifteenth-century bell said to have been used before the Reformation. This Sanctus could not be heard during the day as its faint echo of the great bell was drowned by the traffic's roar, but the Luftwaffe has silenced both.

"I will do one thing more of which London shall not show the Like," boasted Thomas Harris (or Harrys), whose premises were at the Blackfriars end of Water Lane, when Tompion's shop was at the brow of the hill leading into Fleet Street. "I will make two hands show the hours and minutes without the church (St. Dunstan's), upon a double dial, which will be worth your observation, and to my credit." Also he proposed to build a portico under which two figures of men with pole-axes would strike the quarters—all for the sum of £80, including free maintenance. The Vestry compromised, gave him £35 and the old clock, and £4 a year for keeping in order the Gog and Magog display which still amuses Fleet Street—the only jack-clock in the City. Fleet Street has long been associated with these mechanisms, for there was a jack-clock on show in 1478, and Stowe describes a conduit in that year near Shoe Lane, with angels having "sweet sounding bells before them" on which hymns were played. Tom Harris's Gog and Magog were taken away when the old church was pulled down, were sold at auction to the Marquis of Hertford for £210, and for nearly a century they worked and chimed the hours and quarters in Regent's Park. But by the generosity of Lord Northcliffe the old figures and part of the original clock were restored to St. Dunstan's—not all of it Harris's work,

HANGING CLOCK

Mahogany case with applied carved and gilt decoration, *c.* 1760

for in 1738 the parish spent £110 for repairs. The *Mirror* of 1828, then published from Fleet Street, complained of the rival attraction of the Fleet Street clock jacks, saying: "one would really suppose they were in league with the pickpockets," for many a passing Londoner had his pocket picked or his watch stolen while gaping up at Harris's moving figures. Two years later the clock was sold at auction to the Marquis, but one might quote the motto of the Clockmakers' Company, *Tempus Rerum Imperator*—Time the governor of all things—for now the clock is back again in Fleet Street, and the *Mirror* is published from an office in a side-thoroughfare.

While Langley Bradley, Tom Harris, Daniel Delander, Christopher Gould, Charles Gretton and many another fine maker were following in Tompion's footsteps, Tompion's own nephew and chief apprentice, "Honest George" Graham was also following in the steps of the master craftsman, and creating a new standard of horological precision and ingenuity.

Graham, a Cumberland lad who found his way to London at the age of fourteen, apprenticed to Henry Aske ("at Ye Cross Keys in Bethlem") the very next year, became not only Tompion's apprentice and disciple, but the forerunner of a line of British clock craftsmen who set out to make clocks and chronometers (a device until Graham's time not considered possible) more exact than ever before. For seventeen years he worked with Tompion at the Water Lane shop, and many of Tompion's late clocks made just prior to his death in 1713 and signed "Thos: Tompion, Londini," were probably the work of Graham. Seven years after Tompion's death Graham moved to a better shop a little nearer Fleet Bridge—premises which passed into the hands of Mudge, and subsequently Mudge's son in partnership with Dutton, and so stayed as a clock shop until about fifty years ago. Graham's trade in watches was considerable, and his inventions for watchmaking improvements were almost as revolutionary and beneficial as his discovery of the "dead-beat" escapement for precision clockwork. Yet his trade reputation in his day must have been built up more on showy goods, for the *London Magazine* of 1753 in a satire "Ingredients required for the Manufacture of a Fop" lists:

> A repeater by Graham, which the hours reveals
> Almost over-balanc'd with knick-knacks and seals.

As the years progressed, Graham devoted more of his time to the perfection of timekeeping than to immediate profits from the merely commercial run of clocks and watches, and in the same year that he took over the new shop, next the Duke of Marlborough's Head Tavern, he was elected to membership of the Royal Society. Becoming engrossed in precision work and astronomical research, he was a valued coadjutor of Halley and Bradley. His scientific inventions include the first application of the timepiece to the telescope, in the form we know to-day as the transit clock, for

DEAD-BEAT ESCAPEMENT
Model of the escapement invented by George Graham, *c.* 1715

keeping an equatorially-mounted telescope fixed upon a star. Indeed the first transit clock in Greenwich Observatory was Graham's handiwork. If the seconds hand of an ordinary long-case clock be watched carefully, it will be seen that the anchor mechanism of the escapement permits a slight recoil, and in addition to ticking away the seconds the hand appears to bounce slightly in even the best set-up clock. This source of error and friction could not be overcome until Graham invented the non-recoiling dead-beat escapement, which at the time appeared to be the necessary perfection for astronomical timepieces. Although the observatory clock to-day has far surpassed Graham's limits of tolerance, the dead-beat escapement is still in use, and most watchmakers have as their standard regulator a weight-driven timepiece with a dead-beat escapement. Another landmark in horology was reached by Graham in the devising of the cylinder escapement. Although at that time a Fellow of the Royal Society, and anxious to devote his major energies to pure scientific research, Graham was determined to reduce the errors in timekeeping of pocket watches brought about by the use of the simple verge escapement. The result of his researches described in several papers read before the Royal Society was the cylinder escapement, which has remained unchanged for some 220 years, and is the standard escapement now in all mass-produced pocket- and wrist-watches. The discovery was made about 1725 and in a letter to his Paris colleague, Julien Le Roy, he communicated the invention and so introduced it to France. The mercury-compensated pendulum was another Graham innovation, first given to the world a year after the cylinder-escapement discovery, and in his paper, read to the Royal Society in 1726, Graham described it as "A Contrivance to Avoid Irregularities in a Clock's Motion by the Action of Heat and Cold upon a Pendulum"—basically, the substitution of a container of mercury for the solid metal bob of a pendulum, to counteract errors caused by the expansion of the pendulum rod and associate mountings in warm weather.

Despite these high-flights into scientific research and horological improvement, Graham made many clocks and watches and a comparatively large number exists to-day. That he was a popular maker of domestic clocks is shown by the inclusion of a characteristic Graham ebony-veneer mantel clock in Hogarth's famous family portrait of the Graham Family. Thirty-eight years after the death of the Father of English Clockmaking, the Tompion grave near the western entrance of Westminster Abbey was opened to receive the body of his nephew. The inscription reads: " . . . George Graham of London, Watchmaker and F.R.S., whose Curious Inventions do honour to Yᵉ British Genius." Graham, Honest George from Cumberland, had achieved more than skill in craftsmanship. He had begun a new era, and shown the way to real precision in timekeeping—that precision which was soon to become vital in ensuring Britain's supremacy at sea, through accurate marine navigation.

CHRISTOPHER GOULD'S SIGNATURE

TIME IS PRECIOUS

*When we consider all the achievements of science to-day and
the aid we derive from them in measuring time, it becomes a
matter of marvel how the old scientists and astronomers . . .
were able to get any degree of accuracy.*

H. Alan Lloyd's *500 Years of Precision Time-keeping*, 1938

BEFORE George Graham opened up a new field in precision timekeeping with the compensated pendulum and the dead-beat escapement, the pioneer English clockmakers had resorted to a number of
tricks to compensate for the errors. The Fromanteel family were among
the first to use the device of a spring-loaded maintaining-power to keep
the clock running during the few seconds taken by winding, when the
clock might otherwise be slowed down as the weight would be taken by
the hand and would not be available to drive the clock. Such an error,
though small, would be cumulative in a thirty-hour or eight-day clock; so
to ensure that the maintaining-power mechanism is brought into play each
time the clock is wound, shutters are arranged to cover the winding-holes
preventing the insertion of the key until a cord is pulled or a trigger (or
"bolt") moved aside, this simultaneously applying the spring-loading to
keep the movement running. Hence the term "bolt-and-shutter maintaining-power" as applied to such fittings on early long-case clocks: and very
occasionally the same device was applied to mantel clocks, although the
short pendulums and verge escapement of these gave such rough-and-
ready timekeeping that the unnecessary refinement of the bolt-and-shutter
was merely the clockmaker boasting. Another device used to improve
the quality of timekeeping was the second and a quarter pendulum. The
standard one-second pendulum needs to be approximately thirty-nine
inches long, and any minute adjustment for timekeeping can usually be
made by screwing a wing-nut up or down on a screw-thread at the end of
the pendulum rod, so making slight variation in the position of the brass-
faced lead pendulum bob. If the pendulum could conveniently be
lengthened then it would swing fewer times each minute and every hour,
and if there is any error in length, as there is sure to be with the periodic
changes of temperature, then it will not be magnified so much. A one-
second pendulum swings the surprising number of 86,400 times every
twenty-four hours, so the slightest error will be magnified that number
of times. Somewhere about the year 1675, William Clement, one of the
grand company of early makers and a contemporary of Robert Hooke and
Isaac Newton, realised that a convenient portion of the hour for a clock
movement would be a second and a quarter, instead of one second, and a
pendulum to beat this time would need to be precisely 61·155 inches long—

a convenient length to accommodate in the conventional long-case trunk if the pendulum bob may swing close to the ground. Such a pendulum beats only forty-eight times a minute instead of sixty, so there is a considerable reduction in magnification of error.

But all such horological tricks were elementary. Errors of a second or more were not serious in a workaday world *sans* telephones, *sans* television, *sans* B.B.C. pips and the chimes of Big Ben. Most important makers sold their clocks together with a "dyall" (i.e. a sundial) to check the time, together with an equation table to show the relation between Sun time and Mean time. From this it is to be assumed that clocks were not often given sun-testing during the English winter, and the accuracy even from May to September was dependent on the vagaries of the English summer, with only a sundial as a corrective.

Errors of this magnitude were hopeless for astronomers, and when Charles II appointed Flamsteed Astronomer Royal, with a stipend of £100 a year, there were no clocks at Greenwich to make even elementary astronomical calculations reasonably accurate. Tompion built a set of clocks, one of which had a 13-foot pendulum (making a single beat in two seconds), and to reduce errors caused through winding, the movement was arranged to run for a year. After Flamsteed's death, and the consequent family squabbles about the clocks he had owned at Greenwich, they were taken by his widow and eventually sold. A few years ago a private collector discovered the "13-foot" clock in the vestry of a chapel near Greenwich. In some 250 years it had been taken out of its frame in the Greenwich Observatory Octagon room, fitted in a plain oak case, and of course converted to a one-second pendulum, though it still runs for a year. Mr. Courtenay Ilbert who now owns the clock does so with justifiable pride, as it is no doubt the original timepiece on which Greenwich Time was first recorded at Greenwich. Accurate identification is possible for, on account of the acrimonious disputes between the Royal Society and the Flamsteeds, the astronomer's name as well as that of Tompion are engraved on the dial, and the appearance of the dial tallies closely with the engraving of the Octagon Room from Flamsteed's own *Historia Coelestis*.

Wallace Nutting, the American writer on horology, points out that "It was natural that Britain, being an island, and therefore necessarily a maritime power, should devote more attention than other nations to chronometers. The reflex stimulus upon clockmaking in general is obvious." Much of course might be said with equal truth of Holland, and indeed Christiaan Huygens had proposed mounting a clock in gimbals: that other great envier of maritime greatness, Louis XIV, invited Huygens to Paris to demonstrate this new mechanism for finding longitude with precision. But the clock swung badly, and temperature changes at sea made the whole thing useless. Philip III of Spain had offered a large reward for a workable marine chronometer at the close of the sixteenth century, without avail, but

CHIMING MANTEL CLOCK WITH MOON-WORK
IN RED AND GOLD LACQUER CASE
Thomas Turner, *c.* 1760

ENGLISH WATCHES

Gold watch with outer case of carnelian. Made by Strigner for James II. *c.* 1687
(top and bottom left)

Enamelled and jewelled gold watch. David Bouquet, *fl.* 1628-65
(bottom centre)

Gold repeating watch in open-work case. Thomas Tompion and Edward Banger, 1701
(top and bottom right)

the promise of genius from English clockmakers induced the British Government in 1714 to offer the then very considerable sum of £10,000 for a method of ascertaining a craft's longitude at sea *to within one degree* on a voyage to the West Indies. The prize was to be increased to £20,000 if the clock gave longitude within thirty minutes, but such an accuracy was hardly considered possible (though now an everyday occurrence at sea and in the air), for thirty minutes of longitude correspond with two minutes of time—and it was never considered possible for a marine clock to err by less than two minutes after a six-weeks' journey to the Indies.

The prize was such an encouragement to British clockmakers that one, John Harrison, decided to give up his whole life to the task. He was a Yorkshire carpenter from Pontefract, and all his earliest clocks had wooden wheels. But on hearing of the £20,000 prize he came to London, at the age of thirty-five, bearing drawings of a timepiece which he felt would satisfy the Board of Longitude's requirements, and these drawings were eventually shown to George Graham. The advice Graham gave was probably encouraging. We have no written record. But Harrison went back to his job of making and repairing clocks, and spent the next seven years perfecting his marine chronometer. When he next came to London it was not only in search of the prize. He had determined to set up business with the London clockmakers, and took premises in Red Lion Square.

Halley the astronomer accompanied Harrison and George Graham on tests with the new "No. 1 Timekeeper" on a barge, and later the clock was used on a voyage across the Bay of Biscay to Lisbon. A navigational error of only five miles was shown on this occasion, a revolutionary degree of accuracy for those days thus having been achieved, and Harrison was awarded £500 as some encouragement for his work.

Britain's war with Spain prevented more tests being made for a considerable time, as it was feared Harrison's improved chronometer might be captured and duplicated by the enemy. There is a startling parallel here with the invention of the magnetron valve which produces very high-frequency pulses for radar, and also for electrical observatory timekeepers. Although the magnetron was urgently needed during the war, officials were fearful of using it lest the precious device were captured intact by the enemy; and as the magnetron is in a wall of steel it could not be detonated in an emergency. But Harrison's period of waiting was not one of idleness. In the waiting years he made improved versions of a marine chronometer now only five inches in diameter. By 1759, exactly thirty-one years after George Graham had seen the Yorkshireman's first drawings, the chronometer was ready for trials for the £20,000 prize. On the first voyage an error of only one and a half miles was achieved, such a startling degree of accuracy that the Board refused to pay out the award until further verification could be made. Three years of bickering ensued. The chronometer

HARRISON'S FOURTH MARINE CHRONOMETER, 1759
Winner of the Admiralty's £20,000 reward

was tried again, and then showed an error of less than one minute in five months' navigation on the high seas: and it is amusing now to record that the skipper of the *Deptford* used for these trials made an error in navigation which nearly ruined the whole test. After eighteen days at sea the skipper maintained his position as 13 degrees 50 minutes west of Portsmouth. The Harrison chronometers showed the position to be 15 degrees 19 minutes. If the chronometer were really so much in error it would be useless continuing the voyage, and the skipper was intent on putting back to port. Harrison's son, entrusted on this voyage with the precious timepiece, insisted that there was no error, so they sailed on and found Madeira next day as predicted by chronometer and calculation. That they did so, a news-letter of the times records, "was a matter of great relief to the ship's company, who were then in great scarcity of beer."

Quibbling between the Board, Harrison, the Astronomer Royal, and many officials, as well as rival clockmakers, was not at an end. £10,000 was paid in two instalments on account, but an appeal had to be made to George III for the final grant of £8,750, and Harrison never had the full benefit of the prize in his lifetime. Even after his death the wrangling went on, and his son and daughter even quarrelled about the inscription for his tombstone in Hampstead Church.

One of the quibblers was also a great clockmaker, Thomas Mudge. He was one of the first committee-men appointed to examine Harrison's chronometer in 1765. Mudge, a Graham apprentice, was son of a clergyman

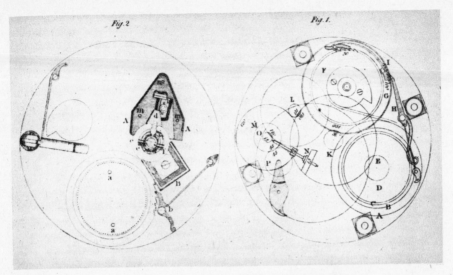

MOVEMENT OF THOMAS MUDGE'S TIMEKEEPER
Engraving from *A Description of the Timekeeper Invented by Mr. Thomas Mudge*, 1799

and schoolmaster in Exeter. After establishing a successful clock and watch business in London he set his heart on capturing the Longitude award. He did not, but he was paid some £3,000 for his trouble, and his marine chronometers were sent on voyages to Newfoundland under the care of Admiral Campbell. As in Harrison's case, the bickerings continued after the clockmaker's death. Mudge's son Thomas published in 1799 *A Description With Plates of The Timekeeper invented by Mr. Thomas Mudge*, with extracts of letters to the Astronomer Royal, Dr. Maskelyne, to the patron Count Bruhl, to Dutton (another famous clockmaker of Georgian times) and others in the controversy.

John Arnold and Thomas Earnshaw also determined to win part of the Longitude prize. Like Mudge, Arnold was a Westcountryman. So proud was he of his work that when asked to submit his "No. 1" chronometer for test he boasted to the Board: "I have made upwards of 900 chronometers, but never two alike so long as I can see room for any possible improvements. I have twenty No. 1 timepieces!" Like Mudge, again, he was eventually paid £3,000 for his discoveries, and on his second voyage in 1772 Captain Cook took Arnold's "No. 3" chronometer aboard the *Adventurer*. Thomas Earnshaw, a young watchmaker from Ashton-under-Lyne, at last in 1789 persuaded the Astronomer Royal to have one of the new chronometers tested. At the close of the eighteenth century Earnshaw was paid an encouraging £500, but he did not get the balance of £2,500 until 1803. The wrangling, again, continued, and *five years after* he had

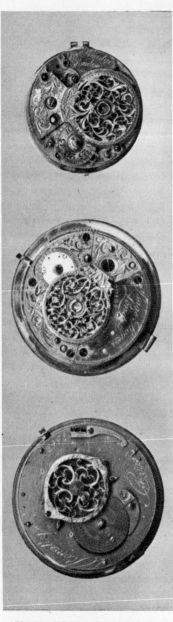

VERGE WATCH MOVEMENTS
c. 1700
Mudge, Rogers and Weston

been given the balance, Earnshaw published an angry "Appeal to the Public" telling how he had been wronged!

Earnshaw taught some of his secrets of jewelling and precision work to William Frodsham, who though not the greatest of the pioneer chronometer craftsmen was probably the most prolific, and the firm of Frodsham's exists to-day, still setting a standard in craftsmanship. William Frodsham's first chronometer shop was in Red Lion Square, where he sold marine chronometers to the skippers of steamers plying from the Thames. The little shop was at its zenith in 1790, but between the years 1822 and 1835 the next generation of Frodshams was engaged in the pursuit of precision timekeeping of a far greater order than dreamed possible by the elder Frodsham or his contemporaries Earnshaw and Arnold. Greenwich tests in 1830 showed that one of the Frodsham chronometers gave an error of only 57/100ths of a second.

Twenty years later Edmund Denison Beckett, Q.C., whose profession was the law but whose hobby was horology, devised the gravity escapement for Big Ben's clock movement, and although this did not render the Graham dead-beat escapement obsolescent it did revolutionise turret-clock construction, and on becoming Baron Grimthorpe this amateur horologist carried on with his investigations into the free pendulum, the type of construction not liable to variation in timekeeping when the force of heavy winds, rain or snow is applied to the large hands of public clocks. Vulliamy, Dent and others were working along similar lines, but the next great step forward in British horology was made in 1895 when F. Hope-Jones made the first practical application of electricity to time-keeping. Fifty-five years previously the Scots inventor, Alexander Bain, had been granted a patent for an

HARRISON'S FIRST MARINE TIMEKEEPER
Constructed 1729–1735

electric relay device to operate a number of dials from one master key-wound clock, and in 1843 a pendulum driven by an electro-magnet was described, and indeed his electric clock was just one of his notions developed in toying with the quest for perpetual motion. Electric power for his clock was obtained by Bain's sinking metal electrodes into moist earth underneath the clock, the potential difference being applied to the magnetic coil driving the pendulum.

TURRET CLOCK MOVEMENT FROM ST. GILES'S CHURCH, CAMBRIDGE
Originally designed for King's College, Cambridge, by William Clement, 1671

This device made no practical step forward in precision horology, but the invention of Hope-Jones's "Synchronome Remontoire," although primarily, like Bain's, developed as a master-and-slave-dial system, did introduce a new principle of making alternate electric contact without checking pendulum motion. R. J. Rudd made the next step three years later when he developed the free pendulum getting its electro-magnetic impulse at zero position of swing, but his ideas were stillborn and there was a gap in this British development until the year 1921, when W. H. Shortt completed his experiments with the "hit-and-miss" synchroniser, and a test made at Edinburgh's Royal Observatory by Professor Sampson showed that the Shortt clock was superior to any other type of observatory clock then in use. Not only had a great step forward been made in the electrical drive and follow, but the whole pendulum mechanism was encased in a copper cylinder evacuated, so eliminating interference in the swing caused by stray air currents. The Shortt clock soon became the observatory standard, but in this chronicle of British timekeeping it is interesting to record that two of the greatest contributions have been made by amateurs—by Grimthorpe for the gravity 'scapement used in Big Ben and several other famous London public clocks, and now by Captain E. Craig who, working on the basic model of the Shortt clock, has devised what experts such as H. Alan Lloyd believe to be the only really free pendulum device in existence to-day.

In the Grimthorpe gravity 'scapement the early English clockmakers such as Clement, Harris, Tompion and Graham would have seen the fulfilment of their dreams—a high degree of accuracy attained by purely mechanical drive for a pendulum. They could never have contemplated the marvels of the Shortt and Craig electric clocks, with their errors of less than 0.002 seconds. Now even the twentieth-century workers on the electrically-driven pendulum observatory clocks are confounded by the onward surge of electric development. The clock craftsman of to-day is not an accurate cutter of clock wheels and pinions, but a handicraft man in the cutting of quartz-crystals, for now our latest clocks have no "works," no weights, no pendulum—and in some instances not even a dial but a cathode-ray tube screen as in a television or radar frame. They are driven by a quartz-crystal-controlled electric oscillator.

While the Royal Observatory still treasures its Shortt clocks (though regrettably having sold, a few years ago, its now priceless Arnold Nos. 1 and 2 Regulators, which had been made for £1,010 in 1774 and are now historic), transit time to-day is checked not by pendulums but by high-frequency electric oscillations. The whole mechanism is an application of electronics to horology, and is akin to the oscillating-crystal drive used to keep B.B.C. broadcasting stations rigidly to their allotted wavelengths, and to the radar mechanism used to time world-record flights of jet-propelled aircraft. It is a fascinating new chapter, and a great credit to British inventors, notably those at the National Physical Laboratory, and the

Royal Aircraft Establishment at Farnborough. But it is, so the old crafts-men would feel, not clockmaking. It may be electronics, and the triumph of brain over craftsmanship. The world has rushed ahead too far from the day when, as Aristophanes told us, man measured the hour by the number of times his shadow was greater than the length of his own feet. For 350 years until the Victorian era of mass-production, we made fine clocks. Now, in our observatory devices which tell time to within one-thousandth of a second, we make good electronics. But that's another story.

ENGLISH POPULAR

AND TRADITIONAL ART

BY

MARGARET LAMBERT & ENID MARX

INTRODUCTION

POPULAR and traditional art, in the sense here intended, is hard to define though easy enough to recognise when seen. It is the art which ordinary people have, from time immemorial, introduced into their everyday lives, sometimes making it themselves, at others imposing their own tastes on the products of the craftsman or the machine, in contrast to the more sophisticated art made by specialists for wealthy patrons. Its very lack of sophistication makes popular art one of the most revealing expressions of national characteristics. Because it is more conspicuous amongst simple non-industrial societies, many people have supposed that its only genuine form is peasant or folk art. This book is an attempt to show that in England too, although peasants may no longer exist, we have a long and living tradition of popular art, which not only survived the industrial revolution, but in some cases, such as fair-ground decoration (or, to take an earlier example, printing) even drew new inspiration from the potentialities of the machine. Whatever the causes for the present very noticeable decline in aesthetic standards, they certainly seem to go far deeper than the generally accepted explanation that machinery and mass production destroy individual taste. A curious fact which seems to emerge from this brief survey is that the last great impetus to popular art came from the Romantic Movement in the early years of the nineteenth century; there has been nothing comparable since.

It is not, of course, possible in so small a compass to cover the whole field, and selection has had to be most arbitrary. We have tried to give some idea of the many forms, however simple, in which English popular art has manifested itself and to show its distinctive qualities: forthrightness, gaiety, delight in bright colours and sense of well-balanced design. For convenience and brevity the examples have been roughly grouped by the materials used and types of decoration.

PAPER AND PRINTING

STREET literature, the literature of the masses, provides some of the most interesting forms of popular art in England. It owes its existence to cheap printing, but printing, once discovered, was surprisingly quickly adapted to the popular traditions. The ordinary purveyor of literature to the countryside, the itinerant ballad singer, who often combined this with the role of miscellaneous pedlar, could now sell printed copies of his songs as well as singing them, thereby enhancing their value for his simple-minded audience.

Ballads and broadsides, being intended for a not very literate public, needed a strong pictorial appeal. A large woodcut would be printed at the head of a long strip of paper, the length varying according to the amount of matter (often topical verses set to traditional tunes) to be printed underneath. These broadside woodcuts, though often coarsely cut, have in their simplicity, directness and freedom, much of the attraction of primitive paintings; they are done in the same spirit as the grotesqueries and humours of misereres or gargoyles in Gothic churches. Ordinary people have always delighted in the marvellous, the dramatic and horrific. Literal pictorial representation of marvels entailed a glorious juxtaposition of incongruous objects, often producing a much more fantastic effect than the deliberate surrealism of modern painters.

Before dying out in the mid-nineteenth century, broadsides declined in the social scale, circulating mainly amongst the rougher and more brutal sections of society. The ballad-sellers became the Flying Stationers or Running Patterers like Silas Wegg in *Our Mutual Friend*. Until 1839, when this was forbidden on account of the din, they would run through the streets of London blowing a horn and crying excerpts from the latest "bloody battle" or "horrible murder," done into broadside doggerel. When sensations were scarce, an old one would be palmed off as new; hence the title "Catchpenny."

Murder, then as now, was a great attraction. Public executions stimulated a brisk trade in the "Gallows Literature" type of broadside; especially popular were "Last Confessions," in doggerel verse with a high moral tone and written, so the Patterer pretended, "in the condemned cell, with the condemned pen, ink and paper." They were given stock portraits, used over and over again, the wood blocks being recut from time to time from earlier originals. But this lack of factual realism never seems to have worried the broadside public; indeed, though dictated by economy, it suited an audience which, being only partly literate, could more easily recognise stock characters like those of pantomime or melodrama. The conception of realism in art is really quite modern. Orlando Hodgson, for instance, produced an illustration of the Greenacre crime with such brilliant and unnaturalistic colour combinations that the gruesomeness of individual details disappears in the theatricality and artificiality of the whole. The result is superb.

Though sensationalism bulked large, the Running Stationer's stock, even towards the end of his existence, was by no means confined to it. Dialogues of all kinds, humorous, elevating, satirical; political squibs, moral tracts, songs "three yards a penny," comic, serious, religious, love songs, drinking songs, patriotic ballads, all embellished with cuts, some most inappropriate, were printed in great variety. One of the last historic events to be recorded in broadside chronicles was Victoria's marriage to Albert in 1840. Jemmy Catnatch and Johnny Pitts, the two rival printers of the Seven Dials district, produced sentiments to suit all tastes; in some Albert was represented as a Prince Charming, in others as a German sausage merchant. In wartime the ballad-monger was the great patriotic historian.

News purveyor, entertainer, scandal-monger, patriot, he was also, oddly enough, a great moralist. We find broadsides, all through their career, dwelling on the vanities of this world and the imminence of death. Sometimes old verses are given contemporary pictures, as in "Death and Mortality" illustrated here.

The simplicity and directness of the broadside woodcuts made them extremely effective propaganda. George Cruikshank, for instance, in his campaign to abolish the death penalty for forgery, adopts the broadside style with remarkably dramatic effect

Complementary to the broadsides, though originating somewhat later, often produced by the same printers and covering many of the same topics, were the Chapbooks, called after the Chapman who sold them. They were slim, small, paper-covered volumes, easy to fit into a pedlar's pack. Small woodcuts usually ornamented their cover or frontispiece and were interspersed in the text, as pictures and swags. These little cuts constitute the special charm of the chapbooks; they have the naïveté, directness and fantasy of ballad and broadside decorations, but being on a smaller scale, display more delicacy. The paper covers of chapbooks deserve special

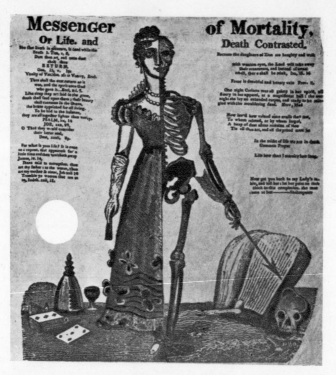

BROADSIDE, c. 1830

mention; they were often gaily coloured (yellow was a favourite ground) with, sometimes, little stuck-on labels for the titles, surrounded with pretty little type ornaments and perhaps a woodcut, hand-coloured. Decorated papers also were used with great effect.

Chapbooks flourished exceedingly from the middle of the seventeenth century onwards. Ranging in price from sixpence to a penny or less, they cover an immense variety of topics. John Ashton, the nineteenth-century antiquarian, made a rough classification, which runs: "Religious, Diabolical, Supernatural, Superstitious, Romantic, Humorous, Legendary, Historical, Biographical and Criminal." The contents can rarely claim any literary merit. The stories, some based on real events, others on old medieval romances, others again crude pirated versions of popular books, such as *Gulliver's Travels,* are generally so hacked about and compressed that at times they hardly make sense. The chapbooks' attraction lies mainly in their illustrations.

Chapbooks specially for children were a late development, as were all children's books not primarily designed as an adjunct to lessons or for moral instruction. Nevertheless, children must have formed a large part of the chapbook public, especially for the fables and romances; Tristram Shandy's Uncle Toby bought them for his schoolfellows. When at last a real publisher of books for children appeared—John Newbery, publisher and friend of Johnson, Goldsmith and Smollett—he followed the chapbook tradition of small pictures and miniature size, with gay covers of Dutch embossed papers, but with the text directly written for children. Even the great Bewick kept to the old chapbook style in his wood engravings for the children's books published, some years after Newbery, by Saint of Newcastle—for instance the delightful *New Lottery Book of Birds and Beasts* (1771).

Chapbooks were frowned on by moralists as putting fanciful ideas into children's heads. Mr. Harvey Darton, the great authority, points out in his *Children's Books in England*, that the battle of the Puritans, the struggle between Penny Merriments and Penny Godlinesses, raged in the chapbook world as elsewhere. Nevertheless, apart from their intrinsic charm, chapbooks made two immortal contributions to our nursery archives; to them alone is due the survival of the Fairy Tale and Nursery Rhyme, which would else have disappeared with the oral traditions which first put them into circulation as children's tales.

Early in the nineteenth century appeared what its publishers called the Juvenile Drama, better known perhaps as the Toy Theatre, or "Penny Plain and Twopence Coloured."

If you bought a Juvenile Drama complete, as you still could till 1944, it would consist of a little book of words, stage directions and instructions; a given number of sheets of scenery—backcloths and wings; a smaller number

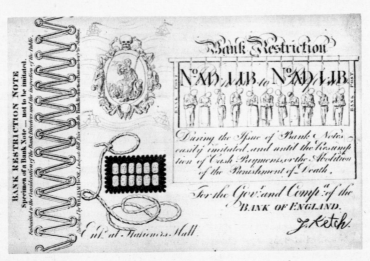

GEORGE CRUIKSHANK'S BROADSIDE AGAINST THE DEATH PENALTY FOR FORGERY

of sheets of characters, and, in the case of a pantomime, a sheet or two of tricks. These sheets would be pictures in outline, either plain for colouring yourself, or, for an extra penny, hand-coloured by professionals with a verve and brilliance the amateur could scarcely hope to emulate. These sheets, to be mounted on cardboard and cut out according to directions, were meant for use on the little wooden frame stages which, complete with gaily coloured proscenium, a real drop curtain and tin holders for footlights, could be bought for about a pound. The stage once set, the characters (in different attitudes according to the action of the plot) were slid on and off from the wings as directed in the book of words. Pantomime "trick" changes were done by dropping little flaps cut in the scenery. For moments of high drama, fireworks might be used; "red fire to burn" is the usual stage direction for the frequent conflagrations required by the plots. Mr. A. E. Wilson, in his fascinating book *Penny Plain and Twopence Coloured*, suggests that the idea of the cut-out model theatre may have come from abroad. The Peepshow was a well-known institution at fairs and the toy theatre is in the same tradition as the peepshow. But whatever its origin, the Juvenile Drama, once arrived, had a great success. The plays and pantomimes presented were taken from the contemporary stage. The characters, especially in the early days, were often faithful portraits of famous players. Stage fronts are, as like as not, taken from well-known theatres. Street scenes, too, are often from life; one of Pollock's shows his own shop. Apart from their intrinsic charm, these little theatres preserve a wonderfully vivid record of the early nineteenth-century stage, even down to the exaggerated gestures, the strut and swagger of the romantic type of acting then fashionable.

This stage lent itself exceptionally well to adaptation for the toy theatre. In literary merit it has probably never been so bad, but action and magnificent spectacle made up for stereotyped characters and artificial plots. The Gothic Revival had merged into the full tide of the Romantic Movement; the stage, like literature, painting and even architecture, was luxuriating in a riot of medieval, Oriental, or otherwise exotic splendour. To meet the demand for what we should now call "actuality," recent events such as the battles of Waterloo and Trafalgar, even the burning of Moscow, were turned into stage and toy theatre dramas, where they provided scope for *tours de force* in scenic display. The first hints of a decline in the toy theatre's popularity coincide with the change that came over the English theatre as a reaction set in towards naturalism and the comedy of manners, dependent for its effect on dialogue rather than on display.

Some publishers dealt only in Juvenile Drama, but the great majority also went in for much else in the cheaper forms of literature; children's books, almanacs, books of fate in the chapbook tradition, coloured engravings and cartoons, Valentines and such-like things. In *Vanity Fair,* Thackeray refers to "West's famous characters," and William West was

CHILD'S INSCRIBED WRITING SHEET

certainly a most prolific producer; Mr. Wilson has found as many as a hundred and seven plays published by him, which gives some idea of the immense vogue the toy theatre enjoyed; West's nautical dramas are some of his most superb and dramatic productions. Another prolific toy theatre sheet publisher was Skelt, from whom Robert Louis Stevenson coined the descriptive word "Skeltery" to epitomise this miniature world of romance. Webb and Pollock (late Reddington) were still carrying on their family businesses until a few years ago, though of course only reissuing old plays.

In their style of drawing and dramatic use of colour, the toy theatre sheets do not break new ground. They follow the same tradition as the coloured engravings, hung on many a cottage wall, or used as illustrations to the various types of cheap paper-covered booklets and pamphlets issued for popular amusement by the same publishers. The frontispiece to the Book of Fate here illustrated, and published by Park, one of the best of the toy theatre publishers, is in the same style of draughtsmanship and colour range.

Many other examples could be cited, such as some of the children's books and games, the coloured borders to their writing sheets, the cheaper type of gardening papers just coming into vogue with their pictures of gaily splashed and speckled "florist's flowers."

The means available for producing these effects were of the simplest; flat washes of water colour on outline drawings, with the minimum of line shading. The basic colours used were usually limited to four—gamboge, carmine, prussian blue and black. Skilful mixing and graduations produced luscious browns, purples, greens, pinks. It is remarkable how sheets over a century old retain their brilliance. Much of the secret seems to lie in the excellent quality of the pigments used and in the imaginative skill shown in juxtaposing one colour with another to set each off to best advantage.

The draughtsmanship too is often of a high order. Some of the earlier publishers, notably West, Jamieson, and Hodgson, used well-known artists. West at one time even employed William Blake. Nevertheless, so strong was the convention, that artists of the most marked individuality seem to fit into it quite comfortably. Partly this is due to the very simple reproductive process used; the artist's sketches were engraved, and the colour hand-painted by teams of children, or perhaps the members of a family. For later productions stencils came in. Stencilling does not give the same tone gradations as direct painting, but has its own attractions in the firmer outline and greater effect of freedom.

If we take a well-known play, such as the melodrama *The Miller and his Men*, and compare the versions produced by the different publishers from the same original, we can easily distinguish one from the other in individualities of style and selection; which shows that the toy theatre artists displayed plenty of initiative and originality. Much of the charm of their work lies in the way the prevailing Romanticism, the passion for things rich and strange, has been interpreted into homely English terms, thereby producing an extraordinary mixture of the real and the fantastic. Just as, half a century later, the village painter, the Douanier Rousseau, was to base his tigers on the ordinary village cat, so the toy theatre artists made up their tropical forests from everyday English vegetation but of a supernatural luxuriance. Robert Louis Stevenson was fascinated by the extreme boskiness of the Skeltonian forests, the excessive gnarledness possible to a plain English oak. The intricately pinnacled castles, washed by rivers of an inky blue, obviously derive from the same originals as the castles still painted on canal barges to-day. Styles of architecture, or costume, Egyptian, Oriental, Central European, are jumbled together in exuberant confusion. The heights of fantasy are reached in the pantomimes. Tradition demands

PICTURE FOR TINSELLING PUBLISHED BY PARK

that Harlequin with his bat, or Clown with the poker, shall turn everyday objects into something unexpected. Toy theatre tricks follow the pantomime tradition, where part of the fun lies in arbitrarily altering the size of ordinary objects; an egg turns into a huge hen bigger than the clown and so on. Tricks were, of course, meant to be cut out, but the sheets as printed, with their juxtaposition of incongruous objects, drawn to different scales and at different angles to fit the paper, give an effect of fantastic inconsequence which would be hard to achieve deliberately.

Closely akin to the Juvenile Drama are the tinsel pictures which reached their heyday about the 1830's. All toy theatre publishers also published these large engravings of celebrities, mostly theatrical but also including royal personages or popular heroes.

Decorating prints with bits of silk, satin or coloured paper was a popular amusement years before it occurred to the theatrical publishers that coloured metal foil, embossed and with a paper backing, would be effective. Tinsel ornaments in immense variety were soon produced and sold in packets for a few pence. These stamped-out tinsels included everything, from stars,

265

dots, spangles, to helmets, breastplates, plumes, even swords, daggers and pistols.

The typical tinsel picture represents the subject in heroic stance; behind him in much smaller scale is a landscape, whilst an explosive sky enhances the general effect. Some of the most attractive prints represent the hero on horseback. Heroines seldom appear: their costumes offer less scope for decoration. Most magnificent of all are the stage villains, stamping and scowling, slung about with an armoury of weapons. Some of the effects achieved with, for instance, Mephistopheles or the Ghost from *Hamlet* are superbly horrific.

Besides these big character portraits, the publishers issued smaller pictures, "fours," "sixes," or even "eights" to a sheet, which could be cut out and decorated separately, and background scenes were sold separately for mounting.

Like the Juvenile Theatres, the success of the tinsel picture depended on the vogue for romantic, unrealistic acting of the barnstorming type. With the vogue for realism and the rise of cheap colour reproductions it lost its appeal.

Not all tinsel pictures are portraits; hand-coloured engravings of highly dramatic scenes, decorated with tinsel dots and stars, may still sometimes be found hanging upon cottage walls. Indeed, any subject seems suitable for tinselling, provided it is sufficiently sensational to lend itself to the brilliancy of coloured foil.

Another form of decorated picture is the Valentine, which was once used by all classes. The idea of a Valentine made by embellishing a set of verses with a picture seems to have arrived at the end of the eighteenth century. At first such Valentines were entirely amateur; verses are composed and arranged to form patterns, and are decorated with pictures, paper cut-outs or stuck-on bits of silk or satin.

The printers soon began to take a hand. They published Valentine Writers like Letter Writers for those who could not versify themselves. Machine-made lace and embossed papers made delightful frames and borders. The hand-painted pictures forming the centres were often posies of flowers, especially the striped and speckled "florist's flowers" surrounded by an appropriate motto. Paper cut-outs in the form perhaps of hearts or true-love knots, would be likewise mounted; sometimes, with admirable skill, the inscriptions too would be cut out of paper in a single piece. Devices for pulling up one picture to show another underneath, or perhaps for opening out or sliding off the top picture, became more and more ingenious; such tricks suggested hidden sentiments which are a great part of the Valentine's attraction.

Besides supplying the accessories for making your own Valentines, printers and publishers also sold them complete. Printed Valentines included all sorts of punning effects—matrimonial ladders, cupid thermometers, pairs of gloves cut out, and adaptations of documentary forms, I.O.U.s, wills,

VALENTINE: HAND-COLOURED LITHOGRAPH, 1845

licences, and bank notes; so realistic was a representation of a £5 Bank of Love note that it provoked action by the authorities for fear it might help forgers.

Some of the most attractive are the trade Valentines, hand-coloured engravings representing the different occupations and trades, in full costume and with suitably apt verses; there are the Chymist, the Barmaid, the Hatter, the Draper, the Pastry Cook, the Housemaid, and so on, one to fit almost any recipient.

In glaring contrast to the sentimental Valentines are the comic ones, which in crudity and brutality remind us of another aspect of English life prevalent a century ago. They consist of caricatures of different types with appropriately insulting rhymes underneath. A favourite comic transformation showed a drawing of a man or woman with a flap, which when folded back, showed the same subject minus hair and teeth. Yet in spite of their

267

crudity one cannot but recognise certain qualities of draughtsmanship and colour, sadly lacking in the modern revival of either comic or sentimental Valentines.

It may be that this ridicule led to the decline of the Valentine. But it seems more likely that they were ousted by the increasing popularity of the Christmas card.

This, as we know it to-day, is just on a hundred years old. Starting as the whim of a few well-known literary figures, who commissioned artists to design them Christmas greetings cards, the idea was promptly taken up by printers and publishers, who saw in it a much more profitable, because universal, market than the Valentine. By the 1860's, the spate of Christmas cards had begun, and they were probably at their best in the last quarter of the nineteenth century. Coming later, they miss much of the simplicity and directness which makes the aesthetic appeal of the Valentine; they are more mechanical and stereotyped, nevertheless they have a luscious exuberance not without attraction. Many of their subjects, suitably modified, are on the same principles as those of the Valentines—sentimental, floral or domestic themes, puns, adaptation of documentary forms, and so on. In variety and ingenuity, as well as in skilful use of the machine, Christmas cards probably reached their zenith in the last quarter of the nineteenth century, which is the date of those here illustrated.

"The paper cut-out, shadow profile, or silhouette, flourished most successfully in England," says Mrs. Nevill Jackson in her enchanting book *Silhouette*: this technique is, she suggests, by its sobriety and restraint, particularly suited to English taste. These shadow portraits filled the need for cheap likenesses before the invention of photography.

Cutting paper to get decorative shadowed effects is a development of missal painting. Paper was cut to look like lace, or letters of initials, or sometimes whole sentences were cut out, leaving the letters solid, in a technique which is somewhere between needlework and carving. Whilst paper was expensive, cut-paper work was mainly confined to the wealthier classes or professionals (for instance, Mrs. Delaney's exquisite flower pictures) but, in the early nineteenth century, it became cheap and accessible to all.

Cut-paper ornamentation was ideal for Valentines, and was also much used for decorating texts and mottoes, as samplers were used in needlework. From hand-made to machine-made lace-papers was a natural step, and some of the early Victorian machine-cut papers are extremely attractive.

In spite of the competition of photography, such is the fascination of the portrait silhouette that it has survived until to-day, and practitioners may still be found at seaside and other pleasure resorts. Cutting lace-paper patterns is still done by street performers to entertain queues.

Akin to cut-paper ornamentation is "pin-prick" decoration, which was also a very popular process. Combined as it usually is with a certain amount of water-colour painting, it produces extremely attractive results.

PEDLAR DOLL SHOWING MISCELLANEOUS WARES
Early nineteenth century
Collection Mrs. Nicholl

TINSELLED ENGRAVINGS USED AS PICTURES IN COTTAGES
Early nineteenth century
Collection Mrs. Nicholl

FRONTISPIECE FROM PARK'S *NEW EGYPTIAN DREAM BOOK*
Hand-coloured engraving of the early nineteenth century
Collection Mrs. Nicholl

PIN-PRICK PICTURE

It depends for its effects on the contrasts between light and shade. By varying the size of the holes, and by pricking now from one side of the paper, now from the other, you can get several different textures and thus build up the pattern or picture.

In England, pin-prick decoration seems to have been first used in religious houses for decorating votive pictures and is, like cut-out silhouettes, a development of the decorated missal. But by the end of the eighteenth century it had become widely popular. The Young Ladies' Annuals which had a great vogue in the 1820's and '30's often gave instructions and suggestions for pin-prick patterns.

271

Cut and rolled or twisted paper is another extremely effective method of paper ornament, especially for heraldic motives; it is, of course, more skilled than the ordinary pin-prick or cut-out technique.

Penmanship is yet another form of decorating paper. The various schools of English calligraphy are outside our scope and may be studied in Sir Ambrose Heal's *The English Writing Masters*. Britain's wide commercial interests naturally gave handwriting special importance. Children were encouraged to write on writing sheets, with printed hand-coloured borders, on the same principle as decorated samplers. Calligraphic styles and ornamentation were reproduced by the printers in, for instance, engraved trade cards, watch verge papers, and the like, with extremely decorative effects.

BROWN EARTHENWARE MERMAID FLASK
Early nineteenth century

POTTERY AND GLASS

SLIPWARE is one of the simplest forms of decorated pottery. The basic technique consists in taking a different coloured clay from the body of the ware, mixing it with water to a cream, and then applying it as a "slip," either all over the body or in patches to form a pattern. There are, of course, many possible variations in the way slip can be applied.

Thomas Toft and his fellows, working in the seventeenth and eighteenth centuries, represent a high-water mark in English slipware and their work is well known. What is perhaps less generally recognised is the high standard of decoration achieved by country potters, many anonymous, in most parts of England, and still sometimes to be found in remoter rural areas. They did most of their work for purely utilitarian local needs, but made special pieces on occasions (harvests, weddings, christenings or to commemorate some event), which have stood a better chance of survival. Each district tends to have its own variations in pattern and shape and its favourite method of decoration.

Typical of such small local potteries are the little group which flourished in North Devon, on the Fremington claybed, lying between Barnstaple and

272

DEVONSHIRE HARVEST POTTERY

Bideford. Best known of these North Devon potters are the Fishley family, established since at least the eighteenth century, and still making decorated wares in the traditional local styles until quite recently. In North Devon, as at Donyatt in Somerset and on many Welsh harvest jugs, the prevalent form of decoration is a coating of slip, scratched and cut away to show the darker ground. A written inscription, enclosed in a panel, often forms part of the decorative scheme.

The pieces illustrated from North Devon are inscribed and dated at the end of the eighteenth century. They are covered with a favourite lead glaze, a rich greenish yellow, which makes the body show up as an ochreous brown and the white slip as honey-coloured. The ornamental heads on the left-hand jug are reminiscent of ships' figure-heads. Besides the usual agricultural motives, nautical ones, ships, mariner's compasses, even mermaids, are favourite subjects, as indeed might be expected in a seafaring country. Local marvels sometimes got special pictures; for instance the birth of twins joined together is commemorated in a dish, bearing their portrait and dated 1680, made at Donyatt in Somerset, and now in the Taunton Museum. This is just the sort of event that the broadside writers delighted to record.

Curiously enough, although each district has its local peculiarities of shape and decoration, the sentiments described on these slipware pieces show little originality. We find the same rustic apophthegms, often in the same words, all over the country. The inscriptions on the jugs illustrated run:

> "He that by the plough must thrive
> Himself must either hold or drive."

And on the right-hand Bideford harvest pitcher:

> "Harvest is come all by itself
> Now in macking of your barley mow
> When men do labour hard and sweat
> Good ale is better for their meat
> Bideford 28 April 1775."

One inscription contains a sort of potter's creed:

> "When I was in my native place
> I was a lump of clay
> And digged was from out the earth
> And brought from thence away.
> But now I am a jug become
> By potters art and skill
> And now your servant am become
> And carry ale I will."

By contrast, each district seems to have had its own set of names for the various utensils. In North Devon, for instance, the pilchard pots shipped to Cornish fishermen were, running from large to small, known as "great crocks," "buzzards" and "gallons." Ordinary red pitchers ran as "long toms," "forty tales," "gullymouths," "pinchgutts," "sixties" and "pennyjugs."

Until quite recently, that is, until the interest of dealers and collectors introduced artificial values, nearly every cottage or farmhouse mantelshelf was decorated with a row of brightly coloured earthenware chimney ornaments or "image toys" as their makers described them. Such ornaments have been the valued family possessions of many generations of country folk, and reflect, in their immense variety of forms, the taste, interests, habits, even the views, of everyday British people. In small country towns, too, it was quite common for such figures to be used for shop window display, especially in dairies, where the produce was liable to spoil in the sun.

Most of these so-called "Staffordshire" figures (in earthenware or stoneware) still to be seen in country cottages date from the late eighteenth and early nineteenth centuries; few earlier ones have survived outside the great collections.

Early stoneware saltglaze figures are now, alas, extremely rare; produced principally in Staffordshire, they are some of the most delightful works of

STAFFORDSHIRE SALTGLAZE STONEWARE FIGURES
Late eighteenth century

English potters, with a directness and humour in the best traditions of popular art. Such are the famous "Pew Groups," where two figures are shown seated on a pew, sometimes a pair of awkward young lovers, sometimes an elderly ogling couple; the groups are white but with details skilfully and wittily picked out in brown clay. Then there are the well-known owl and bear jugs, white picked out in brown, with heads that lift off to form cups. Another effective early method was the so-called "agate ware," made from layers of different coloured clays to give a streaky effect. The discovery of porcelain, however, caused the Staffordshire potters to neglect their saltglaze figures in favour of this more sophisticated material.

Earthenware figures, also made mainly in Staffordshire, held their own against the attractions of porcelain. Earthenware being the coarser and cheaper material became the "poor man's porcelain"; this humbler market naturally influenced the style of modelling, making it less sophisticated Not that porcelain models did not influence earthenware; the grave dogs, with gilt chains, that sit sentinelwise on so many cottage mantelpieces have obviously been derived at few removes from the Meissen porcelain pugs. In the process they have turned into something with a more direct and robust appeal; even with a touch of humour.

275

In looking at some of the early (Astbury Whieldon type) figures, it is curious to notice how different forms seem to get repeated in different countries and even in widely separated epochs. In the little horseman figures the stance of the horses, with their long span, is strongly reminiscent of Chinese and even African art.

All earthenware figures were not necessarily equally simple. On the contrary, some of the later figures, produced for instance by the famous Wood family, are as sophisticated as the porcelain of Chelsea or Bow, and obviously influenced by fashionable foreign models. In their genre they are very successful, but their appeal is different. The elder Ralph Wood is, however, reputed to have modelled the first of a figure which most people think of as being essentially English popular art—the Toby Jug. Variants of the Toby Philpot motive have continued right down to the present day. It is, therefore, all the more odd to find that Ralph Wood most probably derived the idea from a French model and also that the character of Toby Philpot comes from Italy, being derived from the famous mid-eighteenth-century drinking song, "the Brown Bottel," adapted from the Latin verses of an Italian author. Illustrated engravings of the song circulated all over England and thus laid the foundation of a long career.

Independently of famous firms of potters, a host of lesser ones, some

STAFFORDSHIRE SALTGLAZE STONEWARE
Bear-jug of the late eighteenth century

known, some unknown to us to-day, carried on the production of "image toys" in the old popular tradition. Plaster moulds and enamel painting both helped to cheapen production. These wares were peddled by chapmen, or sometimes by the potter himself. A drawing by Rowlandson shows the image seller with his tray of images · arriving in a country town. Mr. G. Woolliscroft Rhead in *The Earthenware Collector* gives many details of how these potters worked and he recalls an old legend current in the Potteries that one of these made the teats of his cows and the Duke of Wellington's nose from the same mould.

It might have been expected that the industrial revolution would have killed off what is after all a very individual art.

STAFFORDSHIRE MILK-JUG

But at first just the contrary seems to have happened. Round about the 1830's and '40's there developed a new style of these figures, with plenty of vitality and robustness, though very simply modelled and obviously produced in large quantities. These are the "Staffordshire figures" most commonly seen about to-day. They are sometimes only fully modelled in front and of a rather flattened shape; the painting, in bright enamel on a white ground, is also often confined to the front only. But this economy in no way detracts from their charm. These figures continued to be made until late into the nineteenth century; their subsequent development falls off: indeed one can watch them deteriorate into the vulgarity of so much cheap gift pottery of to-day.

The subjects represented by these little "image toys" cover the whole range of popular interests and tastes. This is well shown by the Willett collection now in the Brighton Museum which has been assembled, not by names and dates, but by topics. Soldiers and sailors make a frequent appearance; "The Neglected Tar" is a reminder of demobilisation troubles after the Napoleonic Wars. Then there are figures in national costumes; kilted Highlanders; a Welsh couple, the lady in steeple hat, reflecting the beginnings of interest in romantic nationalism.

Amongst popular heroes and famous personages, royalty ranks high. Here we can watch the change in popular feelings towards the throne.

During George IV's reign, Queen Caroline and the King's opponents seem to have captured public sympathy; Princess Charlotte, the Heir Apparent who died young, is also frequently portrayed. William IV is chiefly associated with the Reform Bill. But with the accession of the young Queen Victoria, the domestic virtues come into their own. We can feel the popular upsurge of loyalty and affection, as shown in the lovingly modelled figures of Victoria and her Consort, their court robes giving scope for vivid sweeps of blue and red picked out in gold. Portraits of Wellington and Nelson are frequent, as one would expect. The prevailing sentiment is a robust patriotism. Strange to modern minds is the demand for figures of Napoleon, who is sympathetically presented wearing an expression of romantic melancholy. This is not the age of the illustrated press; portraits did not need to be lifelike. Wellington could at a pinch do service for Nelson. Stranger still is the fact vouched for by Mr. G. W. Rhead that, on occasion, even Wellington and Napoleon were interchangeable. Sympathies with the struggle for democracy in Europe are reflected by the inclusion of foreign patriots, for instance Garibaldi whose red shirt makes a fine show. Political passions are also recorded. From Sir Francis Burdett, Radical M.P. for Westminster, to Mr. Gladstone, popular sympathies ran mainly with the reformers. Indeed we can follow in pottery all the big political struggles of the nineteenth century—Reform Bill, Corn Laws, even Ireland.

Rather surprisingly Crime, which figures so largely in Street Literature, also finds a place in the far more durable form of pottery. An idyllic white cottage with roses growing up the walls is inscribed "Potash Farm," home of Rush the murderer. Portraits of famous highwaymen on horseback are more understandable; they have a romantic appeal.

Biblical and religious subjects offer a fertile field. From time to time we come across an anti-clerical twist, for instance, a group of a farmer and his wife offering the parson their tenth child. No survey, however cursory, of these Staffordshire figures could omit the immense field of sport. Here is a whole gallery of bygone champions, from Tom Cribb the boxer to the famous horse Eclipse. Bull-baiting, bear-baiting and the many field sports are all abundantly represented. Conviviality too fills a large place, whilst drunkenness, then as now, was an endless source of amusement. Nor must we forget the stage. Many of the favourites of the tinsel picture make a simultaneous appearance in earthenware, with the same heroic stance and vivid colour schemes.

Then there are idyllic cottages, churches, castles; they reflect the romantic and picturesque fashion then prevalent in architecture, the toy Gothic of St. John's Wood; and again, the castles are of the same shapes as those still painted on canal barges.

Such are some of the many subjects covered by these image toys. Perhaps the most attractive are those which record nothing special; the multitude of animals and birds, many with oddly human and sentimental expressions,

TOY THEATRE SHEETS

Final Tableau from *The Silver Palace*, published by B. Pollock
&
Scene from *Timour the Tartar*, published by J. Redington

NINTEENTH CENTURY CHRISTMAS CARDS
Page from an old scrapbook

cows, sheep, dogs spotted or plain, cats and little human personages. Often these little figures hit off perfectly some characteristic of their subject, although the representation makes small attempt at literal portrayal.

The idea of making vessels in grotesque human or animal shape must be one of the oldest of potters' jokes. In England "Bellarmine" stoneware bottles with a face on them were known long before they got their name from an unpopular Cardinal. One of the offshoots of the Bellarmine joke is the Toby Jug. Others are the stoneware or earthenware flasks and bottles, ancestors of our present ginger-beer bottles, which were produced in all sorts of grotesque forms.

The Mermaid, made at Rockingham, earthenware glazed a rich chocolate brown like the well-known teapots, is evidently intended to lie in a basket, as her scaly tail curves round so much that she cannot be stood upright; she is to be found with several different faces, but invariably extremely *décolletée*. The Toper is an old gentleman astride a barrel, holding a glass in either hand; his top-hat holds the cork.

The stoneware bottles, made, most of them, at Lambeth, Fulham and Denby, are a much lighter brown, ranging sometimes to yellow ochre, and the details come out more incisively. The Lambeth fish is very handsome; he measures some $11\frac{1}{2}$ inches; he holds the cork in his mouth, and he too cannot be stood upright. There is a flask shaped like a policeman's truncheon to commemorate Sir Robert Peel's introduction of the new police force in 1829. Another is made like an old-fashioned horse pistol, such as travellers habitually carried against highwaymen. Another is the size and shape of a big potato, one of the raw materials of whisky, but also said to have been used for smuggling spirits in a basket of vegetables into the hated new workhouses where alcohol was forbidden. Books, barrels, a railway clock, are some of the other shapes.

The Reform Bill controversy produced a great crop of portrait flasks, half-length representations of the King and the Whig leaders, suitably inscribed—"William IV's Reform Cordial," "The True Spirit of Reform." Rather incongruously the young Queen Victoria features as a full-length flask; wearing her crown and evening dress, she carries a scroll inscribed "My Trust is in My People." More flattering likenesses are obtained in the portrait medallions struck on the sides of square bottles.

During the early nineteen-hundreds an attempt was made to revive these portrait flasks, but the new are nothing like as successful as the old; the modelling seems too careful; it lacks the old dash, vigour and unselfconsciousness.

Transfer printing offers an excellent means of pottery decoration, easily multiplied, yet dependent for its effectiveness on the individual quality of the engraving, done by hand, so that mass production need not necessarily mean a decline in aesthetic standards. It is not surprising to find that transfer printing has been successfully adapted to the needs of popular art.

So great, indeed, is the variety, that we can only arbitrarily draw attention to a few examples.

In a seafaring country, where families are often parted, mementoes are much in demand. By transfer printing, pieces can be suitably inscribed and decorated at small cost. Some of the most attractive souvenir pieces are the Newcastle and Sunderland pink lustre motto pottery which flourished from about the 1780's till well on into the nineteenth century. They are roughly decorated with untidy waves and marblings of pink lustre round the rims and framing the white panels on the front and sides, in which the pictures or verses are transfer printed. The print is decorated overglaze with splashes of vivid colour, red, green and yellow, making little attempt to keep within the outline. Perhaps it is this very feeling of freedom, combined with an extraordinarily sure sense of colour, that gives these things their charm.

One of the subjects most commonly illustrated on the largest jugs, bowls or mugs is the iron bridge across the Wear opened in 1796, no mean engineering feat for those days, and a source of local pride. The Sailor's Return and the Sailor's Farewell very often appear with appropriate verses, as do ships and nautical gear; sometimes a punch-bowl would be specially made to commemorate the sailing of some ship. Masonic emblems, arranged rather haphazardly, form with their cryptic verses pleasantly inconsequential designs for the uninitiated. There are also agricultural motives and some very dashing sporting jugs, sometimes with raised designs.

Smaller pieces generally have pink lustre banding. Sometimes the picture itself is not transferred but roughly hand-painted in lustre, rather like a child's drawing. The plate illustrated belongs to the anti-Corn-Law struggle of the 'forties. The wheatsheaf and agricultural implements are framed in roses, thistles and shamrocks, as befits a national campaign.

Besides political there is also religious instruction. Faith, Hope and Charity appear very charmingly on tea services. More forbidding are the text plaques to be hung up on the walls and bearing in bold letters an admonitory text.

Imaginary arms of various trades, sailor's, farmer's, mason's, were used as transfer decoration by all the big pottery centres, Staffordshire, Liverpool, Leeds, Sunderland, Newcastle and the rest, the idea being presumably derived from inn signs. The opening of the railways produced a crop of railway pieces, with pictures of the Rocket and other famous railway events. Indeed, the history of the early British railways can be traced in these simple wares, and the old patterns may still sometimes be found on new products, though they have lost some of the pleasant quality of the old, through over-careless production.

Election campaigns were excellent opportunities for transfer printing to provide a reasonably good, if rather crude, likeness of the candidate, suitably inscribed. Popular heroes and great events, coronations, victories, supplied other themes. As the nineteenth century advanced the process of porcelain

ENGRAVED GLASS FROM "YE OLDE SWAN," NOTTING HILL GATE, LONDON

making was cheapened, and so we find the increasingly popular "Presents from places" made in cheap china, but with the old decorative tradition persisting. Unfortunately, the decline in taste coincided with the introduction of cheap coloured lithographs for transfers from abroad, and it is this method which has made some of the worst modern atrocities possible.

A joke often found in the old Sunderland lustre and other contemporary mugs is a model of a toad or lizard put at the bottom to give the drinker a fright. Another "surprise" mug is so designed that, when tilted, its contents disappear into the handles, which are hollow. Some of the old inscriptions, too, are curiously discouraging. One runs:

"Women make men love, and love makes them sad.
Sadness makes them drink, and drink drives them mad."

As glass is so fragile, examples of popular art in it have rarely survived except for medieval stained glass, which hardly falls within our scope.

Lustred glass and earthenware were used as cheap substitutes for silver. but, as often happens, they soon ceased to be a crude imitation and developed individual qualities. At one time churches in the poorer parishes used altar vessels of silvered earthenware or glass, which proved very attractive for secular use also—vases, candlesticks and other ornaments, gaily painted on the outside with bright bands of colour and groups of flowers. They were used as prizes in the side-shows of fairs on account of their glitter and cheapness. Glass Christmas tree ornaments, birds with spun-glass tails, little coloured balls and other shapes, are too well known to require description; modern ones are usually imported from the Continent.

283

Some of these glass objects played a special part in country superstitions. Glass balls of varying sizes, silvered and daubed with patches of bright colour, used to be made, amongst other places, at Nailsea, for cottagers to hang in the window against the evil eye. As late as the 1840's, cottagers in Devonshire are described as setting up rods and crooks of twisted glass as a cure for fevers.

Like pottery, glass has been much used for love-tokens. Sailors and soldiers often gave a glass rolling-pin, hollow in the middle, with flowers and appropriate inscriptions painted on the outside, or sometimes a ship, flags, or well-known landmark.

Glass can be worked into all sorts of fantastic shapes, giving great scope to individual skill. Many of the amusing and intricate little ornaments we associate with, say, Nailsea—miniature coach horns which blow a note, bells, bellows, even pipes—were *tours de force* made by individual glass workers.

The Nailsea Glass Workers' Guild even made their own pole-head emblems of blown *latticinio* glass. The elaborate glass fountain, with coloured birds perching amongst a fantastic pyramid of twisting arches, to be seen in the Victoria and Albert Museum, is a remarkable example both of skill and of a sense of beautifully balanced form and colour. Foreign workmen, Venetians and French, introduced many of the decorative techniques to England, but these foreign strains have become pleasantly assimilated to native talents.

During the nineteenth century there developed another form of popular art in glass, the engraved glass screen or window, which now mainly survives in public-houses. Engraved (or "brilliant") glass sparkles but also obscures the view; it thus suited the strong urge for privacy, particularly associated with drinking, which prevailed in nineteenth-century England, whilst helping to create a festive atmosphere, one of the attractions of old-fashioned public-houses to survive long after the bad old days of glittering gin palaces and "drunk for a penny, dead drunk for twopence," though it is now gradually giving way before the new social trends represented in the modern "road-house."

Many of these engraved glass screens have elaborate and very decorative designs of scrolls, festoons, fruit and flowers. Sometimes the sign of the public-house is introduced, a swan, perhaps, or a ship. Often the lower half of the glass panel is frosted and the upper left clear, which throws up the design against contrasting textures. For wall decorations, engraved mirrors are used with the same style of patterns; in pairs these mirrors reflect each other with an enchanting effect of spaciousness and brilliancy. Engraved mirrors were once much used for theatres, shops and other display centres. They may still sometimes be seen in old-fashioned grocers' shops, engraved with pictures of the various spice plants, nutmeg or cocoa; alongside the painted tea tins and jars, they suggest an Oriental abundance.

The decorative motives used in this engraved glass derive from the early

GLASS ROLLING-PIN—A SAILOR'S LOVE TOKEN
By courtesy of the Director of the Victoria & Albert Museum

SILVERED GLASS VASES AS USED FOR FAIRGROUND PRIZES

STAFFORDSHIRE FIGURES AND HEN EGG-DISH FROM A DEVON DAIRY WINDOW
By courtesy of the Topsham Dairy

SUNDERLAND LUSTRE MOTTO PLATE—THE ANTI-CORN-LAW CAMPAIGN, C. 1840

SUNDERLAND LUSTRE TEXT PLAQUE
From water colour sketches by Enid Marx

Victorian hotchpotch of styles which reached its zenith at the Great Exhibition of 1851. A tangle of conventionalised twists and twirls, rococo and pseudo-Gothic, combine with extremely naturalistic fruits and flowers. As the century progresses, the curves begin to lose their spring, the patterns grow more stereotyped, the Gothic motives more obtrusive; they lose their playful picturesque qualities, become pinched and stiff, and take on a machine-made look; not that they are machine-made, but because gaiety and spontaneity are lost as the Gothic Revival ousts the Romantic Movement.

BONE STAYBUSK AND CARVED WOODEN ROLLER
Pencil drawings by Enid Marx

PAINTING, CARVING AND METALWORK

CARVING is comparatively durable. We can trace a long tradition of popular art in it, ranging from the early Christian era of the great stone Northumbrian crosses, or even from pre-Christian times if we include the White Horses or Cerne Abbas giant cut out in the chalk of the Downs, on through the wealth of medieval and renaissance carvings to the ships' figureheads and roundabout horses of the nineteenth century. With such an abundance, we can only pick a few examples.

The figurehead is one of the most characteristic forms of wood carving in England, and has lasted from Tudor times, when sailing-ships developed a beak, right down to the beginning of this century, when iron replaced wood for shipbuilding. In its heyday, the carving ran right round the ship to finish in a blaze of magnificence at the stern. The changes in style and type of the "carved works" on English ships, together with the long struggle between the sailors who insisted on them and the economising tendencies of the Admiralty, may be studied in Mr. L. G. Carr Loughton's *Old Ships' Figureheads and Sterns*.

We can no longer see figureheads placed as their carvers meant, but they may often be found, set up in seaports or as inn signs, as well as in special collections like that of the Royal Maritime Museum, Greenwich.

Figurehead of H.M.S. *Centurion*

In the West Country, figureheads of lost ships might be set up as a memorial to the crew, as in Morwenstow churchyard or Bude, whilst a great many are to be found in the Scilly Isles, a grim reminder of past wrecks.

Few of these surviving figureheads are earlier than the nineteenth century, by when single figures of simple design were common, especially on naval vessels; they grew in size, till by the 1850's a three-quarter length figure might be fifteen feet high. With the arrival of the clipper, the position of the figure inclined more to the horizontal, which, together with the graceful lines of these fast sailing-ships, again affected their design. The vogue for realism led to portraits of royal personages or popular heroes. An attractive example is the fifteen-foot figurehead of the *Royal Albert*, dating from 1854, and now at Chatham. The Prince Consort, complete with sidewhiskers, looks surprisingly like his little Staffordshire figure portraits. The many Oriental figures recall British interests in the East Indies. Portrait figureheads on merchantmen named after their owners sometimes give strange results; the *James Bains* is carved buttoned up in a frock coat; the *Samuel Plimsoll* actually had a top-hat. We can get some idea of the great variety, both in size and subject, if we recall that these nineteenth-century figureheads were carried by vessels of all sorts and conditions, from the man-o'-war and elegant clipper to the humble paddle-steamer.

What the figurehead was to the ship, the sign once was to the shop or inn. At a time when few could read, all shops displayed their signs, pictures or effigies or both. Shop signs are now comparatively rare, but most inns maintain them though sometimes in sadly degenerate form.

Signs may be painted on wood, carved in wood or stone, moulded in plaster or fashioned in metal. Mostly they were produced by local craftsmen, though during the late eighteenth and early nineteenth centuries, signmaking was a recognised industry. The subjects of signs, with some famous exceptions in the case of inns (usually derived from local corruptions of an older name) keep to a pretty definite range, though local design and execution often show much variety. There are historic, heraldic, religious and classical motives, emblems of various trades and professions, and, amongst inns especially, sporting motives, jokes and puns, commemorative and geographical subjects.

Few inn or other signs, in whatever material, survive from earlier than the late seventeenth century, though the stone carved and gilt angel's head bracket above the doorway of the Angel and Royal inn at Grantham is much older. Effigy signs, carved in the round, are usually placed over porticos, but sometimes, like the magnificent White Hart sign at Salisbury, on the gable of the roof. They are often

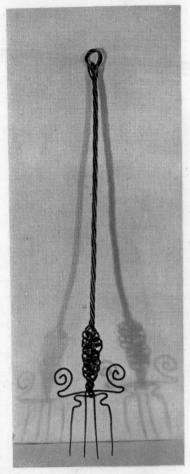

TWISTED WIRE FORK

beautifully carved with an economy and vigour admirably suited to their purpose. Plaques, carved or moulded in relief, are often set over doorways, for instance the painted plaster Knights of St. John illustrated here, which dates from the 1820's. Signboards are sometimes hung from a bracket, set up on a post or, in the old "gallows" form of a sign, of which a few examples still survive, slung from an archway across the road. These archways were often surmounted by figures such as the Four Swans at Waltham Cross.

The wrought-iron brackets or frames are often admirable examples of the work of local smiths. Sometimes they repeat in metal the device painted on the board, as in the famous Three Swans bracket at Market Harborough

PEARLIE KING

which dates from about 1700. Abstract scroll-work decoration is more common, sometimes ending in a bunch of grapes. Signboards on posts sometimes have decorative ironwork hoods, like The Bear at Woodstock; sometimes scroll-work frames. Indeed it is surprising how much variety can be put into the simple purpose of hanging up a board.

Much of this ironwork dates from the eighteenth century, but the signboards themselves have usually been frequently repainted owing to the effect of the weather, though the old device has sometimes been preserved. There are a few instances of signs painted by famous artists, Morland, Hogarth, Wilson and so on, but by far the great majority were local work. Examples of work in the same tradition but better preserved may often be seen as decoration in country churches; boards displaying the royal coat of arms, or with symbols of mortality, like the one here illustrated.

Another form of sign which displays the work of local craftsmen is the weathercock or weather-vane. Weathercocks are peculiarly English and were in use before the Norman conquest, as the Bayeux tapestry shows. The weather-vane, properly so-called, derives from the general medieval custom of using pennants or "fanes"; it often has an armorial or other device pierced in it. Interest in wind and weather is understandable in a seafaring country, as witness the wealth and variety of weather-vanes in London, especially on the City churches, before the air-raids. The cock illustrated has his wings, comb and wattles fitted on separately, to show up better from the ground, and tail set at an angle to catch the wind. Cocks are the most frequent, though from time to time we find other symbols, generally of local significance, like the gilded wooden fish on Charmouth church. The little Devonshire village of Spreyton formerly had, over the forge, the figure of a blacksmith hammering on an anvil; it had been most ingeniously made by the smith himself to work in the wind.

To the ingenuity of the country smiths and wheelwrights we also owe one of the latest and most flamboyant manifestations of popular carving and painting (the more remarkable because it arose as part of the industrial revolution), the elaborately carved and decorated roundabouts and swings of the fair-ground. The idea of grotesque figures at popular entertainments is immemorially old. The London Guildhall giants, Gog and Magog (alas,

290

FAIR-GROUND HORSE FROM A ROUNDABOUT AT KEW BRIDGE, LONDON

burnt in the blitz) were originally Lord Mayor's Show effigies, replacing those lost in an earlier conflagration. The hobby-horses of folk-dancing and mumming, once widespread, now survive only in a few country districts. Hobby-horses as children's toys evolved into the often beautifully carved rocking-horses of the eighteenth and nineteenth centuries, as also into the primitive merry-go-rounds with wooden horses on a revolving platform propelled by hand, which were the only entertainment of their kind some seventy years ago. The steam engine revolutionised the fair-ground rides as it did so much else. Most of the credit for applying steam to fair-ground entertainment goes to Frederick Savage, a country blacksmith and wheel-wright of King's Lynn, in Norfolk, where his statue stands to-day, though it must be confessed more for his achievements in developing agricultural machinery.

The extraordinarily elaborate decoration of roundabouts is the more remarkable if we remember that they have to be constantly transported;

METAL WEATHERCOCK ON LYME REGIS PARISH CHURCH
WOODEN WEATHERVANE IN THE FORM OF A FISH ON CHARMOUTH PARISH CHURCH
Pencil and wash drawings by Enid Marx

everything must take to pieces quickly and easily. A steam engine in the middle drives a revolving centre, from which project steel shafts like the spokes of a wheel, to carry horses and platform. Every possible bit of space is flamboyantly decorated. The revolving centre is enclosed by sets of carved and painted panels; at the top these are crowned with elegant scroll-work carving and edged with scalloped or lozenge "droppers," each carved and painted, often with an engraved "brilliant" mirror inset. The curved, or "rounding," boards forming the rim of the wheel are similarly orna-mented, and bear the owner's name in lettering elaborately twirled, shaded and picked out in colours. Where joins occur, as they frequently must, bits of carving hide them.

Such is the background for the horses. Hung four or five abreast from shiny twisted brass rods (nowadays mostly chromium) the outermost "galloper" is usually elaborately carved and painted; the decoration grows progressively less and the innermost one may be painted only. Naturalism is at a discount. Not only harness and trappings, but the whole body of the horse may be patterned with handsome scallops and scrolls, acanthus leaf motives, or roses, thistles and shamrocks perhaps, with portrait medallions or grotesque masks on the flanks. Varnished paint, with details picked out in contrasting colours, heightens the effect. Individual gallopers vary very much; all adopt the traditional flying stance, but they have different decora-tions, as also different expressions. Each horse has his name inscribed on a ribbon round his neck. The rise of ostrich farming in South Africa, which supplied the costermonger's "Donah" with her traditional feathered hat, also suggested rideable birds to the showman. Ostriches took their

MEMENTO MORI. PAINTING ON WOOD IN LYME REGIS PARISH CHURCH
Pencil and wash drawing by Enid Marx

places alongside the horses, and in due course other birds also, turkeys, cockerels, peacocks, and sometimes hybrid creations, with the tail of one and the head of another. The birds mostly have a fierce grotesqueness reminiscent of Tibetan devil-masks, whilst scaly dragons look rather Chinese. The Switchback, cars revolving on an undulating platform, came rather later than the gallopers. The cars—gondolas, dragons and so on—gave less scope for variety in decoration, but the stationary platform is mounted by a magnificent flight of steps with ornamental balustrades, which might have come straight out of a Juvenile Drama palace.

As to the origins of all this decorative exuberance, the bones, as it were, obviously derive from the romanticised rococo of early nineteenth-century theatre decoration, as we may still see it in the Toy Theatre sets. Superimposed on this we find the same inconsequential hotchpotch of styles and underlying sense of the magnificent that characterises the Great Exhibition of 1851. But what is so surprising is the way the old decorative tradition has persisted, assimilating, without undue incongruity, later ideas and motives, widely separated from each other in both space and time. You may find, for instance, a plaque of the head of some Boer War hero, in wide-brimmed hat, alongside a classical mask or an eighteenth-century stylised Britannia. The paintings on the panels, depicting, as they frequently do, the high spot of some terrific adventure, a tiger hunt perhaps, are lineal descendants of the old Raree or Peepshow. They continue the old, simple-minded homely style, whereby tigers take on the appearance of outsize domestic cats. Here and there more peaceful moods prevail; moonlit rocks and waterfalls echo the romantic landscape of the Toy Theatre and the castles painted on barges.

In spite of exotic forms, this decoration remains characteristically English, as may often be seen by comparing it with the style of the richly ornate front of the steam organ, with its dancing automatons, which is usually of foreign workmanship. This form of popular art reached its heyday about the 1900's. From about the 1920's a decline set in; taste changed towards a more mechanical and streamlined style; motor-cars and aeroplanes replaced the horses; portraits of film stars were not, as had been the case with earlier celebrities, assimilated to the rococo spirit of the whole; stereotyped cinema standards began to drive out the much more individual and rich traditions of the music hall. At present the change is proceeding very rapidly, and the old-style decoration is not likely to survive many more years.

By contrast, the painting on English canal barges, which has much in common with fair-ground decoration, still persists in its traditional forms. Attempts to explain these forms in terms of the mystic symbolism attached to boat decoration in other parts of the world are not very convincing; good luck is traditionally associated with the symbols of playing-cards found in barge decoration, but any deeper significance seems doubtful.

The most striking motives are castles and flowers. The castles are set in a little scene on a river. No two pictures must be identical, consequently architectural details vary quite a bit. Nevertheless they all have a recognis-able affinity to a common ancestor both in style and colour—the roman-ticised, picturesque castle that we also find in the Toy Theatre sheets. Nor is this surprising if we remember that English canals were being built apace from the 1760's to about the 1830's, which coincides with the early romantic phase of the Gothic Revival when picturesque castles were all the rage. The canal folk, in the early days, were many of them of gipsy origin, which in

BARGE DECORATION

Painted by Mr. Frank Jones of Leighton Buzzard, 1945

INN SIGN—KNIGHTS OF ST. JOHN TAVERN, C. 1820
Detail from a water colour sketch by Enid Marx
By courtesy of the Pilgrim Trust

MINIATURE CAST-IRON FIREPLACE WITH GRATE, FENDER
AND FIRE-IRONS OF POLISHED BRASS

turn may account for the resemblance between the bright colours and highly polished brass fittings of canal barges and those of caravans and fair-ground decoration.

Much of the attraction of barge decoration is due to the style of painting, which is extremely free, in the true peasant tradition. Deep bottle green or vermilion is a favourite ground for sprays of roses in contrasting colours of red, pink and yellow, with darker shading. The painter puts in the body of the rose with a few deft brush sweeps, adding the shading whilst the paint is still wet, to get a melting quality. Multi-petalled daisies, yellow, pink, red or blue, with contrasting centres, are set off, as are the roses, by light green foliage, elaborately veined and shaded. The lettering of the owner's name and place of origin is full of curls and twirls and elaborately shadowed, like the lettering on old-fashioned farm carts and fair-ground entertainments, with little garlands of flowers filling in the spaces and corners.

Besides castles and flowers, a bright geometrical pattern of circles and diamonds, known as "Scotch plaid," is also used. Each pattern seems to have its traditional place—the tiller bar, for instance, is banded in contrasting colours like a barber's pole, only wider. Inside the cabin, elaborate paint-work bird's-eye graining fills in the background. The equipment is also ornamented; blocks and stands for gang planks, stools, even the large galvanised fresh-water-can and washing-bowl. The water-can often has the owner's name inscribed on a scroll. Everything possible is decorated— one boat painted by Mr. Frank Jones of Linslade, Leighton Buzzard, has as many as two hundred flowers.

Painted decoration of farm carts, which has much in common with barge painting, is, unfortunately, rapidly disappearing. The painting is done on the front and tailboard, and it used to consist of panels, back and front, bearing the owner's and maker's names in shaded lettering, with decorations of scrolls and curls. Costermonger's carts are also often very prettily picked out in colour, a practice which seems to continue.

SAILOR'S PIN-CUSHION

TEXTILES

QUILTING is an old traditional cottage industry in England and was at one time common all over the country, though nowadays it survives directly only in certain regions, Wales and the North, though, through the efforts of the Rural Industries Bureau, it is being resuscitated in areas where it had previously virtually died out. Although the quilter usually designs her own pattern, she is naturally influenced by local tradition, so that experts are often able to identify the place of origin of a quilt by certain regional differences. Thus Mrs. Elizabeth Hake *(English Quilting, Old and New)* who has specially concerned herself with West Country quilting,

298

PRINTED COTTON COMMEMORATIVE HANDKERCHIEF

which was very nearly extinct, suggests that geometrical patterns are particularly associated with Wales, rather formalistic floral ones with the North, and freer flowing floral decoration with the West Country, though of course there can be no hard and fast rule. The different types of centres might also perhaps be attributed to regional traditions, but the revival of interest in English quilting is so recent that the question of comparative designs has been little explored. Nowadays only wadded or padded quilts are still made, though some of the earlier ones, with raised corded designs, are very decorative. Close stitching is sometimes used to throw up certain parts of a design.

In looking at English quilts, what is perhaps most remarkable, besides the utilisation of space to best advantage, is the number of different ways in which a few basic motives—cable, shell, feather, intersecting circles or diamonds and so on—can be used. Floral motives seem to have been studied and adapted from life.

Closely allied to quilting, and often combined with it, is patchwork. Although she is using bits of old material, the patchwork-maker has great scope for her individual decorative sense, not only in the arrangement of colours and textures, but also in the varying shapes into which she cuts her patches.

Smocking was once worn by countrymen all over England, but has now died out. The principle, of making a raised pattern on textiles, is the same as quilting, though the designs and methods are different. They varied, not according to the localities, but according to the trade of the wearer, conventional symbols of which were embroidered on the front, the idea being, apparently, that at country hirings the farmer could recognise the qualifications he required—ploughman, shepherd, dairymaid and so on—though no doubt professional pride also played its part, as with other uniforms. Smocking, like quilting, shows a remarkable decorative sense. Another form of textile decoration is knitting, of which the most interesting living survival in England is perhaps the fisherman's jersey or guernsey as knitted on the Yorkshire coast. Here the design varies according to the village from which the wearer comes, allegedly so that in case of disaster bodies washed ashore could be readily identified, but again local pride is undoubtedly part of the explanation.

Quilting, smocking, knitting, are all crafts which survive, if at all, only tenuously from a glorious past. But there is one form of popular textile decoration which seems to have arisen spontaneously during the last forty-five years. This is the costermonger's pearlie suit, which is decorated with fantastic patterns in pearl buttons. The traditional coster costume of the 'eighties and 'nineties was a square-cut jacket, with velvet collar and pocket flaps, a waistcoat, and bell-bottomed trousers, with a brightly coloured scarf and a bowler hat. The buttons on the coat and waistcoat were the usual number but made of pearl, or sometimes glass: the celebrated "Road to Ruin" buttons were glass with, inset, the traditional symbols of wine, women and song—horse, dog, wineglass, woman's head, etc. The women wore bright velveteen dresses, coloured scarves, pearl button boots and the huge ostrich-feather hat. This special costume has now disappeared. In order to have some sort of a fancy-dress for collecting for their various hospital societies, costers took to decorating ordinary suits with patterns made of pearl buttons, inventing the designs themselves. At one time they even adopted a version of Wild West cowboy suits. Many of the "pearlie" patterns show a pleasantly fantastic sense of decoration and are extremely effective. The custom is one more example of the urge to create popular art whenever opportunities allow.

Soldiers and sailors had their own forms of textile decoration, rugs, and above all, large and elaborately tasselled pin-cushions, usually heart-shaped and decorated with buttons, beads and pin heads. They were made as a pastime and for presents. Indeed, pin-cushions provide some of the most

PATCHWORK QUILT IN SILK, SATIN AND VELVET
Mid-nineteenth Century

interesting examples of popular taste, commemorative, political, or simply
as a pretext for decorative exuberance.

Tattooing, though not exactly textile decoration, is so akin to it in motives
and design that we cannot forbear to mention it here. As a practice it is
very old and is found in many parts of the world. It seems to have been
rediscovered by sailors and soldiers in the East, which would account for

the prevalence of exotic Oriental motives, especially dragons, amongst the hearts, linked initials, flowers, butterflies, anchors and other homely symbols of luck, fidelity and affection which we find repeated over and over again in other forms of popular art.

Printing has also been applied to cheap textile decoration. The printed cotton handkerchiefs and scarves of the nineteenth century really belong more to street literature than to textiles, with their commemorative, sporting and political pictures. Even the ornaments for borders are often more reminiscent of typography than of textile traditions, although they sometimes combine both together.

CHILDREN'S PENNY TOYS
Nineteenth Century

MISCELLANEOUS HANDIWORK AND DECORATION

THE desire to give presents, especially love-tokens, has stimulated much popular art, often in the simplest materials. A bit of bone, for instance, might be shaped into a staybusk, in the days when women of all classes wore these formidable articles of dress, and be decorated with hearts, arrows, linked initials or other devices, scratched in outline and coloured. Apple-corers or cheese-tasters, with the same sort of patterning, use the knuckle for the handle. Whip or walking-stick handles in wood or bone, and many other small objects show much ingenuity and decorative sense in exploiting natural forms; indeed, a living branch might be carefully trained for years to grow the right shape for a special bit of carving. A *tour de*

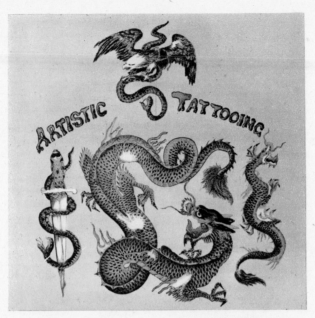

PROFESSOR BURCHETT'S DESIGNS FOR TATTOOING

force was to cut a spoon and fork linked together by a wooden chain all from the same piece. Carved knitting sticks, butterpats for stamping butter, gingerbread rollers, tobacco pipes, are a few examples of simple materials skilfully used. Sailors have always been great adepts at this, and one of their favourite and most ingenious achievements is the fitting of a model ship into a bottle, by jointing it so that it will pull upright on threads fixed in the cork.

Apprentices, too, had special forms of handiwork. The shoemakers' apprentices are responsible for many of the little wooden shoe-shaped snuff-boxes, often exquisitely carved and decorated with minute brass studs in the soles; they are also made in beaten pewter. So careful is the workman-ship that we can trace a whole century or more of changing fashions in shoes from them. Apprentices would also make little replicas in the actual materials of their trade, for practice and samples; many miniature pieces of furniture are their work. The little cast-iron fireplace here illustrated, complete with brass fender and fire irons, is one such, and also shows the decorative possibilities of cast iron, in which there is a long tradition. Earlier examples of it are the elaborately ornamented firebacks made in Sussex. The big iron-foundries carried on the tradition, so that we even find them casting chimney-piece ornaments in iron, as well as semi-utilita-rian objects, grotesque door-stops, scrapers, and so on. Such things were

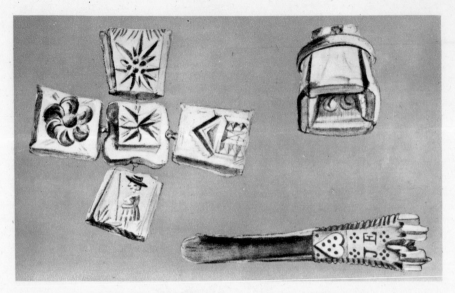

CARVED WOODEN BUTTER-PATS AND BONE APPLE-CORER

partially mass-produced, by contrast to the forged iron latches, hinges, fire-irons and innumerable other everyday objects where local smiths delighted to exercise their individual skill and pleasure in ornament.

The brasses or "medals" once worn by cart-horses on high days and holidays are another example of metal decoration. Originally pierced by hand from sheet metal, these brasses were at their best when cast in solid brass and polished, as they were till towards the end of the nineteenth century. The later phase of stamping them in brass detracts greatly from their appearance, although the traditional devices are preserved. Some of these devices, such as the crescent moon, the sun in various forms, and stars, are believed to be very old; others have been added from time to time; indeed, we often find topical allusions, such as a railway engine or even the portrait of a popular hero. Some of the same motives, crescents, stars, a hand, appear in the brass polehead emblems formerly carried in processions by local guilds and associations, which gave great scope for fantastic invention. The metal trade-tokens, once issued in lieu of small change by shops and inns, often preserve the old sign devices. A strange essay in the grotesque are the so-called "Billy and Charlie" fakes of the 1850's, when two illiterate workmen started making spurious medieval antiquities, medals and the like, and passing them off as discoveries during building excavations in London, thereby puzzling antiquarians not a little. The resultant hotch-potch of quasi-medieval motives, though without rhyme or reason, has surprising charm and vivacity.

Straw, too, has great decorative possibilities, as used, for instance, by the country thatcher. Plaited straw "dollies" still form part of harvest celebrations in some parts of England. The cross of plaited wheat-ears illustrated was made by a country labourer for harvest festival church decoration. More ephemeral are the flower posies still sold in country markets—Barnstaple for one. In the selection and arrangement of colours, they carry on the old traditional taste of the "florist's flowers" of a century ago, once carefully cultivated in cottage gardens for their bright contrasting stripes, speckles and lacings, as Mr. Jason Hill describes in *The Curious Gardener*. The artificial wreaths of white china flowers, still sometimes seen in country churchyards, preserve something of the same quality.

Toy-making, not the expensive kind, but penny toys for street hawkers to sell, had become a full-time family occupation by the mid-nineteenth century, and often produced delightful examples of popular art; this in spite of the miserable poverty of toy-makers, as the competition of imported foreign toys drove down wholesale prices. Jointed "Dutch" dolls, horses and carts, birdcages, soldiers, money boxes and much else besides were made in wood, in the traditional forms; children especially delighted in things they could see in the streets—garden rollers, for instance, were said to be less popular, since so few poor children had ever seen a real garden. Toys in tin and pewter, doll's house equipment and sets of toy soldiers were slightly more expensive. Early nineteenth-century toy soldiers, two-dimensional and gaily painted, often give scenes of camp life, like those here illustrated. The workmanship of the toys and other cheap objects sold by hawkers is often of a high level, as witness the penny toasting-fork here illustrated.

The attraction of souvenirs from places has also stimulated popular art, at first amateur, later professional. The use of sea shells for decorating boxes and frames, or of coloured sand for making patterns in glass weights, are but two examples which could be multiplied indefinitely.

MINIATURE TIN SOLDIERS, C. 1815

PLAITED STRAW DOLLIE
FOR HARVEST THANKSGIVING

LIST OF ILLUSTRATIONS

PLATES IN COLOUR

BRITISH CRAFTSMEN

PAGE

AN ENGLISH STAINED GLASS WINDOW, *c.* 1400. Detail from the Jesse window in the Choir of York Minster   17

SLIPWARE DISH MADE BY SAMUEL MALKIN, BURSLEM, STAFFORDSHIRE, *c.* 1726   18

DESIGN FOR A COACH. Late eighteenth century   27

DESIGN FOR A BOOKCASE. Coloured engraving from T. Sheraton's *The Cabinet-Maker, Upholsterer and General Artist's Encyclopaedia*, 1804   28

PAGE

BED HANGING. Designed and embroidered by Miss Morris, daughter of William Morris   33

FORGING BILLHOOKS, SHEFFIELD. Water colour by Thomas Hennell   34

THE CHARCOAL BURNER. Water colour by Vincent Lines   43

A BLACKSMITH'S FORGE. Water colour by C. Conway   44

BRITISH FURNITURE MAKERS

CHAIR OF RAISED VELVET IN THE CARTOON GALLERY AT KNOLE. Seventeenth century. Drawing by H. Shaw from Meyrick's *Specimens of Ancient Furniture*, 1836   61

COMMODE BY ROBERT ADAM. Coloured engraving by B. Pastorini, 1770. From *The Works in Architecture of Robert and James Adam, Esqs.*   62

DESIGN FOR A SOFA. Drawing by Robert Adam, signed and dated, 1777   71

DRESSING TABLE IN SATINWOOD. Coloured engraving from Sheraton's *The Cabinet Maker and Upholsterer's Encyclopaedia*, 1804.   72

DRAWING-ROOM CHAIRS. Coloured engraving from George Smith's *A Collection of Designs for Household Furniture, and Interior Decoration*, 1808   89

MUSIC GALLERY IN THE ROYAL PAVILION AT BRIGHTON. Coloured engraving by John Nash, 1824   90

DESIGN FOR A CUPBOARD, & DESK DESIGNED FOR CARLTON HOUSE. Coloured drawings from a book of sketches made for Gillow's, 1787   99

DRESSING TABLE AND FOLDING TABLE. Coloured drawings from a book of sketches made for Gillow's, 1787   100

ENGLISH GLASS

NAILSEA JUG. Late eighteenth or early nineteenth century   109

BRISTOL WHITE-GLASS ENAMEL-PAINTED VASE. Mid-eighteenth century   110

WINEGLASS PAINTED BY WILLIAM BEILBY. Mid-eighteenth century   119

COUNTRY-MARKET JUGS. Late eighteenth or early nineteenth century   120

NAILSEA JUG AND FLASKS. Late eighteenth and first half of the nineteenth century   137

EARLY-VICTORIAN GLASS FOUNTAIN WITH BIRDS   138

GLASS VASE AND BOWL DESIGNED BY KEITH MURRAY. Stevens & Williams, Limited, Brierley Hill, Stourbridge   147

LARGE GLASS VASE. James Powell & Sons, Limited, Whitefriars Glassworks, Wealdstone   148

PAGE

SLIPWARE DISH BY THOMAS TOFT,
c. 1675   169

STAFFORDSHIRE TEAPOT DECORATED
WITH APPLIED RELIEFS, c. 1755. From
the Glaisher collection   170

PATTERNS FOR TABLEWARE. Designs
from the first pattern book of Josiah
Wedgwood begun shortly after 1759 179

WORCESTER TEAPOT AND BOWL,
c. 1765-1770   180

PAGE

LOWESTOFT MUG WITH SCALE BORDER,
DECORATED WITH FLOWERS. From the
collection of Mr. G. F. Hotblack   185

BOW, POSSIBLY WORCESTER, FIGURE OF
A LADY, c. 1765. From the collection
of Mr. G. F. Hotblack   186

TWO WEDGWOOD MUGS DESIGNED
BY ERIC RAVILIOUS   195

FLOWER POT BY NORAH BRADEN, 1942.
Oil painting by Beryl Sinclair   196

BRITISH CLOCKS AND CLOCKMAKERS

THIRTY-HOUR STRIKING AND ALARUM
BRASS LANTERN CLOCK. Jeffrey Bayley.
Signed and dated 1653   209

THIRTY-HOUR STRIKING HANGING
CLOCK IN INLAID MARQUETERIE CASE.
Christopher Gould, c. 1690   210

EARLY LONG-CASE CLOCKS. Thomas
Tompion, c. 1675. Thomas Harris,
c. 1690. Henry Crump, c. 1670   219

EARLY LONG-CASE CLOCKS. Early
Daniel Quare, c. 1671. Joseph Windmills, c. 1685. John Ebsworth, c. 1690 220

LONG-CASE CLOCKS OF THE EIGHT-
EENTH CENTURY. John Ross of Tain,
c. 1780. Joseph Windmills, c. 1710.
Daniel Quare, c. 1720   237

ALARUM AND STRIKING MANTEL
CLOCK IN EBONY-VENEERED CASE.
Henry Jones, c. 1685   238

CHIMING MANTEL CLOCK WITH
MOON-WORK, IN RED AND GOLD
LACQUER CASE. Thomas Turner,
c. 1760   247

ENGLISH WATCHES. Strigner, c. 1687.
David Bouquet, fl. 1628-1665. Thomas
Tompion and Edward Banger, 1701   248

ENGLISH POPULAR AND TRADITIONAL ART

PEDLAR DOLL SHOWING MISCELL-
ANEOUS WARES. Early nineteenth
century   269

TINSELLED ENGRAVINGS USED AS
PICTURES IN COTTAGES. Early nine-
teenth century, and FRONTISPIECE FROM
PARK'S NEW EGYPTIAN DREAM
BOOK. Hand-coloured engraving of
the early nineteenth century   270

TOY THEATRE SHEETS. (a) Final Tableau from The Silver Palace, published
by B. Pollock ; (b) Scene from Timour
the Tartar, published by J. Redington 279

NINETEENTH-CENTURY CHRISTMAS
CARDS. Page from an old scrapbook   280

GLASS ROLLING-PIN : A SAILOR'S
LOVE TOKEN ; SILVERED GLASS VASES
AS USED FOR FAIR-GROUND PRIZES ;
STAFFORDSHIRE FIGURES AND HEN
EGG-DISH FROM A DEVON DAIRY
WINDOW   285

SUNDERLAND LUSTRE MOTTO PLATE :
THE ANTI-CORN-LAW CAMPAIGN,
c. 1840 & SUNDERLAND LUSTRE TEXT
PLAQUE. From water colour sketches
by Enid Marx   286

BARGE DECORATION. Painted by Mr.
Frank Jones of Leighton Buzzard, 1945 295

INN SIGN : KNIGHTS OF ST. JOHN
TAVERN, c. 1820. Detail from a water
colour sketch by Enid Marx   296

BRITISH CRAFTSMEN

PAGE

THATCHER'S 'DOLLY.' Drawing by Thomas Hennell — 8

SPECIMEN OF PENMANSHIP. Nineteenth century — 9

MEDIAEVAL BUILDING. Illumination from the Guthlac Roll, late twelfth century — 11

BRICKFIELD AT BUSHEY, HERTFORDSHIRE. Wash drawing by A. Monro, 1801-1880 — 12

PURBECK QUARRYMEN. Line engraving by Stanley Anderson — 13

MASONRY. Etching from W. H. Pyne's *Microcosm*, 1806 — 15

SECTION OF A LIME KILN. Engraving by Boyce for the *Compleat Body of Husbandrye* — 16

ROOF OF WESTMINSTER HALL. Detail from an aquatint by Pugin and Rowlandson, 1809 — 21

INTERIOR OF PIGEON HOUSE ROOF. Marshfield, Gloucestershire. Pencil drawing by Thomas Hennell, 1929 — 22

FARM CART UNDER CONSTRUCTION. Pencil drawing by Thomas Hennell, 1930 — 23

THE WHEELWRIGHT. Line engraving by Stanley Anderson — 25

CEILING DECORATION AT 20 PORTMAN SQUARE, LONDON. Designed by Robert Adam, 1775, probably painted by Angelica Kauffmann — 29

TUDOR PAINTING TO IMITATE CARVING. Eastbury House, Barking, Essex. Drawing from T. H. Clarke & W. H. Black's *Eastbury Illustrated*, 1834 — 30

PAGE

PARGETING ON AN ESSEX HOUSE. Drawing by Mary Cregan — 31

DESIGN FOR CHAIRS. Engraving from Chippendale's *Gentleman and Cabinetmaker's Director*, 1762 — 32

WOODEN DOOR WITH WROUGHT IRON HINGES. Fourteenth century. Probably from Dunnington Church, Yorkshire — 37

FACE OF A ONE-HAND CLOCK BY BENJAMIN HIGHWORTH, 1740 — 38

WROUGHT IRON GATE. Early eighteenth century — 39

ART OF MAKING CLOCKS AND WATCHES. Engraving from the *Universal Magazine*, Vol. II, 1740 — 40

SILVERSMITH'S WORKSHOP. Seventeenth-century Advertisement from the Bayford Collection — 41

TILE. Designed by William Morris and painted by Mrs. Morris — 46

TAPESTRY. Designed and woven by William Morris — 49

BLOCKS CUT FOR TEXTILE PRINTING. Designed by P. Barron and D. Larcher, using felt on wood, lino on wood, wood and rubber blocks — 51

DESIGN FOR A COVERED VASE. Water colour drawing by Alfred Stevens — 53

BOWL DECORATED BY ERIC RAVILIOUS AND PLATE BY MICHAEL CARDEW. Oil painting by Beryl Sinclair — 55

BLUE GLAZED COVERED BOWL. Designed and made in the Omega Workshops — 56

Illustrations on pp. 11, 41 are reproduced by courtesy of the Trustees of the British Museum; on pp. 12, 53, by courtesy of the Syndics of the Fitzwilliam Museum, Cambridge; on pp. 13, 25, by courtesy of Stanley Anderson, Esq.; on p. 21, by courtesy of the Parker Gallery, London; on pp. 22, 23, by courtesy of the late Thomas Hennell, Esq.; on pp. 29, 56, by courtesy of the Courtauld Institute of Art; on p. 31, by courtesy of Miss Mary Cregan; on pp. 37, 39, by courtesy of the Director of the Victoria & Albert Museum; on p. 38, by courtesy of the Swindon Museum; on pp. 46, 49, by courtesy of Edward Scott-Snell, Esq.; on p. 55, by courtesy of Mrs. Beryl Sinclair

PAGE

DESIGN FOR A CHAIR. Thomas Hope, 1807 — 59

OAK CHEST. Thirteenth century. Said to have come from a Church in Hampshire — 65

CARVED OAK BEDSTEAD. Middle of the seventeenth century. From Queensbury, Yorkshire — 67

OAK GATE-LEGGED TABLE. Seventeenth century — 69

NONESUCH CHEST. Late sixteenth century. Oak, inlaid with Marquetry — 70

DAY BED IN WALNUT. Late seventeenth century — 74

WRITING CABINET, INLAID WALNUT. Made by Samuel Bennett, c. 1700 — 76

TOP OF A WALNUT TABLE. Marquetry, c. 1680 — 78

WALNUT CABINET. Decorated Marquetry, c. 1700 — 79

WINGED ARMCHAIR UPHOLSTERED IN NEEDLE-WORK, c. 1700 — 80

MID-EIGHTEENTH CENTURY WINDSOR CHAIR. Yew and Oak — 83

FURNITURE FROM DAVID GARRICK'S BEDROOM. Painted in the Chinese manner, c. 1770 — 85

PAGE

CLOCK-CASE — 86
&
CLOTHES PRESS. Engravings after designs by Thomas Chippendale from The Gentleman and Cabinet Maker's Director, 1754 — & 87

RIBBON-BACKED CHAIR. In the manner of Thomas Chippendale, c. 1760 — 88

WRITING DESK. Design by Chippendale from the Society of Upholsterers' Journal — 92

DESIGN FOR A HARPSICHORD BY ROBERT ADAM. Executed in London for the Empress of Russia, 1774. Engraving from The Works in Architecture by Robert and James Adam — 93

SKETCH FOR A CARVED TABLE. Pen drawing by Matthias Lock, c. 1740-1765 — 95

TWO SHIELD BACK CHAIRS. Engraving from G. Hepplewhite's The Cabinet-Maker and Upholsterer's Guide, 1788 — 97

STATE DRAWING ROOM. Coloured aquatint from George Smith's A Collection of Designs for Household Furniture, 1808 — 102

SISTERS' CYLINDER BOOKCASE. Thomas Sheraton's design from The Cabinet Dictionary, 1803 — 103

A CABINET IN ENGLISH WALNUT. From Ernest Gimson, His Life and Work, 1924 — 105

Illustrations on pp. 65, 67, 69, 70, 74, 76, 78, 79, 80, 85, 88, 92, 95 are reproduced by courtesy of the Director of the Victoria & Albert Museum

ENGLISH GLASS

GLASS-MAKER'S TOOLS. Engraving from Haudicquer de Blancourt's The Art of Glass, 1699 — 113

TUDOR MEDICINE-BOTTLES — 115

THE CHESTERFIELD "FLUTE-GLASS," c. 1663. Sir Richard Garton Collection — 117

VERZELINI GLASS, 1583. Hamilton Clements Collection — 122

RAVENSCROFT EWER, c. 1675. Cecil Higgins Collection — 125

BOWL AND COVER IN BAROQUE STYLE. Late seventeenth century. Formerly in the Joseph Bles Collection — 126

BALUSTER WINE-GLASS. Early eighteenth century — 127

GROUP OF GLASSES. Early eighteenth century — 128

GROUP OF GLASSES. Second quarter of the eighteenth century — 129

GROUP OF CUT GLASS. Middle and late eighteenth century — 131

BRISTOL BLUE-GLASS BOX. Third quarter of the eighteenth century — 132

BRISTOL BODKIN-CASE AND SCENT-BOTTLE. Third quarter of the eighteenth century — 133

BRISTOL SCENT-BOTTLES. Second half of the eighteenth century — 135

GROUP OF ENGRAVED GLASSES. Middle of the eighteenth century — 140

<table>
<tr><td></td><td>PAGE</td><td></td><td>PAGE</td></tr>
</table>

GROUP OF CUT GLASSES. Late eighteenth and early nineteenth centuries 141

VASE. Late eighteenth century. Formerly in the Joseph Bles Collection 143

DECANTER-BOTTLE. With medallion stamped : *T. Ridge* 1720 144

MODERN CARBOY. Green bottle-glass 145

DISH DESIGNED AND MADE BY TOM HILL. James Powell & Sons, Limited 150

VASE DESIGNED BY CLYNE FARQUHARSON. John Walsh Walsh, Limited 151

DECANTER AND GLASSES. James Powell & Sons, Limited 152

DECANTER AND GLASSES. Thomas Webb & Corbett, Limited 153

OVEN-GLASS CASSEROLE. Phoenix Glassware Co. 154

BOWL DESIGNED BY BARNABY POWELL. James Powell & Sons, Limited 155

The thanks of Author and Editor are due to the collectors and firms who have supplied photographs for reproduction. Grateful acknowledgment is also made to the Director and Secretary of the Victoria & Albert Museum for facilities granted for photography and the use of photographs, and for permission to adapt and include some passages from the Author's guide to the Museum collection of glass of all countries and periods

ENGLISH POTTERY AND PORCELAIN

LEECHPOT. From Josiah Wedgwood's first Shape Book 157

JUG WITH VERTICAL SLIPWARE DECORATION. From the site of the Bodleian Extension, Oxford. Fourteenth century 159

BALUSTER JUGS. Green glaze with network pattern. Fourteenth century 160

CISTERCIAN WARE BEAKER WITH TWO HANDLES. Dark brown lead glaze. Sixteenth or seventeenth century 161

STAFFORDSHIRE SLIPWARE. Mug with initials R. W. Dated 1695. J. or R. Simpson, Rotten Row 162
&
Mug excavated at Burslem, probably made by J. or R. Simpson, Rotten Row, *c.* 1690. Tankard of so-called *sgraffito* slip, *c.* 1725 163

FULHAM STONEWARE AND LAMBETH ENAMELLED EARTHENWARE. Seventeenth and eighteenth century 165

ENAMELLED EARTHENWARE PAINTED IN BLUE WITH PORTRAITS OF TWO CHILDREN. E. A. Taylor, Bristol. Middle of the eighteenth century 167

'ELERS' WARE. The cup, *c.* 1695. The teapot, *c.* 1750 171

STAFFORDSHIRE SALT-GLAZE PEW-GROUP. Early eighteenth century. Glaisher collection 172

STAFFORDSHIRE SALT-GLAZED STONEWARE. Middle of the eighteenth century 173

STAFFORDSHIRE ENAMELLED SALT-GLAZED STONEWARE. Middle of the eighteenth century 174

STAFFORDSHIRE 'WHIELDON' WARE. Agateware teapot, *c.* 1750 175

DETAIL FROM AN EARLY NINETEENTH CENTURY WEDGWOOD CATALOGUE. Plate engraved by William Blake 176

ARTICLES FOR USE IN THE DAIRY. From Josiah Wedgwood's first Shape Book 177

ARTICLES FOR USE IN THE SICK-ROOM. From Josiah Wedgwood's first Shape Book 181

STAFFORDSHIRE CREAM-JUG IN BLUE JASPER WARE ; CAMEO RELIEF IN WHITE. John Turner. Late eighteenth century 182

CHELSEA FIGURE. Boy in red coat, yellow vest and turquoise breeches 189

STAFFORDSHIRE (NEW HALL) PORCELAIN. Late eighteenth and early nineteenth centuries 190

'CHELSEA-DERBY' PORCELAIN. Made at Chelsea under the management of William Duesbury, *c.* 1775 191

LONGTON HALL PORCELAIN, *c.* 1755　193
BIRD FOUNTAIN. Earthenware with Copper Lustre Motif. Early nineteenth century　194
LUSTRE VASE BY WILLIAM DE MORGAN　200
TWO JUGS AND A COVERED DISH BY BOURNE　202
CIDER BOTTLE BY MICHAEL CARDEW　203

STONEWARE BOWLS MADE BY B. LEACH, NORAH BRADEN AND W. STAITE MURRAY　204
SALT-GLAZE WARE BY WILLIAM GORDON　205
SOME EXAMPLES OF EARLY MARKS ON ENGLISH PORCELAIN　206

Illustrations on pp. 159, 160, 161 are reproduced by courtesy of the Visitors of the Ashmolean Museum, Oxford ; on pp. 162, 163, 171, 174, 175, 193, 194, by courtesy of the City Museums, Stoke-on-Trent ; on pp. 165, 167, 173, 182, 190, 191, 200, 202, 203, 204, by courtesy of the Director of the Victoria & Albert Museum; on p. 172, by courtesy of the Syndics of the Fitzwilliam Museum, Cambridge; on pp. 157, 176, 177, 181, by courtesy of Josiah Wedgwood & Sons Ltd.; on p. 189, by courtesy of G. F. Hotblack, Esq.; on p. 204, by courtesy of W. N. Edwards, Esq., and Henry Bergen, Esq.; on p. 205, by courtesy of William Gordon, Esq.

The groups on pp. 165, 173, 190, 191, 204 have been taken from English Pottery Old and New *by W. B. Honey, published by the Victoria & Albert Museum*

BRITISH CLOCKS AND CLOCKMAKERS

WELSH WATCH CLOCK. Eighteenth century　207
INTERIOR DIAL OF WELLS CATHEDRAL CLOCK SHOWING JOUSTING KNIGHTS　213
NICOLAUS KRATZER, ASTRONOMER TO HENRY VIII. Oil painting by Hans Holbein, 1528. Louvre, Paris　215
WATCH IN CASE AND COVER OF SMOKE CRYSTAL WITH DIAL OF ENAMELLED GOLD. Michael Nouwen of London, 1609　216
STRIKING CLOCK IN ENGRAVED SILVER-GILT CASE. Bartholomew Newsam, *c.* 1590　217
JEFFREY BAILEY'S SIGNATURE. Engraved on the brass lantern clock shown on page 209　222
WATCH SHOWING THE SIGNS OF THE ZODIAC, MOON-PHASES AND DATE. Benjamin Hill, d. 1670　224
LARGE SILVER WATCH INSCRIBED 'PRO F.B. M.D.' James Markwick of London, 1720　225
VERGE WATCH MOVEMENTS, *c.* 1700. Quare, Fromanteel and Clarke　226
BRASS TABLE CLOCK. Daniel Quare, 1648-1724　227
ENGRAVED DIAL OF A STRIKING CLOCK. Edward East, 1610-1673　228
BRASS LANTERN CLOCK. John Hilderson, *c.* 1665　229

MOVEMENT OF A VERGE STRIKING CLOCK. Design engraved by J. Mynde from W. Derham's *Artificial Clockmaker*, 1696　231
TAVERN CLOCK IN TRUNK CASE, *c.* 1760　233
HOOD OF LACQUERED LONG-CASE CLOCK. James Markwick, *c.* 1720　237
HANGING CLOCK. Mahogany case with applied carved and gilt decoration, *c.* 1760　241
DEAD-BEAT ESCAPEMENT. Model of the escapement invented by George Graham, *c.* 1715　243
CHRISTOPHER GOULD'S SIGNATURE. Engraved on the hanging clock shown on page 210　244
HARRISON'S FOURTH MARINE CHRONOMETER, 1759　250
MOVEMENT OF THOMAS MUDGE'S TIMEKEEPER. Engraving from *A Description with Plates of the Timekeeper Invented by Mr. Thomas Mudge*, 1799　251
VERGE WATCH MOVEMENTS, *c.* 1700. Mudge, Rogers, and Weston　252
HARRISON'S FIRST MARINE TIMEKEEPER. Constructed 1729-1735　253
TURRET CLOCK MOVEMENT FROM ST. GILES'S CHURCH, CAMBRIDGE. Originally designed for King's College, Cambridge, by William Clement, 1671　254

ENGLISH POPULAR AND TRADITIONAL ART

PAGE

SPECIMEN OF ORNAMENTAL PENMANSHIP by John Crocker, 1867   257

BROADSIDE, c. 1830   260

GEORGE CRUIKSHANK'S BROADSIDE AGAINST THE DEATH PENALTY FOR FORGERY   261

CHILD'S INSCRIBED WRITING SHEET   263

PICTURE FOR TINSELLING PUBLISHED BY PARK   265

VALENTINE. Hand-coloured lithograph, 1845   267

PIN-PRICK PICTURE   271

BROWN EARTHENWARE MERMAID FLASK. Early nineteenth century. Drawing by Enid Marx   272

DEVONSHIRE HARVEST POTTERY   273

STAFFORDSHIRE SALTGLAZE STONEWARE FIGURES. Late eighteenth century   275

STAFFORDSHIRE SALTGLAZE STONEWARE. Bear-jug. Late eighteenth century   276

STAFFORDSHIRE MILK-JUG   277

ENGRAVED GLASS FROM "YE OLDE SWAN," NOTTING HILL GATE, LONDON   283

BONE STAYBUSK AND CARVED WOODEN ROLLER. Drawings by Enid Marx   287

FIGUREHEAD OF H.M.S. CENTURION   288

PAGE

TWISTED WIRE FORK   289

PEARLIE KING   290

FAIR-GROUND HORSE FROM A ROUNDABOUT AT KEW BRIDGE, LONDON   291

METAL WEATHERCOCK, LYME REGIS PARISH CHURCH ; WOODEN WEATHERVANE, CHARMOUTH PARISH CHURCH. Pencil and wash drawings by Enid Marx   292

MEMENTO MORI. Painting on wood in Lyme Regis Parish Church. Pencil and wash drawing by Enid Marx   293

MINIATURE CAST-IRON FIREPLACE WITH GRATE, FENDER AND FIRE-IRONS OF POLISHED BRASS   297

SAILOR'S PIN-CUSHION   298

PRINTED COTTON COMMEMORATIVE HANDKERCHIEF   299

PATCHWORK QUILT IN SILK, SATIN AND VELVET. Mid-nineteenth century   301

CHILDREN'S PENNY TOYS. Nineteenth century. Rough sketch by Enid Marx   302

PROFESSOR BURCHETT'S DESIGNS FOR TATTOOING   303

CARVED WOODEN BUTTER-PATS AND BONE APPLE-CORER   304

MINIATURE TIN SOLDIERS, c. 1815   305

PLAITED STRAW DOLLIE FOR HARVEST THANKSGIVING. Pencil and wash drawing by Enid Marx   306

SHORT BIBLIOGRAPHIES
BRITISH CRAFTSMEN

Building Craftsmanship by Nathaniel Lloyd. 1929, Cambridge University Press.—*The Wheelwright's Shop* by George Sturt. 1923, Cambridge University Press.—*The Village Carpenter* by Walter Rose. 1938, Cambridge University Press.—*Made in England* by Dorothy Hartley. 1939, Methuen.—*Old English Household Life* by Gertrude Jekyll and Sydney R. Jones. 1939, Batsford.—*Fifteen Craftsmen on Their Crafts*, ed. by John Farleigh. 1945, Sylvan Press.—*Country Craftsmen* by Freda Derrick. 1945, Chapman & Hall.—*English Country Crafts* by Norman Wymer. 1946, Batsford

BRITISH FURNITURE MAKERS

Thomas Chippendale by Oliver Brackett. 1924, Hodder & Stoughton.—*Early English Furniture and Woodwork* by Herbert Cescinsky and Ernest Gribble. 2 vols. 1922, Routledge.—*English Furniture* by John Gloag. 2nd ed. 1944, A. & C. Black.—*The Englishman's Castle* by John Gloag. 1944, Eyre & Spottiswoode.—*Measured Drawings of Old Oak English Furniture* by J. W. Hurrell. 1902, Batsford.—*History of English Furniture* by Percy MacQuoid. 4 vols. 1904-08.—*The Dictionary of English Furniture* by Percy MacQuoid and Ralph Edwards. 3 vols. 1924-27. Country Life.—*History of Oak Furniture* by Fred Roe. 1904, The Connoisseur.—*Furniture and Furnishing* by John C. Rogers. 1932, Oxford University Press.—*Old English Walnut and Lacquer Furniture* by R. W. Symonds. 1923, Jenkins.—*English Furniture from Charles II to George II* by R. W. Symonds. 1929, The Connoisseur.—*Furniture Mouldings* by E. J. Warne. 1923, Benn.—*A History of Domestic Manners and Sentiments in England during the Middle Ages* by Thomas Wright. 1862, Chapman & Hall

ENGLISH GLASS

Curiosities of Glass Making by Apsley Pellatt. London 1849.—*Old English Glasses* by Albert Hartshorne. 1897, Edward Arnold.—*Glassmaking in England* by Harry J. Powell. 1923, Cambridge University Press.—*Old English Glass* by Francis Buckley. 1925, Benn.—*A History of English and Irish Glass* by W. A. Thorpe. 1929, Medici Society.—*English Glass* by W. A. Thorpe. 1933, A. & C. Black.—*Glass in Architecture and Decoration* by Raymond McGrath and A. C. Frost. 1937, Architectural Press.—Victoria and Albert Museum. *Glass : A Handbook for the study of Glass Vessels of all Periods and Countries, and a Guide to the Museum Collection* by W. B. Honey. 1946

ENGLISH POTTERY AND PORCELAIN

The Ceramic Art of Great Britain by Llewellynn Jewitt. London 1878.—*English Porcelain* (1902) and *English Earthenware and Stoneware* (1904) by William Burton. Cassell.—*Staffordshire Pottery and its History* by J. C. Wedgwood. 1913, Sampson Low.—*English Pottery* by Bernard Rackham and Herbert Read. 1924, Benn.—*Catalogue of the Schreiber Collection* by Bernard Rackham. London 1928.—*Old English Porcelain* by W. B. Honey. 1928, Bell.—*English Pottery and Porcelain* by W. B. Honey. 1933, A. & C. Black.—*Catalogue of the Glaisher Collection (Fitzwilliam Museum, Cambridge)* by Bernard Rackham. 2 vols. 1935, Cambridge University Press

BRITISH CLOCKS AND CLOCKMAKERS

Observations on the History and Practice of Watchmaking by Octavius Morgan. (*Archaeologia*, vol. xxxiii, 1849.)—*Curiosities of Clocks and Watches* by Edward J. Wood. 1866.—*A Handbook and Directory of Scottish Clockmakers from 1540 to 1850 A.D.* by John Smith. 1904.—*English Domestic Clocks* by Herbert Cescinsky and Malcolm R. Webster. 1913, Routledge.—*Chats on Old Clocks and Watches* by Arthur Hayden. 1917, Fisher Unwin.—*The Marine Chronometer* by Rupert T. Gould. 1923.—*Some Clocks and Jacks, with Notes on the History of Horology* by R. P. Howgrave-Graham. (*Archaeologia*, vol. lxxvii, 1928.)—*Watches : their History, Decoration and Mechanism* by G. H. Baillie. 1929, Methuen.—*Old English Clocks and Watches and their Makers* by F. J. Britten. 6th ed. 1933, Spon.—*The Old English Master Clockmakers and their Clocks* by Herbert Cescinsky. 1938, Routledge.—*The Evolution of the Long-case Clock* and other articles in *The Antique Collector* (from 1940 onwards), by Percy Dawson

ENGLISH POPULAR AND TRADITIONAL ART

The Earthenware Collector by G. Woolliscroft Rhead. 1920, Jenkins.—*London Tradesmen's Cards* by Sir Ambrose Heal. 1925, Batsford.—*Old Ship Figure-Heads and Sterns* by L. G. Carr Laughton. 1925, Halton & Truscott Smith.—*Children's Books in England* by F. J. Harvey Darton. 1932, Cambridge University Press.—*Penny Plain, Two Pence Coloured* by A. E. Wilson. 1932, Harrap.—*English Quilting Old and New* by Elizabeth Hake. 1937, Batsford.—*Silhouette* by Mrs. E. Nevill Jackson. 1938, Methuen.—*English Smocks* by Alice Armes. 2nd ed. 1930, Dryad Press

INDEX

ADAM BROTHERS, the, 32; their factory, 199

Adam, James, 94, 96; influence of, 77

Adam, John, 96

Adam, Robert, 94, 97; influence of, 77, 94, 98; furniture designed by, made by Chippendale, 91; artists assisting, 97

Adam, William, 96

Affairs of the World (1700), 232

"Agate" ware, 164, 275

Ainsworth, William Harrison, 214-215

Akerman, John, 135, 136

Aldridge, John, wall-paper designer, 51

"Amen glasses," date of, 134

Ammonites or fossil shells, 14

Anglo-Venetian glass, 149

Antique Collector, The, quoted, 235

Antiquities of Freemasonry (Gould), quoted, 232

Antiquities of Rome (Palladio), 78

Antwerp, an active glass-making centre, 118

Apprentices, replica-making by, 303

Archer, Henry, first warden of British Clockmakers' Company, 225

Architecture, classical, of Rome, 65; and a gentleman's education, 83

Arnold, John, and the Longitude prize, 251

Arte Vetraria (Neri), 123, quoted, 124

"Artificial," change of meaning of the word, 232

Artificial Clockmaker (Derham), 232

Art Nouveau, Japanese inspiration of, 150

Ashton, John, antiquarian, and the chapbook, 260

Astbury, John, and Staffordshire salt-glaze, 172, 174

A true Certificat of the Names of the Straungers residing and dwellinge within the City of London, 222

Ayckbowm, glass cutter, 142

BACON, John, potter, 184

Baillie, Lady Grisell, 135

Bain, Alexander, electric devices of, 253, 255

Ballad-monger, as moralist, 259

Ballads and Broadsides, 258

Barnsley, Sidney, furniture designer, 104, 106

Barometers, the first made in England, 230, 233

Barri, Gerald de (Giraldus Cambrensis), 63

Basketwork armchair, early example of, 63

Bath Assembly Rooms, chandeliers in, 143

Bawden, Edward, wall-paper designer, 51

Beckett, Edmund Denison, *see* Grimthorpe, Baron

Beds, early British, 63; later elaboration of, 68, 75

Beilby family, painters on glass, 139-40

Belfast, glass factory, 142

"Bellarmine" stoneware, 281

Billingsley, William, 197

Benfield, Eric, on stoneworking, 12

Bennett, Samuel, 77

Bere Regis Church, 30

Betew, Panton, 184, 188

Betts, Thomas, glass-maker, 136

Bewick, Thomas, 261

Bexley, William Morris's home at, 150

"Billy and Charlie" fakes, 304

Bishop, Hawley, Ravenscroft's successor, 127

Black basalt stoneware, 178

Blake, William, on builders of Gothic churches, 12; his illustrations for Wedgwood catalogue, 178; and toy theatres, 264

Bles, Joseph, collection of glass, 123

Blue glass, use of, for scent bottles, 142

Blythburgh Church, 29

Blythburgh Man, the, clock-jack, 214

Board of Education, the, and art teaching in schools, 154

Bone-china, mass production of, 197

Book of Fate (Park), 264

Bottle-glass, 144, 146

Bottles and jugs, 144-146

Bourne, Joseph, of Denby, 204

Bouverie, Miss Pleydell, 201

Bowes, Sir Jerome, 118

Bow porcelain factory, 183, 188; work of Tebo (Thibaud), 184, 192; closing of, 184

Box, near Bath, quarrying at, 10

Braden, Norah, 201

Bradford-on-Avon tithe barn, 19

Bradley, Langley, 239, 242

Brain, William, 203

Brick-making, 15-16

Brighton Museum, the Willett collection of "image toys," 277

Bristol porcelain, 191-192

Bristol white glass, 140-142

Britannia, figures of, engraved on glass, 139

British History (Geoffrey of Monmouth), quoted, 63

British Museum, clocks and watches at, 218, 221

Broadsides, 259

Brunt, country farrier, 35-36

Buckley, Wilfred, collection of glass, 123, 134
Building materials, local, 24
Burlington, Earl of, works published by, 78 ; influence of, 84, 96
Burne-Jones, Sir Edward, 21
Byng, the Hon. John, later fifth Viscount Torrington, 87

CABINET AND CHAIR MAKERS' REAL FRIEND . . . (Manwaring), 94
Cabinet Dictionary (Sheraton), 101, 102
Cabinet - Maker, Upholsterer and General Artist's Encyclopaedia (Sheraton), 101
Cabinet Maker and Upholsterer's Guide (Hepplewhite), 98, 101
Cabinet Maker's and Upholsterer's Guide (Smith), 103
Cabinet Maker's London Book of Prices and Designs of Cabinet Work, plates by Shearer, 94, 98
Caerleon, 63
Canal barges, paintings on, 294, 297
Canal folk, gipsy origin of, 294
Caravaggio, Michelangelo da, 20
Carboys, 146
Cardew, Michael, 201, 202
Carving, durability of, 287
"Catchpenny," origin of the term, 258
Catnatch, Jemmy, printer of broadsides, 259
Caxton, William, 211
Chairmaker's Guide, The (Manwaring), 94
Chair-making industry, 82
Chairs, 64, 68, 70, 74-75, 81 ; Windsor, 82 ; ladder-back, 83 ; rush-seated, 83
Chambers, Sir William, 91
Chance, Robert Lucas, 146, 149
Chance Brothers, 155
Chandeliers, Regency, 143

Chantry Bequest, the, 54
Chapbooks, 259-261
Chapman, George, glass engraver, 134
Charcoal burners, 14-15
Charmouth Church, curious weather vane, 290
Chaucer, Geoffrey, on clocks, 211
Chelsea-Derby tableware, 188
Chelsea factory, 184
Chest, 63, 64
Chest, mule, 68
Children's Books in England (Darton), 261
Chiming Clocks, working of, by water, 211
Chinese lacquer painting, 32
Chinese wares, imported, 172
Chippendale, Thomas, 86-88, 91 ; craftsmanship of, 60, 81, 91 ; books by, 35, 85, 88 ; and Harewood House, 91, 98
Christmas cards, 270
Chronometers, 230, 242
Cipriani, Giovanni Battista, 32
"Cistercian" ware, 161
Clement, William, clockmaker, 245-246
Clepsydrae (water-clocks), 207, 211
Clock, John, 221
Clocke, Petter, 221
Clock-jacks, 212, 214, 240
Clockmakers' Company, see Worshipful Company of British Clockmakers
Coach builders as painters, 20-21
Coalport works, 199
Cobb, John, 92
Cobbett, William, 70
Cole, John, 201
Commonwealth Mercury, The, 232 ; advertising in, of the Fromanteel Regulator, 236, 239
Complete Body of Architecture (Ware), 95
Compton Pottery, Surrey, 53
Cook, Captain James, and Arnold's Chronometer, 251

Cookworthy, William, 183, 188
Coster, Samuel, and the Huygens pendulum, 236
Costermongers, 298, 300
Cotswold stoneworkers, 14
Cottage Economy (Cobbett), quoted, 70
Cotton-prints from patterns cut by children, 54-55
Country wood-crafts, 20
Craig, Captain E., his free-pendulum device, 255
Cripplegate Church clock, 240
"Crisselling," 124
Crome, John, of Norwich, 20
Cromwell, Oliver, glass dedicated to, 134
Cruikshank, George, adoption of the broadside style by, 259
Crystal Palace, the Great Exhibition at, 149, 156, 199
Cupboard, 68
Curious Gardener, The (Hill), 305
Cut-paper ornamentation, 268

DAILY ADVERTISER, The, 232
Daily Post, The, 232
Darton, Harvey, 261
Day-bed, invention of, 74
"Death and Mortality," 259
Decanters, 139, 144, 146
Delander, Daniel, clockmaker, 242
Delaney, Mrs., flower pictures by, 268
Delft ware, 165, 166, 167 ; see also Liverpool-Delft
Denon, Baron de, 103
Derby factory, 184, 188 ; amalgamation with Chelsea, 188 ; biscuit figures and groups, 188
Derham, Canon William, D.D., 223, 232
Description of England (Harrison), 66

Description with Plates of the Timekeeper invented by Mr. Thomas Mudge, 251

Designs (Jones), 78, 91

Designs for Household Furniture (Shearer), 94

Designs of Chinese Buildings, Furniture, Dresses, Machines and Utensils (Chippendale), 91

Dover Castle, connection of, with horology, 211

Dromore glass factory, 142

Drulardy, clockmaker, 216

Dublin, glass-makers at, 142

Duesbury, William, potter, 175; and the Derby factory, 184, 188 ; his specialities, 192

Dufy, designs of, for Lyons silk-weavers, 52

Dunvegan Castle, glass found at, 134

Dwight, John, of Fulham, 168, 171

EARNSHAW, Thomas, 230 ; and the Longitude prize, 251 ; and the testing of the new chronometers, 251-252

Earthenware Collector, The (Woolliscroft Rhead), 276

East, Edward, 230, 232, 233

Edkins, Michael, glass-painter, 141, 142

Edwards, Benjamin, glass merchant, 142

Egyptian glass, 115

Elers brothers, the, 168, 171

English glasses, engraving of abroad, 135

English Quilting, Old and New (Hake), 298

English Writing Masters (Heal), 272

Evelyn, John, and the Duchess of Portsmouth's apartment, 73 ; on Charles II's clocks, 236

Exeter Cathedral, connection of, with horology, 211 ; clock-tenders, feeding of, 214

"FACT AGAINST SCANDAL," pamphlet, 240

Fairgrounds, effect of the steam engine on, 291

Fairy tale, the, survival of, 261

Farm carts, painting of, 298

Farquharson, Clyne, glass designer, 153

Fashion and War (Laver), 64

Fennemore, T. A., and industrial design, 52

Ferg, Paul, 188

Figureheads, 287, 288

Fishley family, potters, 273

Flamsteed, John, Astronomer Royal, 223, 246

Fleet Street, home of fine clockmakers, 231 ; Thomas Harris clock, 214

Fleury, C. M., 134

Flint-glass, term adopted for Ravenscroft's productions, 124

Flint-knapping, 10

Flute glass, 121, 123

Foliot bar, introduction of, 212

Fortunes of Nigel, The (Scott) quoted, 221

Frederick the Great, portraits of, engraved on glass, 139

Freestone, working of, 10 ; seasoning of, underground, 10

Fremington pottery, 272

Frodsham, William, 252

Fromanteel, Ahasuerus, clock-maker, 225-226

Fromanteel family, clock-makers, 236, 239, 245

Fry, Roger, and the Omega workshops, 55 *et seq.*

Frye, Thomas, 183

Furniture, style in, 60, 64-65, 66 ; in town and country houses, 67 ; effect on, of Puritanism, 68 ; revival, 70, 73 ; influence of Inigo Jones, 73-74 ; day-bed and love-seat, 74 ; chairs, new designs, 74-75, 81; regional styles, 75, 77 ; cabriole leg, 80, 81 ; Huguenot and Dutch influence, 81 ; veneering, 81 ; Chippendale, Hepplewhite and Sheraton, 91 *et seq.*

Furniture and Furnishing (Rogers), quoted, 92

GALLOWS LITERATURE, popularity of, 259

Gawdy Hall, dining-room tapestry, 221

Geares, Wenijfrid, name on a Verzelini glass, 121

Gentleman and Cabinet-Maker's Director (Chippendale, 1754), 85, 91

Gentlemen's or Builders' Companion (Jones), 95

Geoffrey of Monmouth on the cities of Britain, 63

Gesso, use of, 96

Gibbon, Edward, on architecture, 84

Gibbons, Grinling, 30, 31, 168

Gibbs, James, books by, 96

Gill, Eric, 12

Gillow, Richard, architect, 86

Gillow, Robert, craftsman designer, 85-86, 98

Gimson, Ernest, furniture designer, 104, 106

Glaisher, Dr., and the Wrotham potters, 164

Glass, early, 107, 108, 115, 116, 118 ; technique and decoration of, 108, 111-114; trunk-beakers, 115-116; coloured window-glass, 116 ; Venetian glass-workers in England, 118 ; substitution of sand for flint, 124; English baroque, 129 ; German influence, 130; the baluster period, 130-131 ; increased excise duty, 131, 142; engraving and cutting, 133-139; enamel painting, 139-141; Anglo-Irish style, 142-143, 150 ; nineteenth-century cut glass, 144 ; pressed glass, 149 ; transfer printing, 150 ; mass-produced, 154; use in architecture, 156; engraved screens and mirrors, 254, 287

Glass Excise, the, 131, 142, 149

Glastonbury Abbey, connection of, with horology, 211

Glastonbury tithe barn, 19

Gog and Magog, Guildhall giants, destruction of, 290

Gordon, William, and salt-glaze ware, 204

Gothic Architecture . . . Geometrically Expressed (Langley), 91

Gothic revival, 294

Gould, Christopher, clockmaker, 232, 242

Gouyn, C., and Sprimont, Nicolas, owners of Chelsea factory, 184

Graham, "Honest George," 238, 242, 244, 245; and Harrison, 249

Grandfather clocks, 75, 236

Granger, Hugh, cabinet-maker, 91-92

Great Exhibition of 1851, 149, 156, 199

Greene, John, and Michael Measey, glass-sellers, 118, 129-130

Gretton, Charles, clockmaker, 242

Grimthorpe, Edmund Denison Beckett, 1st Baron, 232, 252

Gulliver's Travels in chapbook form, 260

HAEDY, Bohemian glass-cutter, 135, 136

Hake, Mrs. Elizabeth, on quilting, 299

Hallett, William, 92

Halley, Edmund, and Graham, 242

Hancock, Robert, and transfer printing, 190

Handiwork and decoration, miscellaneous, 302-305

Hannover, Dr., on commercialisation of the Potteries, 197

Harewood House, Yorkshire, Furniture for, designed by Adam, 91, 98

Harley, Thomas, member of the Clockmakers' Company, 227

Harris (Harrys), Thomas, 240, 242

Harrison, John, clockmaker, 249, 250

Harrison, William, 66

Hartshorne, Albert, on de Lysle, 121

Heal, Sir Ambrose, furniture designer, 106

Heath, John, 188

Henry VIII's clocks, 214-216

Hepplewhite, George, 91, 92, 94, 98; pattern-books of, 35

Herbert, Sir Alan, on B.S.T., 208

Herbert, Sir Thomas, and Charles II's watch, 232

Higgins, Cecil, collection of glass, 128

Hilderson, John, 230, 234, 235

Hill, Jack, Stourbridge glass-maker, 142

Hill, Jason, quoted, 305

Hill, Tom, glass designer, 151

Historia Coelestis (Flamsteed), 246

Hobby-horses, rarity of, 291; as children's toys, 291

Hobhouse, Miss, work of, after the Boer War, 48

Hodgson, Orlando, 259, 264

Hogan, James, glass designer, 151

Holkham Hall, 96

Holmes, Arthur, smith, 36 *et seq.*

Hooke, Robert, 223; diary of, 232

Hope, Thomas, and the English Empire style, 103

Hope-Jones, F., and the application of electricity to time-keeping, 252

Horacudii, hour-striking clocks without dials, 208

Horological Dialogues (Smith, 1675), 232

Horse-brasses, 304

Horse Guards, Whitehall, 96

Household Furniture and Interior Decoration (Hope), 103

Household Furniture in the Genteel Taste (Society of Upholsterers), 94

Hubble, Nicholas, and slip-ware ceramics, 164

Huguenots and the silk industry, 81

Huygens, Christiaan, and the pendulum, 236; mounting of a clock in gimbals, 246

"IMAGE TOYS," 274, 276; the Willett collection, 277; personages represented, 278

Imperial Chemical Industries, earthenware vessels made for, 54

Ince, William, work of, 92

Industrial Revolution and the decline of crafts, 41

Inlay, veneer, marqueterie, development of, 32

Inn signs, 289, 290

Italian marble and the English mason, 10

Italian Renaissance in Europe, 65, 73

"JACKS," 212, 214, 240

Jackson, Sir Thomas, architect, 150

Jacobite glasses, 134, 136

Jacobs, Isaac, and Bristol glass, 142

Jacobs, Lazarus, 142

James, John, horologist, 235

Japanese art, vogue of, 199

Japanese clock, ancient, 208

Jasper ware, 178

Johnson, Dr., on Scotland, 77

Johnson, Jerom, cut-glass dealer, 135

Johnson, Thomas, 96

Jones, Frank, of Linslade, barge-painter, 298
Jones, Henry, clockmaker, 230, 233-234
Jones, Inigo, 30, 73-74, 77 ; and the Palladian style, 235
Journey to the Western Islands of Scotland, A (Johnson), quoted, 77

KAUFFMANN, Angelica, decorations of, 32
Keney, Vincent, 216
Kent, William, architect, 60, 81, 96
Kilpeck Church, 11
King's Pottery, Verwood, 53
Knibb, John and Joseph, 32, 239 ; and the Clockmakers' Company, 226 ; and Sir Richard Legh, 235
Knitting, local traditions in, 300
Kratzer, "the Astronomer," clockmaker, 218

LANE, Mrs. Jane, and Charles I, 234
Lantern clocks, 218
Lavenham, St. Mary's Church, 11
Laver, James, on costume and architecture, 64
Leach, Bernard, 54 ; his work in Japan and at St. Ives, 201
Leeds ware, 181
Legh, Sir Richard, 235
Lemnius, Dr. Levinus, 67
Le Roy, Julien, 244
Liberty's clock, Regent Street, 214
Lime-burning, 14
Littler, William, 192
Liverpool-Delft ware, 166-167, 192 ; *see also* Delft
Lock, Matthias, 96
London Gazette, The, 232, 233
London Glass-Sellers' Company, 118, 123-124 ; protest against import of cut glass, 135

London Magazine, 232 ; and a satire on Graham, 242
Longitude, determination of, 246, 249-250
Loughton, L. G. Carr, on old ships' figureheads, 287
Louis XIV, and Huygens, 246
Lowestoft factory, 192-193
Lucas, John Robert, 146
Lustre, use of, 199
Lustred glass, 283, 284
Lysle, Anthony de, 121

MAHOGANY, introduction of, 35, 82
Maiolica, 165, 166
Mairet, Mrs. Ethel, weaver, 49
Mansell, Sir Robert, and the glass industry, 118
Manwaring, Robert, 92-94
Marquetry, 69, 81
Marx, Enid, and her end-papers for the Curwen Press, 51
Maskelyne, Dr., Astronomer Royal, 230
Mason's "Ironstone" china, 199
Masterpieces of English Furniture and Clocks (Symonds), quoted, 82, 92
Mayhew, Thomas, 92
Mazzola, Paolo, maker of *verres ornés*, 121
Medici colour prints, 54
Meissen, influence of, 187
Memoirs of William Hickey, quoted, 84
Mermaid, the, earthenware figure, 281
"Metropolitan" ware, decoration of, 164
Millwright's trade, 21
Milne, Jean, 49
Minton factory, 52, 198
Mirror, The, quoted, 242
Mirrors, 75
Model ships in bottles, 303
Modern English glass, 150-156
Monks as potters, 161
Moore, Sir Jonas, 232

Morgan, William de, 199
Morris, William, 46 *et seq.*, 104, 106 ; on applied art, 150
Mudge, Thomas, 242, 250, 251 ; his work for the Longitude award, 251
Mudge, Thomas, Jr., 251
Mumford, Lewis, on wood, 23
Murray, Keith, architect and glass designer, 152, 153, 203
Murray, Kenneth, and stoneware pottery, 54
Murray, W. Staite, 54, 201

NAILSEA, bottle-glass factory at, 146, 149, 284
Nantgarw, 197
Nash, "Beau," and Tompion's clock for the Pump Room at Bath, 236
Nash, Paul, industrial designer, 51
National Physical Laboratory, inventors at, 255
Neri, A., author of standard Italian book on glass-making, 123, 124
Newbery, John, publisher, 261
New Hall, Staffordshire, hard paste made at, 194 ; use of lustre, 194
New Lottery Book of Birds and Beasts (1771), 261
Newsam, Bartholomew, 218, 232
Newton, Sir Isaac, and the building of a water clock, 223
Nollekins and his Times, 184, 188
"Nonesuch" chests, 69
Northwood, John, and his reproduction of the Portland vase, 150
Norwich, seventeenth-century jacks at, 214
Norwich Cathedral, connection of, with horology, 211
Nottingham salt-glaze, 173

Nursery rhymes and chap-books, 261
Nutting, Wallace, American horologist, 246

OAK, in Gothic buildings, 16; use of, by woodcarvers, 26
Oak trees, planting and growth of, 19
Old Clocks and Watches (Britten), 230
Old Ships' Figureheads and Sterns (Loughton), 287
Omega Workshops, the, 55

PACQUET FROM WELLS, A (1701), 232
Paine, James, 96
Paper, materials of, 24
Paradiso (Dante), quoted, on the horologe, 211
Pargeting, 16
Parker, William, of Fleet Street, 143
Paston, Sir John, letter by, concerning return of his clock, 214
Patchwork, 300
Peacock, Elizabeth, weaver, 49
Pecock, Reginald, Bishop of Chichester, on clocks, 211
Pellatt, Apsley, glass designer, 144, 149
Pendulum, introduction of, 212
Penmanship, 272
Penny Plain and Twopence Coloured (A. E. Wilson), 262
Penrose, George and William, glass merchants, 142
Perfume bottles, English and French, 155
Pergolesi, Italian designer, 32
Peterborough Cathedral, connection of, with horology, 211
Philip III of Spain, and a workable marine chronometer, 246

"Phoenix" glass oven-ware, 155
Pilkington Bros., St. Helen's, and glass bricks, 156
Pincushions, made by soldiers and sailors, 300
"Pin-prick" decorations, 268; first use of, 271
Pinxton porcelain factory, 197
Pitts, Johnny, printer of broadsides, 259
Planché, Andrew, 188
Pleydell Bouverie, Miss, 201
Porcelain, English, 183; early marks on, 206
Portrait flasks, 281
Portsmouth, Duchess of, 73
Potteries, the, commercialisation of, 173, 197
Potters, status of, 198
Pottery, early, 160-161, 205; local variations in, 273; transfer printing on, 281; use of, for recording political comment, 278
Powell, Barnaby, glass designer, 151
Powell, Messrs. James, and Sons, glassmakers, 112, 150, 151
"Prince Rupert's drops," glass toys, 112
Printing on textiles, 302
Prints, decorated, 265
Public executions and "Gallows Literature," 259
Purbeck Shop (Benfield), 12
Puritan period, the, effect of, on furniture design, 68, 69
"Pyrex" oven-ware, 155

QUARE, Daniel, Quaker clock craftsman, 230, 232, 235
Queen Anne period, 77
Queensware, 178
Quilting, 298-299
Quivil, Bishop Peter, 214

RAMSAY, David, 221, 232; elected first Master of the Clockmakers' Company, 225

Ravenscroft, George, chemist and glass-maker, 123, 124, 127, 128
Ravilious, Eric, glass designer, 52, 153, 203
Regency furniture, 103-104
Richardson, George, and slipware ceramics, 164
Rockingham pottery, 199
Rococo decoration, 132
Rogers, John C., quoted, 91
Roman furniture from Pompeii, 80
Roman glass-blowing, 115
Romano-British furniture, 63
Roofing slats in the Cotswolds, 14
Ropford, Roger de, bell-founder, 214
Rossetti, Dante Gabriel, 21
Rotterdam, great windmill in the Oostpleine, 21-22
Roundabouts and swings, 290, 291 *et seq.*
Rowlandson, Thomas, 276
Royal Aircraft Establishment, Farnborough, 256
Royal Observatory, Shortt clocks in, 255
Royal Society, the, founding of, 123
Rudd, R. J., designer of electric pendulum, 255
Running Stationer, the, 259
Ruskin, John, on engraving of glass, 113; on "applied art," 150
Russell, Gordon, furniture designer, 106
Rye Church, the high quarter-boys on the tower of, 214

SAER, Joseph, 230
Sailors as handicraftsmen, 302-303
St. Albans, Abbot of, and his astronomical clock, 41
St. Clement Danes, Strand, 240
St. Lawrence Church, Reading, history of, 212
St. Paul's Cathedral clock, 239, 240

St. Vedast Church, Foster Lane, 240

Saint of Newcastle, publisher of children's books, 261

Salt-glaze, 168, 172, 203-204; use of, for busts and figures, 168; contrast of, in white, with coloured clays, 174; and transfer printing, 175; drawbacks of, 176

Sampson, Professor, and the Shortt clock, 255

Sand hour-glass, 207

Savage, Frederick, blacksmith, and the application of steam to the fairground, 291

Scottish furniture, 77

Seven Years' War glasses, 139

"Seynt Martynplace," Gloucester, 212

Shearer, Thomas, 92, 94

Shelton, Sampson, first warden of British Clockmakers' Company, 225

Sheraton, Thomas, 92, 94, 98, 101-102; pattern-books of, 35

Ships' timbers in barn-building, 20

Shop signs, 289, 290

Shortt, W. H., and the "hit-and-miss" synchroniser, 255

Sidney, Sir Philip, 218

Silhouette (Jackson), 268

Silhouettes, 268

Silva (John Evelyn), quoted, 31

Skelt, toy theatre sheet publisher, 263

Slipware, 162, 163, 272, 274

Smith, George, quoted, 103

Smith, William, glass engraved for, 121

Smocking, 300

Soane, Sir John, designer, 32

Southwold, "Jack-Smite-the-Clock," 214

Spode, Josiah, and the pumping of water, 178; first printed ware produced by, 181; and the use of bone ash, 183

Spode, Josiah (2nd), and bone china, 197, 198

Spreyton Village, the figure over the forge, 290

Sprimont, Nicolas, 184, 188

Staffordshire slipware, 164

Staffordshire ware, 171, 172; porous moulds, 172; pew-groups, 174-175, 275; other figures, 274, 276, 277; painting of, 181

Staybusks, decorated, 302

Stevens, Alfred, 52

Stevens and Williams, Messrs., of Brierley Hill, Stourbridge, Murray's designs for, 152-153

Stone, crafts of, 10, 11

Stone-breaker, the, 10

Stoneware, 168, 172; salt-glaze figures, 274

Stone-workers, 12, 14

Stourbridge School of Art, 149

Stowe, John, 240

Straw, decorative possibilities of, 305

Street literature, a form of popular art, 258

Sunderland ware, 199

Sutherland, Graham, glass designer, 52, 153, 203

Swan, Abraham, 96

Swansea porcelain factory, 197

Sweeting's Alley, 231

Sweetmeat glasses ("dessert glasses"), 135-136

Symonds, R. W., on wood, 82, 92

Synchronome Remontoire of Hope-Jones, 255

Syria, glass industry in, 115

TABLE-CHAIRS, 70

Tables, many - legged, 66; gate-legged, 68

Tash, Alderman Sir John, and the clockmakers, 226

Tattooing, popular designs, 302

Tebo (Thibaud), work of, 184, 192

Thornhill, Sir James, 188

Timber, modern uses of, 24

Timber barns, Gothic tradition of, 19

Timber buildings, essential points in, 20

Time, early systems of measurement, 207; "Punch" on, 208; B.S.T. and D.B.S.T., A. P. Herbert on, 208

Tin-enamelling, 166

Tin Plate Workers' Company, 227

Tinsel-pictures, 265-266

Toby jug, the, 276, 281

Toft, Thomas and Ralph, and slipware ceramic, 163, 164, 174, 194, 202, 272

Tompion, Thomas, 232, 236, 246; and the marqueterie period, 32; and the Clockmakers' Company, 226; and St. Paul's, 239

Toper, the, earthenware figure, 281

Torrington Diaries, The, quoted, 87

Touchstone of Complexions, The (Lemnius), 67

Toy-making for street hawkers, 305

Toy soldiers, 305

Toy theatre, the, 261-265

Transfer printing on china, 189; subjects chosen for, 281-283

Trent-Mersey Canal, 178

Turner, John, and the pumping of water, 178

Turner, Thomas, of Worcester, 181, 191, 199

UNITED GLASS-BOTTLE MANUFACTURERS, 155

Universal System of Household Furniture (Ince), 94

Urseau, Nicholas, clock-keeper, 218

VALENTINE, the, 266-268

Vallin, N., one of the first English clock-makers, 218

Vanity Fair (Thackeray), quoted, 262

Velasquez, Don Diego de Silva y, and carriage-painters' varnish, 21

Velva, Julia, furniture depicted on her tomb, 63

Venice and the renascence of glass-making, 116, 117

Verre de fougère, Northern glass, 116

Verzelini, Jacopo, glass-maker, 118, 121

Victoria, Queen, 259

Victoria and Albert Museum, 21, 77 ; glass exhibits in, 121, 138, 139

Victorian glass, 149-156

Vile, Sir William, 92

Vision and Design (Fry), quoted, 45

WALDGLAS (forest glass), 116

Walking-stick handles in wood or bone, 302

Walpole, Horace, on William Kent, 96 ; and Anne Boleyn's clock, 215

Walsh, John Walsh, Ltd., glass firm, 153

Walton, Allan, designer of fabrics, 51

Waterford, glass-making, 142, 143

Water Lane, now Whitefriars Street, 231

Watt, James, and Wedgwood, 178

Watts, George Frederick, 53

Weathercocks, 290

Webb, Philip, piano case by, 21 ; and William Morris, 150

Webb and Pollock and the juvenile drama, 263

Wedgwood, Josiah, 144, 173, 176, 178, 181, 197 ; and Flaxman, 52 ; and the Trent-Mersey Canal, 178 ; and James Watt, 178 ; imitators of, 181

Weight-driven clock, introduction of, 208

Wellowe, John, first Warden of British Clockmakers' Company, 225

Wells Cathedral clock, 213, 214

West, William, producer of juvenile dramas, 262-263, 264

Westminster Hall, 19

Whieldon, Thomas, 174-175

Whip handles in wood or bone, 302

Whitefriars glassworks, 231-232

Wilfrid Buckley Collection, Victoria & Albert Museum, 123, 134

William III, 77 ; clocks made for, 230

Williamite glasses, 136-139

Wilson, A. E., on West's juvenile dramas, 263

Winchcomb, Gloucestershire, pottery at, 53

Window panes, making of, 114

Wine glasses and goblets, eighteenth - century, 130, 132, 143

Wolsey, Cardinal, letter to, on Kratzer, 218

Wood family, and their earthenware figures, 276

Wood, Aaron, block cutter, 174

Wood, Ralph, his Toby jugs, 175

Wood, use of, 23, 24 ; limitations of, 82

Woodall, George and Thomas, designers of cameo glass, 149-150

Wooden roofs, 16 ; building of, 20

Woodman, the, his knowledge of his job, 26

Woodworkers, 26, 59 *et seq.*

Worcester china factory, 188, 190, 191, 198

Worshipful Company of British Clockmakers, 223-228

Wren, Sir Christopher, 77, 223, 232, 235 ; and the English Renaissance, 30

Wrotham ware, 164

Wyatt, James, classic designs by, 103

YORKSHIRE MUSEUM, early examples of furniture shown in, 63, 80